Building a
Virtual Library

Ardis Hanson and Bruce Lubotsky Levin
University of South Florida, USA

INFOSCI **Information Science Publishing**
Hershey • London • Melbourne • Singapore • Beijing

Acquisitions Editor: Mehdi Khosrow-Pour
Managing Editor: Jan Travers
Development Editor: Michele Rossi
Copy Editor: Jane Conley
Typesetter: Amanda Appicello
Cover Design: Integrated Book Technology
Printed at: Integrated Book Technology

Published in the United States of America by
        Information Science Publishing (an imprint of Idea Group Inc.)
        701 E. Chocolate Avenue
        Hershey PA 17033-1240
        Tel: 717-533-8845
        Fax: 717-533-8661
        E-mail: cust@idea-group.com
        Web site: http://www.idea-group.com

and in the United Kingdom by
        Information Science Publishing (an imprint of Idea Group Inc.)
        3 Henrietta Street
        Covent Garden
        London WC2E 8LU
        Tel: 44 20 7240 0856
        Fax: 44 20 7379 3313
        Web site: http://www.eurospan.co.uk

Library of Congress Cataloging-in-Publication Data

Building a virtual library / [edited by] Ardis Hanson and Bruce Lubotsky Levin.
        p. cm.
    Includes bibliographical references and index.
     ISBN 1-59140-106-2
        1. Digital libraries--Planning. 2. Libraries--Special collections--Electronic information
resources. 3. Academic libraries--Automation. 4. Digital libraries--United
States--Planning. 5. University of South Florida Virtual Library. I. Hanson, Ardis. II.
Levin, Bruce Lubotsky.

ZA4080 .B85 2002
025'.00285--dc21   2002068799

eISBN 1-59140-114-3

British Cataloguing in Publication Data
A Cataloguing in Publication record for this book is available from the British Library.

NEW Titles
from Information Science Publishing

- **Web-Based Education: Learning from Experience**
  Anil Aggarwal
  ISBN: 1-59140-102-X: eISBN 1-59140-110-0, © 2003
- **The Knowledge Medium: Designing Effective Computer-Based Learning Environments**
  Gary A. Berg
  ISBN: 1-59140-103-8; eISBN 1-59140-111-9, © 2003
- **Socio-Technical and Human Cognition Elements of Information Systems**
  Steve Clarke, Elayne Coakes, M. Gordon Hunter and Andrew Wenn
  ISBN: 1-59140-104-6; eISBN 1-59140-112-7, © 2003
- **Usability Evaluation of Online Learning Programs**
  Claude Ghaoui
  ISBN: 1-59140-105-4; eISBN 1-59140-113-5, © 2003
- **Building a Virtual Library**
  Ardis Hanson & Bruce Lubotsky Levin
  ISBN: 1-59140-106-2; eISBN 1-59140-114-3, © 2003
- **Design and Implementation of Web-Enabled Teaching Tools**
  Mary F. Hricko
  ISBN: 1-59140-107-0; eISBN 1-59140-115-1, © 2003
- **Designing Campus Portals**
  Ali Jafari and Mark Sheehan
  ISBN: 1-59140-108-9; eISBN 1-59140-116-X, © 2003
- **Challenges of Teaching with Technology Across the Curriculum: Issues and Solutions**
  Lawrence A. Tomei
  ISBN: 1-59140-109-7; eISBN 1-59140-117-8, © 2003

Excellent additions to your institution's library! Recommend these titles to your Librarian!

Building a Virtual Library

Table of Contents

PART II:
SERVICES & FUNCTIONS

PART III:
ADMINISTRATION & EDUCATION

Foreword

Virtual libraries are organic. Understanding the challenges of development is ongoing. These challenges range from content to interfaces, from digital video to geospatial infrastructures, from staffing to marketing. This book explores the dynamics of building a virtual library at the University of South Florida within the context of national developments and standards. This illustration will assist the reader in understanding and developing similar resources and services for his or her library.

Issues presented in this book are complex. The simple question "What is information" depends upon your current role. Do you need a quick definition of "genetics" or guidance in using Worldcat or need to know that the *New York Times* has a searchable archive? The qualification of "current" is equally important, since even as information professionals, we navigate as experts and as novices. At one and the same moment, we have a subject expertise and a passing knowledge of many others. Further, we have immediate needs and longer timeframes depending upon the context. However, as information professionals, there are concerns about our own roles as *librarians* and how we interpret what this means. Are we seeking to reinforce our brick presence as we expand our click presence? Where is the "teachable moment" in the electronic environment? Are we visible or invisible mediators in the provision of information? Can anyone *see* us? Do we *need* to be seen?

The taxonomy of the Internet currently includes websites, email (one-to-one or one-to-many), asynchronous discussion forums (newsgroups and mailing lists), synchronous chat (Instant Messenger, including MSN, ICQ, AIM, and IRC), MUDS (including MOOs and MUSHs), metaworlds (Virtual Reality), interactive video and voice, and is still expanding (Wallace, 1999a). This taxonomy exacerbates issues of authority, permanence, and accessibility, and introduces other issues, such as provenance. In many ways, the issue is the same: people need access to answers.

In response, libraries of all types have tried to reposition themselves in a virtual world, from providing access to their repositories and services to undertaking massive and successful digitization efforts of text, images, sound, and datasets. The response from the commercial sector includes enterprises such as About.com, Amazon, and Google. Concurrently there is the wholesale ability of everyone to self-publish. In this digital environment, GIGO (garbage in, garbage out) has emerged as the greatest challenge, with cognitive miserliness as the second challenge (Wallace, 1999b). Humans seek to filter information; we seek to reduce cognitive inputs, and we will accept immediacy over accuracy or even relevancy.

Once upon a time, computer users debated the superiority of Macintoshes and PCs. The debate focused on control vs. surface and simulation. As librarians, skilled in command line and/or fielded searching, the ability to manipulate online catalogues and databases has remained an important value even as our catalogs have migrated to web-based interfaces. However, the majority of our users have valued surface, immediacy, and depthlessness (Jameson, 1984). They value tools which allow them to skim along the surface. This isn't to say that either end-users or these tools are second class. It simply acknowledges a preference by the user.

Each click-effort nudges another effort. We have moved our catalogs to the Web and provided access to every imaginable database either locally or remotely. However, in the process, we have created silos. Our traditional framework has required the researcher to develop an idea, articulate that concept to a librarian or simply to a card catalog, and mediate the topic in search of answers. The difficulty of this framework is that it shifts focus from the need to the resource, from the idea to the navigation. Our click-libraries have sought to replicate place and service – a difficult architecture. Each technology, however, affords us the opportunity to re-examine the matrix as we work toward a convergence of format and access.

Central themes in this dynamic involve four major issues. First, there are inter- and intra-institutional cooperative collection efforts and reference services with colleagues at different institutions in different nations, whom we may or may not ever meet. These cooperative efforts also have an impact on the relationship between distance educational resources and the libraries' role in collection development. Second, multi-modal presentations (RealAudio and MPEG3 formats next to sheet music), the integration of formats far beyond that of items held in our catalogs, and the merger of archive and access through digital formats require an increased emphasis on metadata to both describe and link resources and collections. Third, the growing awareness of a user-centered rather than system-centered perspective has an impact on both technology and services. Finally, a cognitively flexible work-force with technical skills is critical to ensure effective, reliable services to library users, regardless of where they are located.

These are merely four of a number of major themes found in this volume. The chapter contributors have done an excellent job presenting both conceptual approaches and case illustrations in building a virtual library within an academic environment. Librarians will have a greater understanding of how technology and change impacts their environments. Staff in the traditional functional areas of libraries will see examples of how emerging technologies can be most efficiently and effectively utilized within their respective organizations. In addition, librarians in administrative positions will greatly benefit from the discussion of organizational change, the emergence of work teams, and staffing and personnel. In addition, the chapters on marketing, and statistics provide a clear picture of the importance of both of these activities to both libraries and their larger institutions. Finally, library and information science faculty will be interested in how the development of virtual libraries will re-engineer library education. This book is essential reading for those individuals currently planning or implementing virtual library services and resources within their academic environment.

Amy Tracy Wells, M.L.S.
Belman-Wells Information Services
East Lansing, Michigan
6 March 2002

REFERENCES

Jameson, F. (1984). Postmodernism, or the culture of late capitalism. *New Left Review*, 146(July-August):59-94.

Wallace, P. (1999a). *The psychology of the Internet.* New York: Cambridge University Press, 4-9.

Wallace, P. (1999b). *The psychology of the Internet.* New York: Cambridge University Press, 19.

Preface

The organization, functioning, and the role of libraries in university communities continue to change dramatically. Cummings, Witte, Bowen, Lazarus and Eleman (1992), in a report prepared for the Andrew W. Mellon Foundation, underscored four emerging trends in academic libraries that, a decade later, remain critical issues:

1. The library traditionally has been the most important facility within the university supporting advanced scholarship and has been essential for the ability of colleges and centers within universities to support distinguished programs;
2. Libraries consume large quantities of the monetary resources of universities and compete with other valuable facilities and academic initiatives for limited funds;
3. Scholarly information needs (until very recently) have been based upon a culture of print, with these information needs served almost exclusively by technology created more than 500 years ago; and
4. Many new technologies have been employed simply to automate *existing* functions.

These emerging trends for 1992 are even more relevant in the new millennium. While academic research libraries continue to acquire information, organize it, make it available, and preserve it, the critical issues for their management teams in the twenty-first century are to formulate a clear mission and role for their library, particularly as libraries transition to meet the new information needs of their university constituents. Michael Buckland, of the University of California at Berkeley, has defined the library's role to include facilitating access to information, while its mission is to support the overarching mission of its parent organization (Graham, 1995).

Therefore, it is critical for the university to make longstanding financial commitments to support the library's role in the academic online environment. This includes innovative funding initiatives and commitments for resources that the library and university together must identify and establish. In addition, a digital academic research library requires sustained operational funding over many years. Almost any other library activity can survive a funding hiatus of a year or more. For example, funding for acquisitions, building maintenance, and staffing can be temporarily reduced, and the physical collections of the library will more or less survive. However, like the online catalogue, digital collections require continual maintenance to provide access to scholarly materials.

In paper-based libraries, the definition of a core collection is material that is purchased. In the digital environment, the emphasis is on access rather than ownership. Libraries no longer own materials, they license them. However, new means of publication (such as electronic pre-print services and depositories of scholarly publications) promise to transform the methods by which scholars exchange and preserve the results of their work, and, in turn, transform academic libraries. Interactive media increasingly is used as curriculum and research support. The rise of distance learning initiatives has also radically changed the access to and demand for scholarly information.

Wilson (1998) acknowledges that until now, libraries have been most successful in mechanizing manual processes, but have been slow to embrace new modes of electronic information delivery and to incorporate new methods of teaching and learning. Above all, Wilson feels that it is the changing nature of user needs and the changing nature of scholarly communication that forms the impetus for academic libraries to re-evaluate services. Libraries should identify user (staff, students, and faculty) needs, and design work processes to reflect organizational goals, and to support frontline performance (Janson, 1992).

As electronic information increasingly becomes part of their charge, the organization of academic libraries has also changed. Some libraries locate the responsibility for electronic information distinct from print information. Other libraries see the information as inseparable, and include electronic responsibilities along with existing (print) responsibilities in assignments for collection development, cataloging, and public service. This new breed of academic librarians will require many skills and knowledge areas that demand increasingly diverse library personnel. Woodsworth et al. (1989, p. 135) provided a persuasive list, including: "...subject specialists, technicians, and professionals from other information fields — e.g., programmer/analysts, network designers and managers, marketing specialists, and experts in artificial intelligence and the cognitive sciences."

Rapple (1997) has suggested that users of academic libraries will face difficulties in adjusting to recognizing a world where information seeking is without spatial and temporal constraints. However, the development of virtual or digital research libraries brings this vision closer to fruition.

ORGANIZATION OF THE BOOK

The contributors of this volume attempted to provide a framework for the creation and maintenance of these new services and resources, now an essential component of academic libraries. This was accomplished through a case presentation of how one academic library at the University of South Florida (USF) re-engineered its collections, services and functions, administration team, and educational environment in the design and implementation of a virtual library.

In the introductory Chapter (One) in this volume, Hanson, Levin, Heron, and Burke examine the history and emergence of information technology and its implications for the academic library. The remainder of the book is divided into three major sections: Collections (Part I); Services & Functions (Part II); and Administration & Education (Part III).

Part I (Collections) consists of Chapters Two through Four. Acquiring electronic resources from a library's perspective is more than just placing an order through a vendor. In Chapter Two, Pettijohn and Neville examine the issues involved in establishing collection development and evaluation policies for electronic collections. Libraries are going beyond the acquisition and maintenance of traditional printed information sources to becoming information providers, in order to meet the information needs of their local communities and to make their in-house collections more accessible to remote users.

Kearns in Chapter Three discusses the teaching and research uses of video materials in academic environments. He goes beyond a description of video formats to argue for a comprehensive implementation plan when considering the distribution of video resources. The chapter also includes an illustration of how one academic library employed database technology to create a video card catalog accessible from the Internet.

In Chapter Four, Abresch examines the development and implementation of a Geographic Information Systems (GIS) Research and Data Center within a virtual library. He reviews specific organizational, design, and technical aspects of three model centers, as well as federal data standards and issues for cataloguing geospatial data.

Part II (Services & Functions) of this book consists of Chapters Five through Ten. The library operation commonly called "access services" is addressed by Burke in Chapter Five. This operation is in the midst of change on three levels: structurally, economically, and technologically. Burke examines interlibrary loan, electronic reserves, licenses and contracts, and the impact of distance learning on access to electronic resources and services.

Heron and Gordon in Chapter Six provide an overview of current cataloging principles, issues in handling evolving formats, and challenges for academic online catalogs. They also examine the model created by USF in determining best practices in the creation of records for shared, online academic environments.

In Chapter Seven, Wells and Hanson discuss the age-old predicament of the information seeker – to whom and how does one ask a reference question now that the reference department is ensconced within an electronic environment? After a brief overview of the evolution of e-reference, the authors then examine the functional requirements, costs, and growth of synchronous e-reference software. Finally, they review the requirements for information literacy within an "information literacy competency" taxonomy.

In Chapter Eight, Caggiano discusses the fact that acquiring library resources and moving library services to an online environment is critical as universities move to a 24-hour-a-day, seven-days-a-week paradigm. Although all websites want a pretty front end, the critical issues are usability of the site and seamless integration for the user.

Grohs, Reed, and Allen in Chapter Nine briefly examine marketing issues in academic libraries, how those issues were dealt with in marketing the USF Virtual Library, and where marketing for academic libraries may be going in the future as the physical and virtual worlds shift, meld, and merge.

After a brief review of the history of distance education and the impact of this technology on higher education, Burke, Levin, and Hanson in Chapter Ten explore the role of libraries and librarians in providing the variety of services, resources, and technology necessary to support this steadily growing facet of academic institutions. A case illustration of how one university has incorporated its virtual library as a critical element in its distance learning educational initiatives is also provided.

Part III (Administration and Education) of this book consists of Chapters Eleven through Fourteen. Arsenault, Hanson, Pelland, Perez, and Shattuck in Chapter Eleven discuss the responsibilities of management in handling such a sea change within a fairly conservative operational setting. The authors also discuss how to manage these new work paradigms and overcome barriers in effecting change.

As libraries move into new working and service delivery environments, new ways of working, either organizationally or technologically, require retraining, retooling, and ongoing staff development and training. In Chapter Twelve, Chavez presents the necessary elements to keep an organization moving ahead to create an environment that encourages professional development, and identifies emerging trends in library staffing.

As the public and the state demand more accountability from their academic institutions, and as administration requires bottom-line interpretations for its scarce dollars, the ability to establish a sound case for capturing those dollars for library resources is critical. Bland and Howard in Chapter Thirteen explore the need for integrating and streamlining statistical gathering and establishing standards across a multi-campus library system.

Finally, what skills and education will the next wave of librarians need in order to provide critical information services and resources to the academic community? In Chapter Fourteen, Gregory examines four major professional areas: collection management and maintenance, reference services, technical services, and library administration. She also suggests that, within the profession of librarianship, academic librarians will need to ensure that continuing education remains a high priority.

ACKNOWLEDGMENTS

There never would have been a book about the USF Virtual Library without the vision of the late Samuel Y. Fustukjian, the director of the Tampa Library at the University of South Florida from 1980-1999. Mr. Fustukjian greatly enhanced the University of South Florida Libraries, especially in terms of technology. In 1995, *Florida Trend* magazine reported that at USF, "Continuing growth and an emphasis on innovation helped create one of the nation's most sophisticated electronic libraries." Although Mr. Fustukjian died in 1999, he was able to see the inception and the implementation of many of the initiatives of the USF Virtual Library Project. We believe he would be most pleased with the continuing evolution of the USF Library System that he deeply loved.

We would also like to thank the Directors of the USF Library System who supported the efforts of the many USF faculty, staff, and students who contributed to this volume. A special note of thanks is given to the staff at Idea Group Publishing, particularly to Michele Rossi, Jan Travers, and Mehdi Khosrow-Pour, for their enthusiasm and tremendous support during this book project. We would like to extend a heartfelt thank you to Amy Tracy Wells for her Foreword that sets the tenor of the volume so well. Two other individuals deserve appreciation for their assistance on this volume: Denise Darby for her role as the "naïve" reader of the manuscripts and Walter Cone for his assistance in the transmission of the finished works to the publisher.

Finally, on a personal note, we would like to thank as well as dedicate this text initiative to our families for their unfailing love, patience, support, and comic relief during the writing and editing of this book.

Ardis Hanson and Bruce Lubotsky Levin
The de la Parte Institute
University of South Florida
Tampa, Florida

REFERENCES

Cummings, A. M., Witte, M, L., Bowen, W. G., Lazarus, L. O., & Ekman, R. H. (1992). University Libraries & Scholarly Communication: A Study Prepared for The Andrew W. Mellon Foundation. Chicago, Ill.: The Association of Research Libraries. [also available online: http://www.lib.virginia.edu/mellon/mellon.html]

Graham, Peter S. The Digital Research Library: Tasks and Commitments. Digital Libraries '95. [http://csdl.tamu.edu/DL95/papers/graham/graham.html]

Janson, R. (1992). How reengineering transforms organizations to satisfy customers, National Productivity Review, Dec. 22: 45

Rapple, Brendan A. (1997). The Electronic Library: New Roles for Librarians. CAUSE/EFFECT, 20(1): 45-51. [http://cause-www.colorado.edu/ir/library/html/cem971a.html]

Wilson, T.D. (1998). Redesigning the University Library in the Digital Age. Journal of Documentation, 54(1): 15-27.

Woodsworth, A., Allen, N., Hoadley, I., & et al. (1989). The Model Research Library: Planning for the Future. The Journal of Academic Librarianship, 15 (July): 135.

Chapter I

Technology, Organizational Change and Virtual Libraries

Ardis Hanson and Bruce Lubotsky Levin
The Louis de la Parte Florida Mental Health Institute at
the University of South Florida-Tampa, USA

Susan Heron and Merilyn Burke
Tampa Campus Library at the University of South Florida, USA

Change has become a way of life for most organizations in the 21st century. In order to withstand profound change, an organisation must be flexible and incorporate the ability to adapt and respond to its external environment and its many stakeholders (Kanter, Stein, & Tick, 1992). At the same time, in an era of increasing fiscal constraints, new technologies, and an explosion of information, informatics plays an increasingly important and prominent role in society, in knowledge exchange, in communication, and in commerce between organizations. Accordingly, the most remarkable opportunities and challenges have emerged within academic libraries with regard to the incorporation of technology into daily functioning. Academic libraries only achieve real change when every person, from staff to administrator, is willing to examine functions, strategies, goals, and processes and to participate in free discussions of the critical issues. This chapter examines such a landmark shift in an organization's operation and culture with the creation of a "virtual library" at an urban university. It will review the planning, development, and implementation process of the virtual library. It will also examine the barriers and successes within the organizational role of a multi-campus, autonomous university library system. The chapter will conclude with a discussion of future issues and opportunities for the role of technology in organizations and organizational change.

THE USE OF TECHNOLOGY IN SOCIETY AND ORGANIZATIONS

There has been an astounding evolution of technologic advances in the development of information infrastructures at various levels of society (e.g., organizational, governmental, and human service systems). These infrastructure components encompass a variety of elements including: the physical facilities to store, process, and transmit information; the hardware; the information itself; the applications and software that allow access, structure, and manipulation of information; and the network standards and transmission codes that facilitate inter-organizational and cross-system communication.

Also included in the infrastructure are the individuals responsible for creating and developing the information (National Telecommunications and Information Administration, 1998). For example, the development of computer-based patient records, personal health information systems, and unified electronic claims systems utilize various electronic communication technologies to streamline and centralize databases (National Telecommunications and Information Administration, 1998; National Rural Health Association, 1998). Furthermore, behavioral telehealth and telemedicine strategies continue to broaden health and mental health clinical care, education, and services delivery for at-risk populations in rural America (Levin & Hanson, 2000). Nevertheless, the development, management, and integration of these increasingly sophisticated information infrastructures remain largely uneven and diverse in their organizational structure, complexity, degree of implementation, and functioning.

However, it is within the field of education where the most remarkable opportunities, challenges, and obstacles have emerged in relation to technology initiatives. Historically, institutions of higher education have been a community focal point for creative activities, generating new knowledge, and advancing scholarship through scholarly communication. While academic libraries have traditionally served as the repository of written records of intellectual achievement for faculty and students, these organizations are facing a number of major and complex challenges. These challenges include the escalating costs of scholarly publications; the exponential increase of academic information; compliance with copyright laws; issues of intellectual ownership; and the dramatic changes in the external environment, most notably the rapid technologic change in telecommunications (Cummings, Witte, Bowen, Lazarus & Ekman, 1992; *Towards a New Paradigm*, 1995).

Thus, questions have begun to surface regarding the viability of maintaining the traditional model of research libraries at universities. With emerging advancements in telecommunications technology, a new paradigm has evolved. It requires a reconfiguration of libraries that places a greater emphasis and priority on access to scholarly information. In order for libraries to deal with these changes, the traditional workplace is no longer viable. Academic libraries with their host institutions must rethink their structure, operations, and processes in order to meet the changing environment in higher education. New work methods (e.g., cross-functional work teams) have become necessary in order to incorporate changing technology and communication.

EMERGENCE OF WORKTEAMS

Studies have indicated that successful organizations are often those that are less reliant on formal decision making and more reliant on the ability to develop effective communication both up and down the management chain using less structured decision-making techniques (Adams, 1995). These informal communication networks and the decentralization of decision making are becoming more common in organizations with a high degree of computerization (Travic, 1998). The use of technology as a tool often had been limited to relatively independent or isolated work environments. Virtual technology has expanded the potential of team working to more collaborative work segments by enabling participation across remote locations.

Work teams have the potential not only to enhance organizational outcomes but also to enhance member motivation, production, and satisfaction. The interdependence of the individual team members is a defining characteristic of groups (Yan & Louis, 1999). Although work teams contain jobs that are interrelated through project tasks and milestones, they also contain a social structure linking the individual team members in such a way that successful completion of each member's job is necessary to achieve the larger goals and desired outcomes (Kling, 1993).

Emergence of Technology in Teams

Telecommunications technology has removed the need for physical proximity and allows new work teams to form and reform according to interests, particular tasks, or issues. A person may be a member of many "electronic communities," shifting his or her virtual presence from one locus of activity to another with ease (Marshall, Shipman & McCall, 1995).

The relationship between internal communication and cross-functioning teams has been the subject of considerable research (Tushman & Nadler, 1986;

Damanpour, 1991; Ettlie & Reza, 1992; Nonaka & Takeuchi, 1995). Individuals maintain and monitor communications links (e.g., e-mail and voice mail) after hours and away from the office. Increased use of telefacsimile, audio and video conferences, conference calls, and the Internet has dramatically expanded the access of an individual to various sources of information as well as increased the level of participation in various information networks. As a result, virtual teams can be set up as temporary structures with fluid membership, can exist only to complete a specific task, or can be permanent structures working on core business processes.

ACADEMIC LIBRARIES

Academic libraries are witnessing a transition to a new work organization (Neal, 1996; Bauwens, 1994; Kling, 1993). Traditionally, libraries were warehouses of physical pieces of information, and librarians served as the guardians and mediators of the information. Based on the perceived needs of their users, librarians carefully selected materials for the collection, acquired, cataloged, shelved and circulated them, and found information for patrons (or instructed them on how to find information). Scholars and students had to travel to the library to thoroughly research a topic. Librarians set up designated information areas where patrons could query library staff. Telephone reference was limited to those questions that could be answered quickly and briefly. Some journal indexes were available as databases, but as recently as ten years ago, librarians searched them on behalf of patrons because of the complexity of interfaces and the costs of accessing the information.

The demands of emerging models of distance learning, user needs in virtual settings, and new technologies have challenged older organizational structures of libraries (Anders, Cook & Pitts, 1992). Increasingly, information is being created and offered in a digital format (without ever migrating to a paper format). This transition has required significant changes in the tools and roles of libraries (Beard, 1995). These demands require complex intra-organizational coordination, effective patterns of communication across traditional departmental boundaries within organizational work units, and a capacity to respond quickly to contingencies (Galegher & Kraut, 1990; Weick & Roberts, 1993; McClure, Moen & Ryan, 1994). This new informatics environment demands workplace flexibility and team-based competencies (Townsend 1998; Capelli et al., 1997; Appelbaum & Batt, 1994; Heydebrand, 1989).

Library professionals see this transformation as signifying progress toward workplace empowerment and democracy, because such a transformation demands more skills, grants workers more autonomy and responsibility, and involves teamwork (Saunders, 1999; Vassallo, 1999). These team-based groups give upper-level management more knowledge and resources to control and intensify work processes (Tennant, 1995; Travic, 1998).

Technology implementation is an essential component in this new organizational structure. The emergence of the Internet and the migration to client-server architecture have fostered new ways of accessing information resources and the development of new telecommunications-based services. Prominent in the information systems literature is the extent that technology accommodates and influences strategic direction and the functioning of teams, specifically the use of teleconferencing, electronic mail, and web-delivered information (Grover, Fiedler & Teng, 1999; O'Hara & Watson, 1995; Premkumar & King, 1992; Venkatraman, 1991).

A unique characteristic of these inter-organisational partnerships includes shared ownership of assets and, to some extent, shared control of strategic, technological, and application issues (Lavagnino, 1999). The following case study examines the development and implementation of a multi-campus virtual library project within the University of South Florida (USF) Library System.

CASE STUDY OF THE USF LIBRARY SYSTEM

Overview

The Libraries of USF are comprised of five libraries on three campuses located in Tampa, St. Petersburg, and Sarasota, Florida. The three USF campuses serve unique patron groups. The Tampa campus houses three libraries: the main library which serves both undergraduate and graduate students and the research needs of the university faculty; the Hinks and Elaine Shimberg Health Sciences Library which serves students and faculty in an academic health sciences center; and the Louis de la Parte Florida Mental Health Institute Research Library, which serves the students, faculty and staff in a behavioral health services research facility. The Nelson Poynter Library on the St. Petersburg campus also serves both undergraduate and graduate students and their teaching and research faculty. The Jane Bancroft Cook Library on the Sarasota campus serves both New College and the USF-affiliated students and faculty. Two demographic characteristics distinguish USF students from other college students. USF students are generally older than traditional college students and the majority of students commute to campus. USF has implemented a mandate of 24x7 (twenty-four hours a day, seven days a week) access to courses and resources. USF also has made a significant commitment to distance education. Thus, USF Libraries must provide access to their collections and services to an increasingly large number of remote users.

History

Historically, the USF Libraries existed as primarily autonomous units, with little central coordination or project activity. Inter-library cooperation was generally related to policy development for specific library functions (e.g., circulation policy, cataloguing record standards, or sharing of physical resources).

Although the USF Libraries have had access to electronic mail, calendaring, and document sharing applications since the mid 1980s via the university main-frame, few USF librarians used these services. Many librarians considered the systems difficult and unfriendly, and there was little incentive for many of the staff to learn the new technologies.

In 1991, the telecommunications infrastructure of the university changed significantly as it began to move away from the mainframe environment. Central administration, colleges, and departments migrated to client-server architecture. With the advent of Mosaic in 1992, one of the campus Libraries developed a website. Three years later, all the USF libraries had individual websites and utilized PINE as their electronic mail application.

In 1995, the USF Libraries had a total of 458 databases available within the various libraries that required use in-house or on the campus network. However, there were 50 databases available for use over the Internet. Electronic services on the individual websites were also growing, but the databases and access to services for faculty and staff were not utilized in a consistent manner. While one of the USF libraries provided full-text reports and document delivery, another provided full-text documents online via an electronic reserve system (similar to the "reserve" shelf in traditional academic libraries). Four libraries provided inter-library loan services, three libraries provided electronic reference and instruction, and two libraries provided online book renewal services. Two of the libraries were also offering electronic journals access. A more coherent structure was needed for access to the burgeoning electronic resources and services available within the USF Library System.

Creation of the Virtual Libraries Planning Committee

The USF Virtual Libraries Planning Committee (VLPC) first convened in 1995. At that meeting, the committee was charged by the Director of the Tampa Campus Library with the task of preparing a proposal for a university-wide virtual library. The core members of this group included two librarians from both the main library on the Tampa campus and the Poynter Library in St. Petersburg, and one each from the Cook Library in Sarasota, the Shimberg Health Sciences Center Library, and the de la Parte Institute Library. The eighth member was a librarian from Gulf Coast University brought in as an outside consultant.

The charge was somewhat unusual, since it was the first time the USF Libraries had collaborated on a system-wide project of this scope. It would require careful planning, forethought, an extensive review of the literature, and an impact analysis on the current organizational setting to create such a document. The use of technology proved to be a major benefit in the coordination of this effort.

Organisational Role and Use of Technology within the VLPC

Due to the geographical distances of the three campuses, the VLPC agreed to weekly hour-long conference calls to identify and discuss issues, problems, and to relate individual and group progress. Ongoing and shared communications (such as electronic mail and distribution lists) among the members of a group is essential to group cohesiveness (Tennant, 1995).

The VLPC also used its internal distribution list in the development of a "virtual survey" to determine similar development or technological levels among peer institutions. Each member was asked to develop specific questions relating to his or her main area of expertise. The five focus areas of the survey included questions about the online public access catalogue, electronic collections and services, staffing and infrastructure (software and hardware) needs, budget, and future plans. The survey was sent, via postal mail and electronic mail, to 16 peer institutions of higher education chosen on the basis of FTE and academic setting. A master survey form and its subsequent data were published on one of the libraries' servers for access by the VLPC. The feedback from the survey gave the USF library directors needed information to make implementation decisions.

The final planning document, *The USF Libraries Virtual Library Project: A Blueprint for Development*, covered collections and content, interface and infrastructure, organizational structure, and services (Metz-Wiseman et al., 1996). Included in the document were the list of action items identified by the group, the methodology, the questions and subsequent analyses of the focus groups, the survey of peer institutions, recommended standards, a glossary of terms, and a bibliography. After approval by the library directors, all library staff received the site URL via a mass email.

After the library directors adopted the *Blueprint,* which advocated the creation of nine work teams, the VLPC evolved into the Virtual Library Implementation Team (VLIT). As one of their first directives, VLIT had to market the concept of the virtual library and its development teams to the rest of the staff at the USF Libraries. Based upon the successful use of technologies by the VLIT members, the decision was made to use this same model within and among the teams.

Use of Technology in the Virtual Library Implementation Process

The website publicizing the USF Virtual Library was the natural place to link each of the new virtual library team sites. The use of the web allowed each of the teams to have a public place to post team goals and objectives, meeting minutes and "to-do" lists, draft and working documents, and a list of working and completed projects. Since the web was a public venue, anyone who had an interest could review project or team information.

During the development of the virtual library interface page, the members of the Interface Design Project Group reviewed the types of questions and feedback sent by users to the USF Libraries via the "help page". Based on an analysis of these user responses and the most frequently asked questions, staff developed a four-level feedback page that separated queries and routed questions or comments to the appropriate personnel.

IMPLICATIONS OF THE USE OF TECHNOLOGY

O'Leary (2000) states that it will never be sufficient to define new roles as specific technical or administrative skill sets. In fact, new roles must be examined and understood as a set of capabilities that can be quickly and effectively applied to whatever new need or opportunity arises.

Implementing successful change in technology, in teams, or in the overall organization can be daunting, but when it involves all three, the challenges can be overwhelming. New teams and technologies also mean new ways of dealing with change at the level of day-to-day work experiences.

Library administrators have to be educated to understand that, like Websites, technology and its associated resources must be nurtured. The use of technology requires a significant investment in time, money, and training for both staff and patrons. Staff skills and competencies must be continually upgraded and maintained to make the best use of these technologies as well as to increase organizational capacity and communication (Lamont, 1999; Szeto, 2000). For example, two VLIT members located on different campuses were successful in establishing and using NetMeeting (a software application that allows multiple users to establish voice connections and interactive programs over the Internet) to work on documents and large-scale editing of web pages.

For the USF Libraries, there was 'newness' to the environment: the libraries were not just tiptoeing into the sea of electronic media, they were diving in headfirst. While there were old concepts in new bottles, such as the paper reserve room becoming available electronically, others, such as the digitization center, were new initiatives. Staff now faced a paradigm change. The traditional committee structure was no longer effective. No longer based on job positions or status, staff members self-identified their interests and helped build assignments. Location no longer governed the composition of the teams. The electronic environment allowed multi-campus teams to meet with minimal disruption.

Previously, two factors had led to problems with effective cooperation among the USF Libraries: the time needed to travel between campuses for face-to-face meetings and the disproportionately larger size of the main library on the Tampa campus (TCL). The decision making and leadership often defaulted to the TCL. The advent of teleconferencing allowed the creation of a more democratic VLPC, with nearly equal representation from all libraries. The other libraries viewed this as a welcome change. However, the size of TCL worked against it in one way. The smaller libraries had no choice but to enlist all or most of their staffs in order to cover the multifunctional teams that VLIT created, while TCL had a large percentage of staff who chose not to participate at all, and therefore did not enjoy the resulting staff cohesiveness engendered by the shared experience.

External Organisational Impact

Research relationships or coalitions with universities are another form of supplier relationship. Increasingly, the world's academic institutions are major suppliers of advanced technologies. Because the transfer time from theory to application is rapidly shrinking, academic contributions are directly shaping the form of new product development.

Partnerships between the libraries and the university's computing departments, with academic units, or with businesses and local government, can further the interests of all participants (Ferguson & Bunge, 1998). University administrators have already developed partnerships with other organizations to combine resources and expertise. The USF Libraries were part of a National Science Foundation high-speed, high-bandwidth Internet2 grant proposal by USF. As part of their meritorious application, the USF Libraries displayed a streaming video database of mental health training and education videos at the Internet2 national meeting (see Chapter 3 in this volume). Other applications include the USF Libraries Digitization Center Project, which is mounting full-text image files of the *Florida Sentinel,* an African American newspaper that traces its history back over 100 years (Doherty, Bernardy & Rowe, 2000). Since these are "web deliverables," this is another example of the use of technology that has larger pedagogical implications for training and education.

CONCLUSION

As organizational theorist Claudio Ciborra argues, users "tinkering" with their new technologies can produce creative applications that may have profound strategic impact over time (Mankin, Cohen & Bikson, 1997). The new convergence of technologies (such as desktop video-conferencing, collaborative software, Internet and intranet-based systems) enables organizations to reconstitute teams from historically dispersed staff, thereby combining the productivity of team-based work with the benefits of a flexible and geographically dispersed workforce. The use of technology has also compressed the time that it takes to accomplish projects. Larger populations can be included in a 'workspace' so that there are new perspectives, which allow for more innovative solutions. Finally, the electronic inclusion of geographically divergent populations has a significant benefit: it allows members of teams or organizations to become a community with common goals, skills, rewards, and expectations despite the physical separation.

The USF Libraries currently use or will be implementing the use of several technology initiatives, particularly as the Libraries move toward achieving ARL status and satisfying requirements for university reaccreditation. User input and satisfaction will drive both of those assessment reviews. Analyzing use statistics and queries also provide organizations with a powerful tool to profile its existing user base and to create and retain stronger relationships within it, as well as to find new potential collaborators (Spethman, 1993; Zineldin, 1998).

FUTURE ISSUES

The impact of technology on marketing practice warrants further investigation. In the future, how should academic libraries relate to their users, suppliers, partners, and competitors? Technology's impact is much broader than advertising, data collection, home pages, selling products/services, direct mail, databases, or public relations. It influences communication and coordination processes within a network of alliances and other collaborators (Zineldin, 2000).

Electronic environments can provide a considerable amount of information to libraries on user interactions and library resources and services. As the use of electronic services delivered directly from outside the library becomes routine, the electronic collection of information will become a vital tool for library management. Patron feedback will be critical in order to operate effectively (Adams, 1995).

In addition, examining changes in use patterns of full-time, part-time, and distance-learning students will provide insights into how resources need to be allocated (Adams, 1995; Anders, Cook & Pitts, 1992). Such information has implications for space, staff, materials and equipment investment.

REFERENCES

Adams, Roy J. (1995). Strategic information systems and libraries. *Library Management*, 16(1):11-17.

Anders, V., Cook, C. & Pitts, R. (1992). A glimpse into a crystal ball: academic libraries in the year 2000. *Wilson Library Bulletin*, 67(2):36-41.

Appelbaum, E. & Batt, R. (1994). The new American workplace. Ithaca, NY: ILR Press.

Bauwens, M. (1994). What is cyberspace? *Computers in Libraries*, 14 (4):42-47.

Beard, K. (1995). Digital spatial libraries: A context for engineering and library collaboration; *Information Technology and Libraries,* 14(2): 79-86.

Cummings, A.M., Witte M.L., Bowen, W.G., et al. (1992). *University Libraries & Scholarly Communication.* NY: Association of Research Libraries, 1992.

Damanpour, F. (1991). Organizational innovation: a meta-analysis of effects of determinants and moderators. *Academy of Management Journal,* 34(3):555-590.

Doherty, M., Bernardy, R., & Rowe, W. (2000). *Born Again! The Sunland Tribune and Tampa Bay History Become Electronic Journals.* Presentation at the annual Symposium on 21st Century Teaching Technologies: A Continuing Series of Explorations. Tampa, Florida: University of South Florida, March 24, 2000. [http://www.lib.usf.edu/virtual/ldc/dpg/s-abstract.html]

Ettlie, J. E. & Reza, E. M. (1992). Organizational integration and process innovation. Academy of Management Journal, 35(4):795-827.

Ferguson, C. D. & Bunge, C. A. (1998). The shape of services to come: values-based reference service for the largely digital library. College and Research Libraries, 58(May): 252-65.

Galegher, J. & Kraut, R. E. (1990). Technology for intellectual teamwork. In Galegher, J., Kraut, R.E., & Egido, C. (Eds.), Intellectual teamwork. Hillsdale, NJ: Lawrence Erlbaum, (pp. 1-20).

Grover, V., Fiedler, K. D, & Teng, J. T. C. (1999). The role of organizational and information technology antecedents in reengineering initiation behavior. Decision Sciences, 30(3):749-781.

Heydebrand, W. V. (1989). New organizational forms. Work and Occupations, 16: 323-357.

Kling, R. (1993). Organizational informatics. Bulletin of the American Society for Information Science, 19(5):14-17.

Lamont, M. (1999). Critical human factors in emerging library technology centers.

Library Hi Tech, 17(4): 390-395.

Lavagnino, M. B. (1999). Authentication, bandwidth, and collaboration: the library systems directors' ABCs . Library Hi Tech; 17(4):396-402.

Levin, B.L. & Hanson, A. (2000). Mental health services. In: S. Loue and B.E. Quill (Eds): *Handbook of Rural Health.* New York: Plenum, pp.241-256.

Mankin, D., Cohen, S. G., & Bikson, T. K. (1997). Teams and technology: tensions in participatory design. *Organizational Dynamics,* 26(1):63-76.

Marshall, C. C., Shipman, F. M., & McCall, R. J. (1995). Making large-scale information resources serve communities of practice. *Journal of Management Information Systems,* 11(4):65-87.

McClure, C. R., Moen, W. E., & Ryan, J. (1994). *Libraries and the Internet/ NREN: Perspectives, Issues, and Opportunities.* Westport, Conn.: Mecklermedia.

Metz-Wiseman, M., Silver, S., Hanson, A., Johnston, .J Grohs, K., Neville, T., Sanchez, E. & Gray, C. (1996). The USF Libraries Virtual Library Project: A Blueprint for Development. Tampa, Florida: University of South Florida.

National Telecommunications and Information Administration (1998). *The National Information Infrastructure: Agenda for Action.* Washington, D.C.: The Administration.

Neal, J. G. (1996). Academic libraries: 2000 and beyond. Library Journal, 121(12):74-77.

Nonaka, I. & Takeuchi, H. (1995). Knowledge-Creating Company: How Japanese Companies Create the Dynamics of Innovation. Oxford: Oxford University Press.

O'Hara, M. T. and R.T. Watson (1995). Automation, business process reengineering and client server technology. In Grover, V. & Kettinger, W.J. (Eds.), *Business process change: Reengineering concepts, methods and technologies.* Harrisburg, PA: Idea Publishing.

O'Leary, M. (2000). New Roles Come of Age. *Online,* 24(2):20-25.

Premkumar, G., and W.R. King (1992). An empirical assessment of information systems planning and the role of information systems in organizations. *Journal of MIS,* 9(2), 99-125.

National Rural Health Association (1998). *The Role of Telemedicine in Rural Health Care.* Washington, D.C.: The Association.

Saunders, L. M. (1999). The Human Element in the Virtual Library. *Library Trends;* 47(4):771

Spethman, B. (1993). Marketers tap into tech. *Advertising Age,* 64(4):30

Szeto, E. (2000). Innovation capacity: working towards a mechanism for improving innovation within an inter-organizational network. *The TQM Magazine,*

12(2):149-158.

Tennant, R. (1995), The virtual library foundation: staff training and support. *Information Technology & Libraries*, 14(1):46-9.

Towards a New Paradigm for Scholarly Communication (1995). Ottawa, Canada: Association of Universities and Colleges of Canada.

Townsend, A. M. (1998). Virtual teams: technology and the workplace of the future. *The Academy of Management Executives*, 12(3):17-30.

Travic, Bob (1998). Information aspects of new organizational designs: exploring the non-traditional organization. *Journal of the American Society for Information Science*, 49(13):1224-44.

Tushman, M. & Nadler, D. (1986). Organizing for innovation. California Management Review, 28(3):74-92.

Vassallo, Paul (1999). The knowledge continuum - organizing for research and scholarly communication. *Internet Research*, 9(3): 232-242.

Venkatraman N. (1991). IT-induced business reconfiguration. In *The corporation of the 1990's: Information technology and organizational transformation*. UX: Oxford Press.

Weick, K. E. & Roberts, K.H. (1993). Collective mind in organizations. *Administrative Science Quarterly*, 38(3):357-381.

Yan, A. & Louis, M. R. (1999). The migration of organizational functions to the work unit level: Buffering, spanning, and bringing up boundaries. *Human Relations*, 52(1):25-47.

Zineldin, M. (2000). Beyond relationship marketing: technologicalship marketing. Marketing Intelligence & Planning, 18(1):9-23.

Zineldin, Mosad (1998). Towards an ecological collaborative relationship management: a co-operative perspective. *European Journal of Marketing*, 32:(11-12):1138-1164.

APPENDIX: PEER INSTITUTION SURVEY

One area of importance within the USF Virtual Libraries Virtual Library Project was an analysis of how the electronic resources at the USF Libraries compared to those at similar institutions. Fifteen universities were selected as peer institutions based on ARL (Association of Research Libraries) or ACRL (Association of College and Research Libraries) statistics for enrollment, staff size, collection size, and budget. A survey instrument was prepared and distributed to each institution that had agreed to participate in the survey. The goal of the survey was to determine the status of virtual library development, including the examination of specific details concerning electronic collections and services, the status of cataloging for electronic resources, the hardware available, staffing, and fiscal support for electronic resources.

I. OPAC (Online Public Access Catalog):

A. What type of OPAC do you use? (NOTIS, DRA, CARL, etc.)?
B. How do you use it?
> **1.** Is it command line driven?
> **2.** Does it have a graphical user interface?
> **3.** Is it WWW-based?
> **4.** What kinds of electronic services (other than databases) are available through your OPAC? Please describe. (for example, ILL requests, electronic reserve, online book requests, etc.)

II. Electronic Collections/Services:

A. CD-ROM databases and databases on diskette:
> **1.** Estimate the number of titles of "commercially" produced CD-ROM and databases on diskette available to the end-user:
> **2.** Estimate the number of federal depository CD-ROM titles that are available for public use:
> **3.** How do you provide access to the commercially produced CD-ROM and diskette based products? (check all that apply)
> > **a.** single use on-site workstation
> > **b.** multiple users-on-site
> > **c.** LAN
> > **d.** campus network
> > **e.** restricted dial-up*
> > **f.** open dial-up*
> **4.** How do you provide access to the federal depository CD-ROM titles? (check all that apply).
> > **a.** single use on-site

        b. multiple users on-site

        c. LAN

        d. campus network

        e. restricted dial-up*

        f. open dial-up*

B. Online commercial databases:

    1. How do you provide access to these resources? (check all that apply)

        a. single use on-site workstation

        b. multiple users - on-site

        c. LAN

        d. campus network

        e. restricted dial-up*

        f. open dial-up*

C. Locally produced databases:

    1. How do you provide access to these resources? (check all that apply)

        a. single use on-site workstation

        b. multiple users - on-site

        c. campus network

        d. restricted dial-up*

        e. open dial-up*

    2. Briefly describe the content of the locally produced databases:

D. Full-text databases:

    1. Do you provide access to full-text databases?

    2. If full-text is provided, is it text only?

    3. Text and image?

    4. Text, image and multi-media?

E. Provide basic information on utility software available to the public (word-processing, spread sheet software - database management):

F. Library home page on WWW:

    1. Full-text materials on WWW: Are they:

        a. in-house databases

        b. special collections materials

        c. dissertations

        d. journals, newspapers

        e. other:

    2. Do you use electronic forms on your homepage?

        a. ILL

        b. materials for purchase

    c. holds

    d. reference questions

    e. bi requests

    f. reserve forms

    g. suggestion box

    h. other:

G. E-journals:

  1. Does the library receive e-journals?

  2. Are they cataloged on OPAC?

  3. Are they archived?

H. Electronic Course Reserve:

  1. Do you have a full-text online course reserve system or are you developing one?

    a. If yes, are you including locally produced materials?

    b. Copyrighted materials?

    c. How does the student access the electronic course reserve collection?

I. Document Delivery/Resource Sharing:

  1. What are the "main" commercial vendors that you use?

  2. Do you provide funding to patrons for direct document delivery services? (requests that are not mediated by library staff)

  3. Do you utilize Ariel for resource sharing?

  4. What is the average delivery time for an ILL request?

III. Staffing/Infrastructure

A. Integrated library system:

  1. What integrated library system do you use?

  2. What functions does it support?

  3. Vendor:

B. Describe the staffing that supports your digital library efforts.

  1. Do you have a collaborative arrangement with academic/campus computing at your institution? If yes, describe:

  2. Can you estimate how many FTE staff support the virtual library: (development, maintenance, selection of electronic resources, training, etc.)?

  3. Does your library staff have responsibility for training users on all computer applications in the library? (electronic databases, Internet, utility software, e-mail) Describe:

  4. What percentage of time is trained staff available to assist users?

5. Please describe your staff training program in relation to the virtual library. Include technical and public services programs:

C. Cataloging:

1. Do you classify and catalog digital/electronic materials for your OPAC?

2. If yes, what do you catalog (online databases, CD-ROMs, full text titles available through a gateway service such as LEXIS/NEXIS/FirstSearch, etc.)?

3. How do you classify/catalog these records (title only, holdings, full cataloging, records, in OPAC, etc.)?

4. Who maintains these kinds of records in the OPAC (currency, holdings, location, etc.)?

5. Are you using any metadata standards/analysis for relational databases? If yes, describe:

6. Do you provide enriched MARC records with links to HTML documents (i.e. URL, subject headings, notes field)? If yes, who maintains those records?

7. If you are cataloging resources on the Web, who decides what is added to the collection?

D. Hardware/Equipment/Labs:

1. Do you have a public access computer lab in library?

2. If so, teaching lab only?

3. General patron use?

4. Other:

5. How many terminals are available for:

    a. library staff:

    b. public access:

6. How many PCs/MACs are available for:

    a. library staff:

    b. public access:

    c. Briefly describe the generation of computers (PCs or MACs) you are using (286s, 36s, 486s, Pentium, Power MAC, etc.):

7. How are the public access workstations used? (check all that apply)

    a. online catalog

    b. Internet/Gopher/Lynx

    c. WWW

    d. e-mail

  e. word processing, spreadsheets (utility use of software)

  f. CD-ROM/online/diskette-based resources

  g. electronic kiosk

  h. tutorials/CAI

  i. other, please describe:

 8. Is your network running 10 MBps or 100 MBps?

  a. If 10 MBps, do you have plans to migrate to 100 MBps?

 9. What type of printing capabilities are available to the user?

  a. How many draft printers?

  b. How many laser printers?

  c. Are the printers networked?

  d. Debit/card reader system?

  e. If you charge, how much per page?

IV. Budget

A. What was the total operating budget for your library for the last fiscal year?

B. Budget Categories:

 1. Is there a separate budget for electronic resources?

 2. Databases and software?

 3. Amount allocated last fiscal year?

C. Budget for Hardware:

 1. Is there a separate budget for hardware?

 2. Amount allocated last fiscal year?

 3. If not a separate budget item, can you estimate how much is allocated for electronic resources/databases and hardware?

D. Document Delivery:

 1. Can you estimate how much you are spending on document delivery?

 2. How are you fiscally supporting document delivery?

 3. Amount?

V. A Future Look at the Virtual Library at Your Institution

A. What are your library technology plans for the next one to two years?

B. What resources will be necessary to realize these plans?

C. What forces do you see on the horizon that will help to shape the virtual library at your institution?

(*dial-up=on-campus and off-campus access)

PART I:

COLLECTIONS

Chapter II

Collection Development for Virtual Libraries

Patricia Pettijohn
The Louis de la Parte Florida Mental Health Institute at
the University of South Florida-Tampa, USA

Tina Neville
University of South Florida, St. Petersburg, USA

The evolution from paper to electronic resources transforms the way that information is owned, shared, and accessed. For libraries, the commodification of digital information has long-term implications for the acquisition and development of library collections. As licensing replaces purchasing, and the business practices of software companies replace those of publishers, access to information on demand supersedes collection building, and cooperative acquisitions supplement local collection development. Growing demand for full-text online content that can be easily searched and remotely accessed has led libraries to depend on a host of intermediary agents and cooperatives. Within this landscape of proliferating information and diminishing buying power, it is not surprising that when the Digital Library Federation launched an informal survey of the major challenges confronting research libraries, respondents identified digital collection development as their greatest challenge (Greenstein, 2001).

In this chapter, we will look first at how libraries have responded to this paradigmatic shift by pioneering new collection development strategies, and then examine the changing responsibilities of collection development librarians in an electronic environment.

ELECTRONIC ACQUISITIONS AND COLLECTION DEVELOPMENT

Collection development represents not just the acquisition of information, but a strategic investment in knowledge. Ideally, the guiding principles, goals, and strategies of this process are formally stated in collection development policies. These policies are based upon an understanding of the strengths and weaknesses of the collection, the availability of shared resources, and the information needs of the community. To define subject coverage, depth, level, and scope, librarians emphasize or exclude specific subject areas, languages, formats, and genres (Evans, 2000). Existing collection development policies may be adapted for use in selecting electronic resources or revised to consider additional formats, features, and evaluative criteria. Policies must consider the virtual library from a dual perspective; it is both a dynamic collection in its own right and a hybrid collection created by merging the virtual and physical libraries (Manoff, 2000).

Ultimately, the goals of collection development in academic libraries are unchanged: to meet the immediate and anticipated information needs of users and to serve the research and teaching missions of the university. This is accomplished through strategically selecting, sharing, retaining, duplicating, divesting, archiving, and facilitating access to intellectual content.

Content

The foundation of the virtual library is intellectual content. This includes indexing, abstracting, and full-text databases; electronic journals and books; resources in multimedia formats; numerical and geospatial data; digitized special collections; and free Internet sites. Resources that contain full-text articles, generally selected by the vendor from a variety of sources (including newspapers, journals, standard reference works, and case law), are often referred to as aggregator databases. Some databases are multi-disciplinary, while others offer integrated access to multiple resources by discipline.

Allocations

In academic libraries, the values outlined in the collection development policy, often stated as collection intensity levels, are reflected in budget allocations committed to specific academic programs, disciplines, and departments. Academic library allocations balance the cost of materials and demand for content (which vary widely among disciplines), often using formulas based upon the number and academic rank of faculty and students within departments (Martin, 1995). The increased cost associated with multiple formats, the shift from owning to licensing information, and the aggregation of information in multi-disciplinary databases together threaten to overwhelm traditional allocations. Although additional funding may be available for the initial acquisition of electronic materials, eventually, electronic resources represent a larger and larger slice of the materials budget pie.

The Role of Consortia

Library consortia have grown in tandem with the emerging electronic publishing industry through negotiating and licensing contracts on behalf of libraries, promoting shared standards and policies, and leveraging economies of scale to lower costs. Shared resources encourage consensus and mutual reciprocity among diverse members of cooperative networks. As discounts increase along with the total number of users in most cooperative pricing schemes, the best terms are negotiated for core collections licensed to a large number of libraries. The representatives of individual libraries advocate for the interests of their institutions, and serve as subject area experts within the larger network.

THE ELECTRONIC COLLECTIONS TEAM

The complexity of evaluating and comparing electronic resources, especially in large academic libraries or networks, makes it difficult for one person to select materials. Therefore, many universities have formed electronic collections selection teams (Thornton, 2000; Jewell, 2001). Members of an electronic collections selection team should possess both functional and subject area expertise. Having representatives from technical services and systems will be especially advantageous when comparing similar resources. Other library departments with a stake in electronic collections include media centers, access services, bibliographic instruction, and special collections.

If the virtual library collection will be available to multiple libraries, it is critical that the selection team have representatives from each library or branch. In addition, an individual must be responsible for negotiating price, and modifying/signing the license agreement. An additional person must be identified to interact with vendors' technical staff and be responsible for mounting new resources on the virtual library.

Establishing Preliminary Policies

Before beginning the identification and selection processes, the team should collect background information and formulate preliminary policies and procedures. The team should begin by gathering relevant library and institutional documents including: collection development policies, collection assessments, copyright policies, library liaison policies, interlibrary loan procedures, resource-sharing policies, acquisitions and cataloging workflows, and budget allocations and formulas. These documents reflect the long- and short-term goals of the library, the strengths and weaknesses of the collection, and the immediate and anticipated needs of library patrons. It is both expedient and wise to adopt policies and standards established by national and international organizations. For example, when contemplating a licensing policy, the *Principles for Licensing Electronic Resources* (ARL, 1997) may be used as a guideline).

Establishing the Budget for Electronic Resources

The selections team should begin with a clear idea of the funds available for electronic collections. Electronic resources may be very expensive, and the selection team should eliminate lengthy evaluations of resources they cannot afford. It is important to define how existing allocations will be diverted to fund electronic resources. If funding will come from public or private grants, it is necessary to identify long-term replacement funding. Finally, since endowments may restrict the types of materials purchased, the library may wish to ask for clarification from university counsel before using endowed funds for electronic books or journals.

When vendor price negotiations begin, basic statistical facts about the university are needed. Vendors use a variety of criteria to establish pricing schemes. For example, academic libraries need to provide full-time equivalent (FTE) data for the student population. A succinct description of the organizational structure of the university may be needed, as vendors may ask how libraries are administered to determine if regional campuses should be considered as separate institutions. Information necessary for vendor negotiations may be found in existing reports, such as the Integrated Postsecondary Education Data System (IPEDS), and therefore may not require additional data gathering.

To take advantage of the reduced pricing structures available through consortia, the team should identify which professional associations or systems are affiliated with the library. These include national and regional library networks; city, county, and state educational systems; special-interest groups for special libraries; professional associations; and statewide technology initiatives. Finally, the selection team should obtain basic information on the hardware and software needed to access the resources and existing technology within the library. For example, the cost of new technology must be considered in the development of the budget for electronic resources.

Establishing the Types of Resources Needed

The selection team needs to determine the types of resources it will consider. A frequent issue involves the replacement of print indexing and abstracting materials with online versions. A second issue considers the licensing of aggregated full-text databases or journals that are only available online. Finally, the team should determine if data in other formats is needed, such as numerical and multimedia resources.

Many libraries require an evaluation of a resource even if it is available (without cost) on the Internet. However, there is a cost associated with the time and energy used by professional staff to evaluate, catalog, and maintain these 'free' resources. In addition, Pitschmann (2001) suggests that open access Internet sites are fundamentally different from commercially produced resources. Therefore, these collections require their own practices, policies, and organizational models.

Establishing Workflow

After establishing a selection team, a budget, preliminary policies, and the types of resources to be considered, it is time to create the actual workflow processes. The team must determine what criteria will be used for evaluation, how results will be reported to the team, and what timeline will be followed to ensure consistency in reporting. Individual team members may be assigned responsibility to evaluate resources in specific subject areas. In addition, the team may solicit input from others.

Once the selection team has decided to evaluate a particular resource, members should request free trial access. On-site demonstrations by vendors are informative, but do not replace the product trial. Many vendors offer time-limited discounts and most free product trials are limited in duration. Ultimately, a reasonable timeframe for completing the review must be adopted by the team.

If general faculty, reference librarians, subject area specialists, and library liaisons will collaborate in selection of materials, additional precautions are necessary. Complications arise when selections must be made among imperfect products that are similar in content or purpose, but differ in licensing terms, pricing structure, copyright restrictions, search interface, or accessibility. For this reason, it is a good idea to have electronic resources vetted by librarians before appraisal by general faculty or patrons. This may necessitate two product trials: the first restricted to team members and the second open to subject area experts, members of the general faculty, students, and other stakeholders. When considering comparable products, concurrent trials facilitate a balanced appraisal of resources.

Published reviews of electronic resources have become regular features in both the scholarly and popular press, and both *Choice* and *Library Journal* include "best of" appraisals of electronic resources. *The Charleston Advisor* is especially valuable, offering reviews that utilize both consistent criteria and a rating system, devoted exclusively to electronic resources. Using trial access, published reviews, and vendor documentation, the evaluation should be completed within a given timeframe and presented to the team.

Establishing Evaluative Criteria

Many selection teams create an evaluation form or checklist that will be used to capture information from the vendor (Jewell, 2001). The completed evaluation form is a useful way to summarize key information for the team, allowing comparison of similar databases using consistent criteria (see Appendix A for a sample evaluation form). There are a number of critical issues to be considered, including content, access, timeliness, cataloging, sustainability, usability, usage assessment and statistics, technical performance and service levels, added value, pricing structure, and licensing terms.

CRITICAL ISSUES IN EVALUATING ELECTRONIC RESOURCES

Content

The quality of digital content, like print content, is judged by a number of factors, including the authority of the resource, comprehensiveness, completeness, currency, accuracy, clarity, uniqueness, and conformity to academic standards and conventions. If the product has a print counterpart, it is important to determine if the electronic version contains all of the content that is available in the print version. In some cases, the online version may contain the full ASCII text of an article but exclude any images, tables, or other illustrations. If graphics are included in the electronic version, major concerns focus on the presence of image clarity and consistency. Ideally, the online version will have all the content of the print as well as added features and content unique to the electronic environment. The evaluation should note diminished content as well as any value-added features.

Because publishers of aggregator databases lease content, databases often lose access to a specific title after purchase. If the vendor states that all articles are included, the evaluator must ask if editorials, letters, and reviews are included as well. Another common problem is content overlap. Libraries that license more than one aggregator database will want to determine the extent of duplication. JAKE (Jointly Administered Knowledge Environment) is a freeware metadata management system and online database used to find, link, and compare journal titles and union lists (http://jake.med.yale.edu/). It is particularly useful for identifying duplicate full-text holdings.

Access

Access is a critical component of any web-based resource. Two major issues surrounding access include copyright restrictions (copying, lending or electronic reserve) and authentication of institutionally affiliated computers/networks and remote users. Authentication can include automatic login using ID and password, automatic login using IP address, library authentication, and proxy server login. Library authentication, proxy access, and IP range authentication are preferable to the use of passwords. Since the library's representative will need to know the IP range of their institution at the time of licensing, this information should be readily available to team members.

Many librarians believe that walk-in patrons should have full access to electronic resources without having to worry about whether a user is affiliated with the institution. If this is the case, then it should be clearly specified in the contract. Whether evaluating the product on site or from remote access, consider, not just the view of the content, but the output as well. For example, are users able to print, download, e-mail the content, as well as cut and paste from the resource? Wireless Internet access, offered by more and more libraries, will require specific consideration in a license. Standards of acceptable access should be defined in the license agreement.

Timeliness

Many library patrons assume that an electronic resource will always be more up-to-date than its print counterpart will. This is not always true. For example, the print edition of the latest issue of a journal is often received before the online version has been posted. Therefore, standards of acceptable timeliness should be defined in the license agreement. Since most libraries do not "check-in" issues of their electronic journals, they would not know if one was missing. A similar problem surfaces with reference resources that are available electronically. The problem is exacerbated when full-text databases make use of editions in the public domain (Brockman, Neumann, Palmer & Tidline, 2001). Unfortunately, it is difficult to know how a vendor will perform when it comes to timeliness. The evaluator may ask the vendor for customer references or ask a representative of a peer institution using the resource if he or she is satisfied.

Cataloging

When considering electronic materials, the availability and quality of cataloging records are important. Descriptive information about electronic resources should include adequate item-level descriptive metadata. For example, licensing information lacking metadata is like purchasing a book without a title page, table of contents, or index. This underscores the need for the selection team to include members with expertise in bibliographic control and cataloging. It is often worth the extra fee to obtain item-level MARC (machine-readable cataloging) records from the vendor, particularly if the cataloging staff will be overwhelmed adding item records for a large electronic collection (for more information on cataloging electronic resources, the reader is referred to chapter 6 in this volume).

Cataloging a resource also enhances its visibility. Users dislike having to access multiple gateways to find a pertinent resource. Mainstreaming electronic resources into the online catalog is best, avoiding separate gateways whenever possible (Demas, 1994).

Sustainability

Sustainability requires that the cost of acquiring and maintaining a resource reflects lasting value and contributes to the integrity of the collection. One of the most important factors to determine is the archiving service available from the vendor. In most cases, vendors are licensing access rather than selling content. The evaluator must determine whether the content will be available in perpetuity, or if the library loses all access once a subscription is cancelled.

If the vendor assures perpetual access, the archival format must also be considered. Large CD-ROM archive collections are often unwieldy; electronic files must be maintained by regular migration. This is a responsibility not to be undertaken lightly by vendors or libraries, as the maintenance costs of digital objects are estimated to be considerably greater than their original cost (Kenney, 2000).

The policy on retaining electronic backfiles of online data should also be specified in the evaluation. Some vendors have a rolling archive: as new volumes become available, older volumes may be removed. Large-scale digital journal storage projects enhance access to backfiles. For example, JSTOR, a non-profit organization created to digitally archive major scholarly journals, allows participating institutions to integrate JSTOR's archival holdings into their retention policy, allowing them to cancel micrographic backups and store or dispose of archival paper copies (http://www.jstor.org).

Usability

The product trial is a good time to look at the usability of the resource. Usability includes ease of use, Americans with Disabilities Act (ADA) compliance, graphic design features, and navigability. Innovative products are exciting, but their interface design may not be intuitive to users. Another problem is that sites with lots of graphics may be slow to open. Since patrons' access to resources depends upon hardware, software, and network connections, resources must be evaluated using a mix of operating systems and browsers. The evaluator should note the hardware, software, and browsers used on the evaluation form.

While librarians often look for advanced features of interest to the sophisticated researcher, it is equally important to consider the needs of the naïve user. Both basic and advanced search screens should be available and easily located. In addition, the number of available search fields (title, author, and descriptor) and whether fields can be modified should be noted. Help menus should be well marked and have clear, easy-to-understand information. Usability also plays a major role in determining the number of clicks, views, and errors in database usage logs (for additional information on usability, the reader is referred to Chapters 3 and 8 in this volume).

Usage Assessment Statistics

Usage statistics theoretically offer a quantitative method for evaluating the use of electronic resources. In addition, usage statistics are used in basic cost-benefit analyses to determine cost per use of a resource and to justify its expense. However, vendor-supplied statistics vary widely in their features. At a minimum, the vendor should be asked if it complies with the International Coalition of Library Consortia (ICOLC, 2001) standards for usage statistics. Electronic collections team members should be familiar with the standards (a more complete examination of issues in usage statistics is found in Chapter 13 of this volume). Usage statistics not only reveal whether the resource is being used, but also indicate problems with technical performance.

Technical Performance and Service Levels

If a printed resource arrives in a damaged or incomplete state, the publisher will normally replace the copy without question. With electronic resources, however, it may not be easy to justify what is satisfactory and what is not. According to the 1999 ICOLC guidelines on technical performance, vendors should provide information about performance levels, including response time, server down time, and disconnections. The electronic collections team member with a background in systems and network administration is best suited to assess issues of technical performance, however all team members need to be aware of the technical issues that may affect performance.

While a product trial can be a valuable tool for identifying technical problems, it should be noted that vendors might use different servers or websites for trials. Speed of data retrieval often depends upon time of day as well as the particular day of the week. Evaluators need to access the site several times based upon the time/day parameters. It is a good idea to test functionality by downloading large files and printing images and tables. If the processing time is slow, the vendor should be questioned about the causes. Of great significance is the general system performance and network capacity of the vendor, as well as the quality of documentation and technical support offered.

Features That Add Value

There are a number of valuable interoperable features found in electronic resources that are not possible in printed versions. Chief among these is full-text searching and linking, which directly connects the text or images of one document or resource to the text or images of another document or resource. For example, some interfaces offer advanced search features that allow users to store and combine searches, map search terms to thesauri, and manipulate search results by limitation. Others organize and display search results in particularly useful ways, or allow the user to customize the display. However, the sheer number of features are often problematic for users, who must adapt to different operators, search terms, and screen displays (Brockmann, Neumann, Palmer, & Tidline, 2001).

Internet sites with substantive content increasingly offer a variety of added value services to an identified community of users. These services may include current awareness alerts (via email), continuous revisions, topical online forums, e-mail lists, and options for creating personal profiles online. The availability of these services is often reflected in the pricing structure.

Pricing Structure

Like its corporeal counterpart, the virtual library is both a gateway and a destination, but it is a parallel universe with a twist: here corporations create content, subject headings, and pricing structures dynamically, while libraries struggle to define content and price. Unlike printed materials, which have a set cost with a possible discount, electronic resources are regularly priced in a flexible manner. Negotiating prices becomes easier with experience, but the evaluator should be able to find out how the vendor sets its price.

The cost of adding online access to a print subscription varies considerably, from a nominal charge to more than double the cost of the subscription. The electronic collections team must decide if features like full-text searching are worth the additional expense. The business models of some publishers emphasize e-journal subscriptions, making print copies prohibitively expensive or unavailable. Other publishers increase the price of electronic journals if print subscriptions are cancelled. If branch or regional libraries are included in a single site license, it is important to ask if canceling duplicate print subscriptions affects pricing.

Some publishers market their electronic journals as a 'bundle' with a single fee. Either publishers bundle all of their electronic journal titles together or they bundle together both the print and electronic versions of a title. In the first case, the single fee package is deceiving. Although it appears to offer substantial savings per title, it may require that the library accept all the titles published electronically by the publisher. In the second case, bundling print and online journals defeats the potential for cost and space containment. Despite these problems, periodical subscription bundling plans have become popular. Benefits include use of a single search interface, access to substantially discounted new titles, and consolidation of licensing, accounting, and technical support.

NEGOTIATING THE CONTRACT

Many librarians think of the licensing agreement as the method that the vendor uses to protect its own interests. What many people fail to realize is that the licensing agreement also protects the interests of the purchaser. It is important to remember that many of the clauses in the license agreement can be negotiated. For example, the licensing agreement should clearly state whether the data would continue to be accessible if the publisher ceased operation or was purchased by another company. The information contained on the electronic collections team evaluation form for that specific resource would prove helpful during contract negotiation (see Appendix B for categories of evaluative criteria for licensing considerations).

It is good practice to have the university's legal department approve the licensing agreement before it is signed. However, it may not be possible to have all licenses approved by counsel before signing. Thus, a librarian will usually conduct negotiations leading up to the agreement, working in conjunction with university counsel, to prepare a licensing policy with mandated and recommended contractual requirements. The team can create a checklist based on the evaluative criteria it has developed. At larger institutions, a legal department may have certain riders (amendments) that must be included in every university contract.

Negotiating Perpetual Access

Archival rights may be the most difficult area for negotiation, as the legal principles underlying the ownership and licensing of electronic information remain unsettled (Brennan, Hersey, & Harper, 1997). Fortunately, a number of individuals and organizations have created documents, websites, e-mail lists, and model licenses. For example, the *Liblicense* project is a comprehensive resource that includes an e-mail list, model licenses, and a software program that can be used to generate, modify, and track licenses (www.library.yale.edu/~llicense/index.shtml).

CONCLUSION

Considerable attention has been given to the role of electronic resources in library collections. Less attention has been paid to the widespread reallocation of library funds to acquire and maintain electronic resources at the expense of all other library materials. When library resources are acquired to meet immediate information needs rather than because they contribute to the consistency or completeness of the overall collection, a transition to electronic resources is assumed, with little accounting—financial or philosophical—of the cost to the library collection. Electronic collections teams have been established to oversee the collection development process. Having a thorough knowledge of the library's mission and collection parameters enables the teams to create meaningful criteria for the guidance and development of research quality academic collections.

FUTURE TRENDS

Theories on the future of libraries and electronic publishing abound. In some cases, technology moves so quickly that future trends rapidly become past practices. Nevertheless, three consistent trends are the emphasis on managed information, increased collaboration with vendors, and the creation of intellectual content.

Managed information, like managed healthcare, attempts to contain costs and improve outcomes through a combination of approaches that focus on integrated, networked systems and services. These include cooperative collection development, on-demand publishing, and purchasing by the article. OhioLink, a statewide academic consortium, is attempting to create a statewide shared collection based on document delivery, expanded access to virtual resources, and the elimination of duplication (Kohl, 1997). The California State University System Journal Access Core Collection project confronts the worst features of publisher bundling and aggregating by requesting that vendors bundle only those journal titles integral to a statewide core collection (Helfer, 1999). While different in scope and focus, both projects identify and prioritize the acquisition of shared core collections.

Unfortunately, the identification of core journals creates an inelastic market, leaving publishers with little incentive to modify pricing or licensing (Guédon, 2001). To handle the continuous inflation of journal collections, libraries have collaborated with publishers to return competition to a market controlled by monopolies. The Scholarly Publishing and Resources Coalition (SPARC) sponsors a number of global publishing initiatives, with the goal of creating core journals in all disciplines (http://www.arl.org/SPARC/).

In addition to partnering with publishers, libraries create content in a number of ways, most commonly by digitally converting local, special, and research collections. Libraries also curate collections by linking digital objects from separate collections that complement or complete each other. Integrated library management systems make it possible for libraries: to create user-centered gateways to collections, customize subject-oriented portals for identified user communities, and establish brand identity in the information marketplace (Lakos and Gray, 2000).

REFERENCES

Brennan, P., Hersey, K., & Harper, G. (1997). Licensing electronic resources: Strategic and practical considerations for signing electronic information delivery agreements. Washington, D.C.: Association of Research Libraries.

Brockman W.S., Neumann, L., Palmer, C.L., & Tidline, T.J. (2001). *Scholarly work in the humanities and the evolving information environment.* [Electronic version.] Washington, D.C.: Digital Library Federation, Council on Library and Information Resources. Retrieved 1/3/2002 from http://www.clir.org.

Demas, S. (1994). Collection development for the electronic library: A conceptual and organizational model. Library Hi Tech, 12(3):71-80.

Evans, G. E. (2000). *Developing library and information center collections.* Englewood, Colo.: Libraries Unlimited.

Greenstein, Daniel. (2001). Preface. In T. D. Jewell, *Selection and presentation of commercially available electronic resources: Issues and practices.* (pp. iv-v). [Electronic version.] Washington, D.C.: Council on Library and Information Resources. Retrieved 10/5/2001 from *http://www.clir.org.*

Guédon, J.C. (2001). In Oldenburg's long shadow: Librarians, research scientists, publishers, and the control of scientific publishing. *ARL Proceedings,* 138. [Electronic version]. Retrieved 10/11/2001 from *http://www.arl.org/arl/proceedings/138/guedon.html.*

Helfer, D.S. (1999). Making digital collection development a reality: The CSU JACC project. Searcher, 7(5):57-59.

International Coalition of Library Consortia (ICOLC). (1999). *Guidelines for technical issues in request for proposal (RFP) requirements and contract negotiations.* Retrieved 12/2/2001 from http://www.library.yale.edu/consortia/techreq.html.

International Coalition of Library Consortia (ICOLC). (2001). *Guidelines for statistic measures of web-based information resources.* Retrieved 1/20/

2002 from http://www.library.yale.edu/consortia/2001webstats.htm.

Jewell, T.D. (2001). *Selection and presentation of commercially available electronic resources: issues and practices*. [Electronic version.] Washington, D.C.: Digital Library Federation, Council on Library and Information Resources. Retrieved 10/5/2001 from http://www.clir.org.

Kenney, A.R. (2000). Mainstreaming digitization into the mission of cultural repositories. In *Collections, content, and the web*. [Electronic version.] Washington, D.C.: Council on Library and Information Resources. Retrieved 11/4/2001 from http://www.clir.org.

Kohl, D.F. (1997). Farewell to all that...Transforming Collection development to fit the virtual library context: The OhioLINK experience. In Schwartz, C.A. (Ed.), *Restructuring Academic Libraries: Organizational Development in the Wake of Technological Change, Publications in Librarianship* no. 49. [Electronic version]. Chicago: American Library Association. Retrieved 1/11/2002 from http://www.ala.org/acrl/pil/kohl.html.

Lakos, A. &. Gray, C. (2000). Personalized library portals as an organizational culture change agent. *Information Technology and Libraries*, 19(4):169-174.

Manoff, M. (2000). Hybridity, mutability, multiplicity: Theorizing electronic library collections. *Library Trends*, 48(4)857-876.

Martin, M.S. (1995). Collection development and finance: a guide to strategic library-materials budgeting. Chicago: American Library Association.

Pitschmann, Louis A. (2001). *Building sustainable collections of free third-party web resources*. Washington, D.C.: Digital Library Federation, Council on Library and Information Resources.

Principles for licensing electronic resources. (1997). Retrieved 9/17/2001 from the Association of Research Libraries [ARL] web site at http://www.arl.org/scomm/licensing/principles.html.

Thornton, G.A. (2000). Impact of electronic resources on collection development, the roles of librarians, and library consortia. *Library Trends*, 48(4)842-856.

Yale University Library Council on Library & Information Resources. (2002) *Liblicense: licensing digital information, a resource for librarians*. Retrieved 1/16/2002 from http://www.library.yale.edu/~llicense/index.shtml.

APPENDIX A: A SAMPLE VENDOR EVALUATION FORM

- Name of the person completing the evaluation:
- Name of vendor:
- Contact information for vendor (Address, Telephone, Email address).
- Brief description of the electronic resource's content, including chronological, geographical and language coverage.
- Is a demo available for this resource? If so, where?
- What is the genre of the electronic resource (citation, full-text, full-text image, multimedia, numeric, etc.)?
- Comment on the quality of the search engine, including user-friendliness, access, and speed.
- Describe the pricing structure for the resource. Attach a vendor quote if available. **
- Is the resource available as a subscription or only as a lease (will the library get to retain permanent access to the information)?
- Does the electronic resource overlap or duplicate content already available in another format? If so, what is the cost of the duplicated collection?
- Does the electronic resource provide superior access to other formats/vendors?
- Comment on storage, hardware, software and connectivity issues. Are additional software applications needed to run, download or print data? Attach vendor specifications if available.
- Describe the archiving strategies available for the electronic resource.
- Is the resource Z39.50 compliant?
- Does the vendor supply usage statistics? In what format?
- If applicable, is interlibrary loan permitted?
- Are bibliographic records available for the items included in this resource? Please describe. Include source, cost, and format information if known.
- Is vendor training available?
- Does the vendor provide promotional materials that can be used for marketing purposes?
- What is the feedback from potential users?

* Specific pricing will not normally be available until the contract negotiations have been completed.

APPENDIX B: EVALUATIVE CRITERIA AND LICENSING CONSIDERATIONS

VENDOR VIABILITY

Evaluative Criteria	Contractual Considerations
✓ Years in business	✓ Vendor warranties right to license
✓ Public or private	✓ Vendor agrees to archival rights if business is sold or fails
✓ Publisher or third party	✓ Written license trumps "click-through"
✓ Provides current and comparable references	

ACCESS

Evaluative Criteria	Contractual Considerations
✓ Purchase or lease	✓ Define & describe what is leased/purchased
✓ Years covered	✓ Require notice of substantive change in content
✓ Indexes	✓ Define substantive change
✓ Abstracts	✓ Define minimal notice (30 days)
✓ Full-text	✓ Define option to terminate
✓ % Complete (vs. print)	✓ Define pro-rating of refunds
✓ Graphics	✓ Define timeliness
✓ Quality of imaging	✓ Define extent of backfiles
✓ Value added features	
✓ Release dates for print and online resources	

AGGREGATOR DATABASES

Evaluative Criteria	Contractual Considerations
✓ Number of documents	✓ As above
✓ Titles included	✓ Specify extent or percent of content or title(s) that are integral to the agreement, and that the loss of such content or title(s) is grounds for pro-rated refund and/or cancellation without penalty
✓ Selected or full content	
✓ What is omitted	
✓ What % meets CD mission	
✓ What % duplication	
✓ How are changes communicated and managed?	

CATALOGING

Evaluative Criteria	Contractual Considerations
✓ OPAC integration	See Technical Performance
✓ Item level MARC records available	
✓ Hooks to holdings	
✓ Descriptive metadata	

ARCHIVING

Evaluative Criteria	Contractual Considerations
✓ Content availability past subscription dates	✓ If limited license, specify time period covered
✓ Policy on changes in vendor status	✓ If licensing permanent use, specify right to make & keep own archival copy
✓ Method of archive delivery	✓ If vendor provides archival copies, specify format & delivery method.
✓ Archive retention policy	
✓ Administrative metadata	

Continued on next page

ACCESS

Evaluative Criteria	Contractual Considerations
✓ Copyright restrictions	✓ Define authorized users: students, staff, faculty (adjunct, emeritus, & visiting), walk-ins
✓ Interlibrary loan	
✓ Distance learners	✓ Define institutional IP range/s
✓ Authentication process	✓ Include remote sites (branches, affiliates)
✓ Remote usage/proxy services	✓ Include wireless access; & right to broadcast
✓ Desktop delivery	✓ Include remote users (proxy access)
✓ Wireless access	✓ Define use consistent with Fair Use
✓ Training library faculty & staff	✓ Education (E-reserve; Course packs; temporary passwords/additional simultaneous users for training)
✓ Bibliographic instruction	
	✓ Research (print, copy, download, e-mail, quote)
	✓ ILL within CONTU guidelines for print
	✓ Avoid nondisclosure agreements that require permission for quoting
	✓ Reasonable notice of copyright violation
	✓ Limited liability for users actions

USABILITY

Evaluative Criteria	Contractual Considerations
✓ Navigation sense	✓ Vendor provides reliable online connectivity comparable to similar products
✓ Browser compatibility	
✓ Ability to perform on typical user or library systems	✓ Vendor should be given a specified period of time to correct malfunctions or defects. If not corrected, licensee may opt to return product for pro-rated refund
✓ Quality of online help	
✓ Search functions & ease of use	
✓ Structural metadata	

TECHNICAL PERFORMANCE

Evaluative Criteria	Contractual Considerations
✓ Speed of data retrieval in actual production environment	✓ Licensee performs a timely (30-45 days) evaluation of product upon licensing access
✓ Adequate simultaneous usage allowance	✓ Both parties provide timely notice of technical defects or problems that arise later
✓ Maintenance expectations	✓ Technical specifications should indicate expectations as well as define requirements
✓ Interface requirements	
✓ Service levels for support	✓ Licensor provides a prompt response to requests for technical support
✓ Compliance with ICOLC standards	
✓ Outage time	✓ Permit change in # of simultaneous users at reasonable cost
✓ Print process	
✓ E-mail process	✓ Support agreement should be addendum to license agreement
✓ Ability to copy/paste	
✓ Downloading capability	✓ Specify compliance with ICOLC standards for technical performance and usage statistics
✓ Provision of usage statistics	
	✓ Reference materials or user manuals may be attached to the legal agreement
	✓ Specify penalties for failure to perform
	✓ Specify allowable downtime for routine maintenance and minimum notice
	✓ Specify uptime (continuous service) minimum

Chapter III

Libraries as Publishers of Digital Video

William D. Kearns
The Louis de la Parte Florida Mental Health Institute at
the University of South Florida-Tampa, USA

Dubbed as the next "Killer Application" (Hanss, 2001), digital video's anticipated impact on computer networks is enormous. Few other applications are so severely impacted by networks incapable of delivering quality of service guarantees for the latency and delay with which video stations receive information packets. The goal of this chapter is to briefly discuss the teaching and research uses of video materials in academic environments, inform librarians of the various forms into which video materials may be encoded, the strengths and weaknesses of the media formats, and to argue for a comprehensive implementation plan when considering the distribution of video resources. We will conclude the chapter with an illustration of how one academic library employed database technology to create a video card catalog accessible from the Internet.

ENHANCING THE ACADEMIC ENVIRONS OF RESEARCH AND TEACHING

Video resources have always served as significant enhancements to the classroom as a way of broadening the experience of the student in lieu of expensive or impossible field trips. Early exposure to such experiences can spark a lifelong interest in learning and exploration and can have inestimable value. Digital video is a relative newcomer to multimedia and presents great promise to educators as a vehicle to present existing materials to large numbers of students at disparate locations, create linkages between video and textual materials in a 'real-time collage' of information, and stimulate face to face conversations with students hundreds (or perhaps thousands) of miles away. Psychologists and human factors specialists are interested in the subtle nuances of human interaction over video-enhanced communication to make it more natural and desirable than telephone communications.

Few educators are aware of what tools are often available to them to enhance their teaching and research endeavors. Fewer still are aware of the subtleties involved in selecting the best one for the job or the numerous options each possesses that may dramatically enhance the learning experience of the student. For example, streaming audio technology is used extensively in support of classroom teaching due to the relative ease with which low bandwidth signals are propagated through the Internet (Furr, 2001). Low bandwidth digital video technologies (multiple still images) have also been used successfully (Michelich, 2002) over slow speed modem connections, serving as highly useful adjuncts to classroom learning. The creation and distribution of streaming video is a considerably more complicated process than the transmission of multiple still images. We will begin with a discussion of the major video formats currently supported.

MEDIA FORMATS

The choice of digital media format is perhaps the most salient factor in obtaining acceptable digital video products for use in the library. Information specialists should not enter into this decision lightly, since their choice may likely determine if the project can be accomplished within budget, will be widely or narrowly available to the public, or of sufficient quality that viewers will find it appealing. A format that delivers only 15 frames per second is well suited for the proverbial "talking head" but is poorly suited to action sequences where camera angles and subjects' locations change rapidly. Viewers seldom watch an unattractive presentation, resulting in a waste of resources except as a training exercise on what not to do.

While it is beyond the scope of this chapter to discuss the finer artistic points of video production, it is paramount that academic librarians consult with professionals from their campus television station, distance education departments, or multimedia centers for assistance in their video production. The subtle nuances created by proper lighting, acoustics, camera angles, set design, and tightly written dialogue and continuity can readily make or break a video production and can scarcely be understated in terms of their importance. A high-quality production of dry content may be seldom viewed, while a compelling and moving video may be quite popular even if it is only available in a postage stamp sized window at 15 frames/sec. This field is changing rapidly and many caveats and cautions specific to technologies discussed within this paper may not be applicable at the time of publication.

MPEG2 Format

A discussion of available formats begins with MPEG2. MPEG is an acronym for the Motion Picture Experts Group (see *http://mpeg.telecomitalialab.com/*), an engineering workgroup that establishes standards for the specification and interoperability of digital video technologies. The MPEG2 standard is perhaps one of the most widely known formats and is used extensively in the television broadcasting industry. Agnew (1999) provides an excellent discussion of the specific parameters of all forms of MPEG encoding and contrasts them with proprietary standards developed by other vendors. The bit rate for an MPEG2 product may be as low as 2 Mbit/sec., but it is extensible into the high definition television (HDTV) ranges of 15 Mbit/sec. or more where the sharpest and clearest images are obtained. Frame rates for this standard are typically 29.97 frames/sec., which renders an exceptionally smooth image free of staccato movements typical of lower frame rate video. Materials produced in MPEG2 format are considered the gold standard by which others are measured. However, their creation and use comes with a significant price tag.

Before the creation of any video, it is important to determine one's audience. MPEG2 technology is well suited to wireless and cable broadcast mediums and MPEG2 distribution over Internet Protocol (IP) is presently in its infancy. MPEG2 transmissions from traditional broadcasting facilities are expensive due to the high infrastructure costs associated with their storage and distribution. Distribution over IP includes robotic "video-servers" capable of supplying video-on-demand across the Internet either gratis or for a user fee. Current home technologies for cable modems and distributed subscriber lines (DSL) support in practice less than 1 Mbit/ sec. and are wholly unsuitable for MPEG2 transmission over IP. Currently, MPEG2 over IP is supportable only for organizations capable of delivering 100 Mbit/sec. switched Ethernet to their viewers.

A common misconception is that 10 Mbit/sec. switched Ethernet will supply sufficient network bandwidth to support the reception of a 5 Mbit/sec. video signal to a viewer's computer. Currently, due to inefficiencies in the network TCP (Transmission Control Protocol) stack on some computers, they utilize roughly 33% of available Ethernet network bandwidth. Thus, a 5 Mbit/sec. MPEG2 video signal will require a minimum of 15 Mbit/sec. switched Ethernet local area network capability, which therefore excludes viewers with slower connections. Persons attempting to view MPEG2 over these slow connections will likely receive the video with substantial frame loss and broken audio and may be perplexed as to the source of the problem, resulting in great consternation for library staff charged with resolving the user's difficulty. Organizations incapable of supplying 100 Mbit/sec. switched Ethernet networking between the transmitter and receiver should consider MPEG1 or MPEG4 as alternative formats for distributing video resources over their network.

In addition to the network limitations, it is important to note that the use of MPEG2 over IP is also hindered by the computing capabilities of the receiving machines. Most personal computers presently are not sufficiently powerful to use only software to decode an MPEG2 signal of 5 Mbit/sec., but exceptions do exist. Hardware decoder boards are available, yet sufficient variations exist in the implementation of MPEG2 over IP to enable transmitted materials to be encoded into file formats that are alien to viewing stations decoder boards. Thus, the choice of which decoder board is a critical factor if MPEG2 resources are made available.

A related consideration is the amount of storage space on the viewing machine's local disk drive (in the case of local storage of the video file) or on the robotic video-server consumed by individual MPEG2, MPEG1, or MPEG4 files. File sizes may be determined a priori by defining the following:
1)   The length of the presentation in seconds; and
2)   The bit rate at which the presentation is encoded (Mbit/sec. or Kbit/sec.)

As an example, to ascertain the expected file size of a ½ hour-long video presentation encoded at 5 Mbit/sec, use the following algorithm:
½ hour = 1800 sec.
1800 sec. X 5,000,000 bit/sec. = 9,000,000,000 bits.

There are 8 bits to one byte, and by dividing we find:
9,000,000,000 bits / 8 = 1,125,000,000 bytes (or 1.125 Gbytes).

At over 1 Gbyte per file, it is readily apparent that storing and tape archiving high quality video assets can be an expensive proposition. Maintaining assets on individual workstations carries with it the danger that the resource may be erased. The distribution of MPEG2 video resources via robotic video-servers is in its infancy. Network bandwidth limitations, variations in encoding technologies, insufficiently powerful viewing computers, and the lack of universally interoperable and inexpensive hardware decoder boards have slowed MPEG2's acceptance. Distribution systems such as Callisto Media System's "Voyager" product, Real Media's MPEG2 venture, and IBM's VideoCharger products are examples of attempts to make MPEG2 video over IP universally available to the public over high bandwidth networks. As home network speeds increase, the viability of such distribution systems will become more evident.

MPEG1 Format

The MPEG1 standard provides a number of highly desirable characteristics missing from MPEG2, including the ability to be viewed without special hardware, convertibility to a variety of other formats (Real Media, Microsoft's MPEG4, and QuickTime), and lessened storage requirements. While it is still necessary to acquire separate hardware encoder (but not decoder) boards to translate video material into MPEG1 (and MPEG2) files, it is expected that the next generation of personal computers will support this feature natively. The MPEG1 format's upper limit is 1.99 Mbit/sec. and the frame rate is 29.97 frames/sec., offering smooth rendering and satisfactory viewing. However there is some loss of sharpness in the video, due to the bit rate at which the material was encoded. Similarly, MPEG1's use of bit rates of up to 1.99 Mbit/sec. make it a candidate for delivery over 10 Mbit/sec. switched Ethernet networks, a consideration germane to smaller libraries whose network may not support 100 Mbit/sec. switched Ethernet service. File sizes are proportionately smaller than MPEG2, although the size of the display area for the video on the computer is reduced. The computational overhead for displaying MPEG1 is much lower than for MPEG2 files, enabling the computer to multitask more efficiently. MPEG1 viewers are supplied as integrated components of the Microsoft Windows operating system (Microsoft's NetShow), and readily available players, such as Real Media's product and QuickTime, all support MPEG1.

For all the apparent advantages of the MPEG1 format, materials cannot be easily streamed to sites possessing DSL or cable modem technology. While it is possible to reduce the available viewing area of MPEG1 video materials (by adjusting the aspect ratio and number of pixels in the horizontal and vertical planes) to lessen bandwidth and thus increase availability, it may not be desirable to do so due to the loss of detail in the video. Nevertheless, improvements in home network technologies may shortly render this issue moot. A third alternative format fortunately exists that permits reasonably high-quality video transmission in conjunction with built in "intelligence" which allows bit rates to be modified according to local network conditions.

MPEG4 Format

The MPEG4 standard, unlike that of MPEG2, was a direct outgrowth of the computer industry. Faced with the challenge of producing video worth watching yet of sufficiently low bandwidth that it could be received over a modem connection, several firms (notably Microsoft, Real Media, and Apple Computer) have worked independently to create digital video encoding and distribution software. Microsoft has distributed the server software and other packages freely to the public for use on Intel-based platforms. These products allow the user to select among dozens of options for how the video will be encoded and delivered, ranging from bit rates of 56 Kb/sec. for modems to 1 Mb/sec. for local area network connections. The audio quality can range from that of a primitive telephone connection (lowest bandwidth consumption) to CD-quality sound (highest bandwidth), with corresponding frame rates set from 15 frames/sec. to 29.97 frames/sec. Netterfield (1999) provides an excellent discussion of the use of MPEG4-based streaming media across campus networks to create virtual lecture halls at a major southern university.

Unlike the MPEG2 and MPEG1 standards, the MPEG4 standard is sensitive to movement within the video field and is capable of distinguishing foreground from background. As a result, the video stream sent to a viewer's computer may actually be less than the selected rate at which it was encoded, especially if the subject of the video moves little or not at all during transmission. The impact of this methodology should not be underestimated, for network bandwidth is a precious commodity and products that minimize its use increase their likelihood of traversing congested networks and arriving at their destination intact. It is more difficult to determine the final file size for an MPEG4 presentation since the software encodes only those features in the input video stream that change. For example, a video of a stationary lecturer encoded at the same frame and bit rate as a video of a football game will consume much less disk space even if they are of the same duration.

A particularly clever strategy employed by the Microsoft MPEG4 product allows multiple encoding formats to be supported in a single video file. The strategy allows for a computer on a congested network to request and receive the same video as that of a machine on an uncongested network but at a bit rate that is appropriate to its local network topology. In the first case, the receiving machine will get a video stream that is sent at 15 frames/sec. and perhaps at 64 Kb/sec. with audio quality similar to that of a telephone. In the second case, the same file will be streamed at 29.97 frames/sec. and at 700 Kb/sec., delivering a relatively high-quality image with CD-quality sound. The choice of which format is determined dynamically by the robotic video-server software and is invisible to the user, making it ideal for large-scale distribution across the Internet.

MPEG4 and Active Agent Technologies

With the emerging MPEG4 encoding technologies, Microsoft has introduced an enhancement to the standard to serve as a conduit for meta information. It is possible to encapsulate commands in the stream, that cause the receiver's machine to open web pages associated with the streamed content. Hence, one can automatically provide the viewer all associated materials, including graphics and other video segments, making this delivery mechanism exceptionally powerful. Additionally, Microsoft's MPEG4 standard allows for the creation of unique segments that are the concatenations of other clips extracted dynamically from existing MPEG4 video files. This allows for the creation of new products without having to painstakingly re-encode existing material, saving valuable time for library staff. Bookmarking within the video file allows users to skip to locations within the presentation explicitly earmarked by the librarian.

STREAMING MPEG AND NETWORK BANDWIDTH CONSIDERATIONS

Throughout this discussion, network bandwidth factors have been tangentially referred to without explanation, yet they are a major determinant of the quality of the stream received from a robotic video-server. The reader will recall that a 10,000,000 byte (10 Mbyte or its 80 Mbit equivalent) video file stored on either a local PC's hard disk or on a streaming media server will (ideally) be played back at the rate at which it was encoded, which for the sake of argument we will assume is 5 Mbit/sec. At this rate, the entire file will be played in 16 seconds, assuming either a perfect network connection (in the case of streaming media) or a personal computer hard disk that is capable of delivering the data at the rate of 5 Mbit/sec. to the processor.

In the case of network delivery, the situation is rarely perfect, as congestion within the network by other computers exchanging data consumes available bandwidth in unpredictable ways. Bandwidth is either shared or switched. In those cases where bandwidth is shared, all of the computers on that segment of the network contend for a piece of the 10 Mbit/sec. bandwidth, effectively slicing it into increasingly smaller segments as more machines contribute to the network traffic (see CREN, 2000, for a full discussion of these factors). The result is that high quality video may be received only when most machines are shut off and network traffic is at a minimum. As these conditions are seldom obtained during normal working hours, a change in network topology to switched Ethernet is highly desirable.

Switched bandwidth (10 Mbit/sec. Ethernet) grants each machine a unique 10 Mbit/sec. of bandwidth and carries up to 3 Mbit/sec. of video information to a personal computer with minimal interruption. It must be recognized, however, that for such a strategy to be successful, it is incumbent upon the receiver of the video information to ensure that the entire pathway from the robotic video-server to the receiving personal computer is a minimum of 10 Mbit/sec. switched Ethernet or faster. Many instances exist where video data from a robotic video-server are sent intact to the campus network but fail to arrive at a user's personal computer due to an inadequate local area network infrastructure within the user's building. Such cases are illustrative of the vaunted "Last Mile Problem" that has vexed network engineers charged with developing high bandwidth applications for wide distribution across the Internet.

While MPEG4 offers advantages under circumstances where network congestion is unpredictable (automatically switching the transmission bit rate and frame rate to adjust for the congested network conditions), it cannot compensate for situations where congestion is almost complete. Under those conditions, streaming video transmission is impossible, and network bandwidth must be increased through significant investments in infrastructure.

In addition to the technical considerations for normal delivery, there are two other areas that librarians must take into consideration when developing media content. These are the delivery of streaming video to individuals with disabilities and access to content via search and retrieval mechanisms. Content, format, and hardware/ software considerations must be reviewed to ensure access.

ACCESSIBILITY

The Americans with Disabilities Act (ADA) requires covered entities to furnish appropriate auxiliary aids and services to ensure effective communication with individuals with disabilities, unless doing so would result in a fundamental alteration to the program or service or in an undue burden (see 28 C.F.R. 36.303; 28 C.F.R. 35.160). In addition, the federal government requires accessibility for all federal agencies (and federal grant recipients who create web or digital content) to meet Section 508 of the Rehabilitation Act: Electronic and Information Technology Accessibility Standards (*http://www.access-board.gov/508.htm*). Auxiliary aids include taped texts, Brailled materials, large print materials, closed captioning, and other methods of making audio and visual media available to people with disabilities.

It has been found that low bit-rate video streams at less than 15 frames/sec., making the deciphering of American Sign Language difficult or impossible because of a staccato effect. This is an important consideration when digitizing legacy materials, as significant staff time must be spent in adding textual material to complement the auditory portion of the video stream to make it ADA compliant. The goal of any library attempting to distribute digital video should be to enhance the learning experience of its patrons, irrespective of their abilities. To the extent that a technology disenfranchises any group of patrons, it works against that goal, and its use should be reconsidered. Further, the inclusion of closed captioning in the video stream renders library materials available to a wider audience than might normally be the case. Closed captioning also provides a method for viewers to gain information from a video stream that has audibility problems due to the deterioration of the primary source material and may also provide an avenue for video materials to be used in regions of the library where audio speakers are forbidden due to noise restrictions. For more information concerning accessibility issues, see The World Wide Web Consortium (W3C) site (*http://www.w3.org/WAI/*).

INDEXING AND RETRIEVAL OF VIDEO MATERIALS

There is significant interest in the electronic archiving and retrieval of video materials, although the technology for doing so is in a nascent stage. It is entirely possible to archive materials based upon the mechanical extraction of features, that may only be relevant to a machine but have little meaning to a human viewer. Software exists which will scan a video stream for the presence of relevant objects, persons, or settings and will develop a word list based upon conversations between actors, thus leading to the development of basic retrieval tools based upon these elements (see Virage's system for video archiving and delivery at *http://www.virage.com* and IBM's Videocharger product at *http://www.ibm.com*). Although many such programs can generate an "index", what they are actually generating is a concordance. A concordance has no cross-references, no subentries, and no collocation of terms. A concordance generator scans a file and compares the character strings with an "exclude list" or a "stop list". "Stop words" include articles, prepositions, conjunctions, and common terms. After the files are scanned and the stop words excluded, the final list is presented in an alphabetical order with the reference locator attached. However, these programs do not generate an index file that contains all the important associations between various keywords and the images that make up the video file.

Unfortunately, word lists are not the most reliable mechanism for indexing a specific transaction on a videotape or video file. Words may be taken out of context in the video and result in a given segment being misclassified. The classic example is when a video discussing the economic aspects of the "dinosaurs" of the American auto industry was inadvertently recovered on a search really meant to find videos pertaining to a discussion on the Paleozoic era. The level of artificial intelligence in even the best-automated indexing systems does not approach the simplest analysis by a professional librarian. Librarians trained in classifying and indexing digital video are the best at extracting deep meaning from the materials and will probably retain this position of prominence for many years as artificial intelligence is slowly improved. Currently, it is not realistic to expect artificial intelligence systems to be able to complete one of the highest human functions of extracting subtle meaning from the spoken word and setting variables.

In the project to be described in the next section, a video database whose materials were archived by a professional librarian using the MARC record format was developed in-house for access by Internet2 and Internet1 users.

THE STREAMING VIDEO PROJECT

Part of the mission of the Louis de la Parte Florida Mental Health Institute at the University of South Florida is to inform professionals of new and effective measures for treating mental illness, to foster closer links between service providers and their clientele, and to clearly represent the mental health needs of the citizens of Florida to the State legislature. In support of these aims, the de la Parte Institute established one of the first World Wide Websites in Florida in 1993. Online access to research library holdings were made available to the public in 1995. Numerous direct-submission technologies were developed at the Institute, which allowed Web browsers to place book renewal requests, register for conferences, etc., before E-commerce became a household word.

In 1998, the University of South Florida was awarded an Advanced Networking Infrastructure and Research Grant by the National Science Foundation. Several meritorious applications were developed by the USF Libraries, one located at the de la Parte Institute. The purpose of the Institute's meritorious application was to develop a searchable database of on-line video archives capable of being viewed across a number of network bandwidths ranging from 56 kb/sec. up to 1Mbit/sec. The Institute's interest was in furthering the dissemination of knowledge about various mental illnesses and lessening the stigma associated with them. To that end, the Institute made the decision to deliver mental health information to the public in a video format that would inform the viewer and provide valuable examples of how to deal with delicate interpersonal situations involving persons with mental health problems. The target audience consisted of the general public, mental health educators and practitioners, legislators, and network researchers who might see, in distributed video, a way to better bring people together by using high-speed Internet technology.

As part of the Institute's commitment to enhancing communication with the public, the Institute's Computer Support Center and the Research Library evolved a strategy to integrate streaming video technologies into its outreach efforts. A set of goals were established early in the development schedule to ensure that the system would be:

1.) Universally accessible through low-speed data networks (e.g., modems) and Internet1;

2.)   Capable of providing broadband high quality video if network conditions (such as Internet2 access) were available;

3.)   Easily updated by a librarian using conventional tools (e.g. Procite); and

4.)   Inexpensive to establish and maintain on a conventional server platform (UNIX).

At the time of the project's inception, a number of products were in early development for the real-time extraction of features from streaming video and audio. The indexing of these features provided a retrieval mechanism for video based upon rudimentary scene content. However, since the artificial intelligence of such systems ranked well behind the indexing capabilities of a trained professional librarian, a decision was made to support a manual categorization scheme for video archives that followed the MARC (Machine Readable Cataloging) record format used by the state university system's libraries.

The coding and classification matrices for adding audiovisual materials to an existing library catalog are well defined (Gorman & Winkler, 1998). The processing and classification of all video materials places a heavy burden upon the librarian, who must adhere to strict guidelines while coding the information for retrieval. Important nuances in the material, which are only detectable by a trained observer, must not be overlooked. Fast-forwarding through the video material was not an option since all processing had to be done in real-time. Once the content had been correctly identified and classified, the classificatory textual material was entered into a Procite database on a personal computer for storage and mainte-nance. In addition, fields containing hypertext information regarding streaming video URLs, the location of the viewer(s) on the generated web page, and the relative size of the resulting image were embedded in the Procite database before porting the information to the UNIX (Web accessible) database for public distribution.

At the time of this project's inception, no Web accessible interface had been developed for the use of Boolean operators to retrieve video materials either in Procite or in other database languages. PostgresSQL (Momjian, 2001) was selected as the database to contain the ported Procite library records for several reasons. First, PostgresSQL was a fully relational database capable of storing large volumes of data and large objects. Second, it supported Structured Query Language (SQL) calls. Third, it could be interfaced with web pages via the Practical Extraction and Reporting Language (PERL). Finally, it was freely available to universities.

The porting of data from Procite to the PostgresSQL database was not accomplished without modification of the original field structure. Procite has a record structure that varies, contingent upon the type of material entered.

Figure 1: Sample Catalog Record with Embedded Viewer

author : Burr, Diane W. //Mullins, Larry C.//Rich, Thomas A.//
Roorda, James A.//Boucher, Louisette A.//Zuk, Irene M.//Oliver,
Kimberly R.//Sullivan-Mintz, Judith
title : Older Homeless Adults in America. Part 9: Law enforcement
collection : Webcast (1000kb)
date : 1992
location : System requirements: Internet connectivity (1000kb),
Web browser software, Microsoft Media Player. If you do not see
a viewer in the field below this message, you will need to download
MediaPlayer from this site.
extent : 15:34 minutes
pages :

note :
abstract : This nine-part video series was produced by the Institute's
Department of Aging and Mental Health in 1992. Funded by the
Retirement Research Foundation, the series was developed as
a training program to support education efforts in the state of Florida.
Part 9 (original title: "A Social Problem, Not a Crime: a video guide for
law enforcement") reviews the demographics of the older homeless
adults, the effects of deinstitutionlization and economic conditions,
medications, physical health problems, and the older homeless adult
as a victim of other crime on the streets.
callnumber : In process (In-house collection)
descriptors : webcast 1000/ internet2/ elderly/ staff training/ Roorda,
James R. (scriptwriter)/Roorda, James R. (narrator)/streaming video
webcast -- educational, training narrative/ homelessness/ mentally ill/ grant/
Retirement Research Foundation/ Aging and Mental Health/ AMH/ Aged/
older homeless adults/ social policy/ vignette/ community mental health s
services/ homeless persons -- mental health services -- United States/ homeless
persons -- services for -- Florida/ housing -- United States/ deinstitutionaliza-
tion/ law enforcement/ crisis intervention/ stereotypes/ stigma/ labeling

PostgresSQL, on the other hand, has a fixed record structure that is set up at the time the table is created and is relatively permanent. Discussions with library staff resolved the formatting issue by selecting a template for exporting the data from Procite that maintained the integrity of the information yet allowed for a fixed field template in PostgresSQL. Data transfer between the two systems (Procite and PostgresSQL) was accomplished via tab delimited ASCII (American Standard Computer Information Interchange) and included all hypertext URLs necessary to allow direct access to video resources on the robotic video-server.

The robotic video-server chosen was Microsoft's NetShow MPEG4 streaming media server. This product provided the following options. Video data could be encoded one time in a format capable of using as much bandwidth as was available to the user but could decrease to as little as was available (e.g., 56 Kb/sec. at 15 frames/sec.) if needed. The video stream supported fast-forward, rewind, pause, and an internal reference table that allowed the viewer to select points in the presentation (skip ahead or backwards) without having to view the entire presentation. The MPEG4 format supported random access within a given video stream, allowing a completely new video stream to be made up of fragments created by splicing together the randomly accessed specific locations within other video files. These fragments could be displayed as a single video and archived with a unique MARC record entry if so desired. It was also possible to begin the display of any video file anywhere within its duration. Closed captioning was available for ADA compliance. Active Agent capabilities permitted linked Web-accessible materials to be brought up during the video presentation to enhance the viewing experience of the audience.

The resulting amalgamation of the UNIX and Microsoft systems is very robust (see http://videodb.fmhi.usf.edu). While PostgresSQL is not exceptionally fast database, it is reliable and since all queries are done on sub-string matches (and/or/not) across eight different fields (including Author, Title, Abstract, Collection, Call Number, Extent, Notes, or Descriptors in clusters of as many as three fields), it is possible to be very precise in the use of recall terms. Queries, once submitted, return to the viewer in what appears to be card catalog entries, with a viewer window containing controls for fast-forwarding, pause, play, stop, rewind, a drop down list of topics within the video, and a mute button for the audio. The viewer could play a single video or multiple videos if he or she so desired, although multiple videos consumed significant bandwidth resources (one stream per video) and produced an audio output that was the compilation of several audio streams yielding a cacophony.

CONCLUSION

This project demonstrated that a Web-accessible Unix database supporting structured query language (SQL) calls could return large amounts of high quality video to networked workstations located on the campus network or on other Internet2 university networks. Low bandwidth versions of the video were made available through the Internet as a function of either the deliberate choice by the viewer or through an MPEG4 encoding format that supported multiple bit-rates. This product has been in use continuously since 1999 and was demonstrated nationally at the March 2000 Annual Member Meeting of Internet2 in Washington, D.C. (see http://apps.internet2.edu/demos2000/march00summary.htm for details).

FUTURE TRENDS

Streaming media holds great promise as a way to communicate more effectively over large distances and epochs with an ever-increasing audience. The technology permits encoding based upon numerous factors, including the quality of the network connection and the figure/ground relationship of the subject matter. Further advances in intelligent processing of the video stream will allow for encoding more sophisticated metadata and interactive components into the stream. The cost for network bandwidth will continue to decline in the interim, making access to library video resources ubiquitous.

REFERENCES

Agnew, G. (1999). *Digital Video for the next millennium. Video Development Initiative (VIDE).* [Electronic Resource]. Retrieved 9/11/2001 from http://sunsite.utk.edu/video/1.shtml.

Corporation for Research and Educational Networking (CREN) (2000). *Networked digital video with guest experts Joel Mambretti and Bob Taylor.* [Electronic Resource]. Retrieved 10/11/2001 from http://www.cren.net/know/techtalk/events/netdigvideo.html.

Furr, G. (2001). The educational applications of streaming audio: Accessible, do-it-yourself multimedia. The Technology Source, January/February 2001. [Electronic Resource]. Retrieved 1/11/2001 from http://ts.mivu.org/default.asp?show=article&id=826.

Gorman, M. & Winkler, P.W. (Eds). (1998). *Anglo-American Cataloguing Rules* (2nd ed.). Chicago: American Library Association.

Hanss, T. (2001). Digital video: Internet2 killer application or Dilbert's nightmare? Educause Review Articles. [Electronic Resource]. Retrieved 11/11/2001 from http://www.educause.edu/ir/library/pdf/erm0130t.pdf.

Michelich, V. (2002). Streaming media to enhance teaching and improve learning. *The Technology Source,* January/February. [Electronic Resource]. Retrieved 9/11/2001 from http://ts.mivu.org/default.asp?show=article&id=941

Momjian, B. (2001). The history of PostgresSQL development. [Electronic Resource]. Retrieved 9/11/2001 from http://www.ca.postgresql.org/docs/devhistory.html.

Netterfield, T. (1999). The Building of a Virtual Lecture Hall: Netcasting at the University of South Florida. *CAUSE/EFFECT*, 22(2): 27-29, 33-39. . [Electronic Resource]. Retrieved 9/11/2001 from http://www.educause.edu/ir/library/html/cem9925.html.

Chapter IV

Geographic Information Systems Research and Data Centers

John Abresch
Tampa Library at the University of South Florida-Tampa, USA

The use of geographic information in a variety of research and educational endeavors has created a number of challenges involving data management and dissemination in support of educational processes. Academic libraries, using computing services and virtual libraries, have provided a framework for supporting the use of geographic information within academic communities. This chapter examines the development and implementation of a Geographic Information Systems (GIS) Research and Data Center within the digital environment of a "virtual library" in a large urban university. The chapter will also highlight specific organizational, design, and technical aspects of three exemplary digital geospatial centers, which served as the basis for creating a model GIS Center. In addition, federal data standards and issues for cataloguing geospatial data will be examined. The chapter concludes with a discussion of future issues and technological challenges for GIS Research and Data Centers.

OVERVIEW OF GIS

Geographic information systems programs are more than tools for the production of maps. A GIS can store and manipulate geographic data for spatial analysis in a variety of environments, including urban planning, resource management, transportation networks, and public administration. In addition, GIS applications have been adapted to academic research as academicians find GIS a valuable tool for research grants and projects.

Designed for use on computer mainframes and written in languages such as UNIX, early GIS programs were organizationally complex and not intuitive to the average user. During the 1990s, technological developments in computer hardware and software provided impetus for the rapid growth in the field of GIS, from hardware configurations to the production of maps. A significant impact to the field was the introduction of desktop mapping software programs, such as Environmental Systems Research Institute's (ESRI) *PC Arc/Info*, Arcview, and MapInfo Corporation's *MapInfo* software series. These GIS software programs, designed for a Windows operating environment, broadened the scope of users of the programs and were designed for a variety of user skill levels.

THE DEVELOPMENT OF GIS

In 1990, the Geography Department at the University of South Florida (USF) began offering courses in GIS methods and techniques, using ESRI's desktop software, *ArcInfo*, and *ArcView*. The GIS classes explored the underlying spatial theories of GIS, environmental modeling, and socioeconomic trends in urban analysis. These classes also educated the initial group of GIS users on the USF campus, increasing the computer literacy and use of these programs by other faculty, staff, and students. Soon, GIS programs, data, and applications were being utilized by a number of academic disciplines (Anthropology, Biology, Civil Engineering, and Geology) and in a number of research institutes (the Center for Urban Transportation and Research, the Florida Center for Community Design and Research, and the Louis de la Parte Florida Mental Health Institute). To facilitate access to products, USF procured a university-wide site license from ESRI for a suite of software applications. Faculty began producing voluminous amounts of digital geospatial and other related data in a wide variety of subjects. The data was produced in a range of heterogeneous formats for research projects and for use within classrooms.

Through its Virtual Library, the USF Library System plays an important role in providing support to the university's increasingly networked computing community. The library system offers educational and research support through an online interface that leads the user to a variety of library services, accessibile to electronic databases, and the library catalog. The foundation of the online services and resources are the traditional library strengths of information collection, description, organization, and dissemination. The combination of the traditional and innovative strengths of the library system makes it well suited to support the educational and research needs of the GIS community at the University of South Florida.

By 1999, in response to the growing use of GIS, the Council of Deans adopted a proposal to investigate the feasibility of establishing a library-facilitated Geographic Information Systems (GIS) Research and Data Center. A year later, a task force, comprised of research and teaching faculty in conjunction with public and private sector GIS practitioners, determined that the main mission of a GIS Research and Data Center was data stewardship and management to support the University's GIS research needs as well as to serve as a bridge to external GIS communities (Reader, Chavez, Abresch, et al., 2000). To further define the primary functions of the Center, the Task Force Committee examined both Association of Research Libraries directives and the role of other libraries in the establishment of other regional spatial data centers.

EXEMPLARY DIGITAL GEOSPATIAL CENTERS

Alexandria Digital Library

A significant effort in establishing a digital spatial library was the creation of the Alexandria Digital Library at the University of California - Santa Barbara, funded by the National Science Foundation in 1994. The Library's collection and services focused on georeferenced information: maps, images, data sets, and other information sources with links to geographic locations (Hill et al., 2000). Much of the information in the collection was primarily of the University's service area and adjoining Southern California region.

A key aspect of this collection was the ability to perform data queries and retrieve results by geographic location. The basic means of describing and finding information utilized a *geographic footprint*. A footprint depicts the location on the surface of the earth associated either with an object in the collection or with a user's query. Either a point or a polygon represents the footprint, with latitude and longitude coordinates (Hill et al., 2000). As a user queries the collection through a user interface, the user creates a footprint or an interactive map to indicate the area of interest (the query area). The query area is matched with the object footprints in the metadata to retrieve relevant objects about the query area. This approach to query structure allows the user to choose arbitrary query areas and is not limited to geographic areas with place names. The objects in the collection that fall within a particular query area do not require the names associated with them that the user enters (Hill et al., 2000). By translating a user's text-based query into a footprint query, the user can retrieve all types of information about a location including remote sensed images, data sets, aerial photographs, and textual information. The Alexandria Digital Library configured its catalog for searches to retrieve objects that are in both online and physical formats (Hill et al., 2000).

Idaho Geospatial Data Center

In 1996, building upon the Alexandria Digital Library model, a team of geographers, geologists, and librarians created the Idaho Geospatial Data Center (IGDC) as a digital library of public domain geographic data (Jankowska & Jankowski, 2000). Funded via a grant from the Idaho Board of Education's Technology Incentive Program, the library contained a number of digital geospatial datasets. Much of the collection contained public domain information from federal and state sources. For example, digital line graphs (DLGs) and digital raster graphics were obtained from the United States Geological Survey, and the TIGER boundary files for the state of Idaho were obtained from the United States Bureau of the Census. The site provided an interactive visual analysis of selected demographic and economic data for counties in Idaho. It also provided interactive links to other state and national spatial data repositories.

As a theoretical and practical foundation, the team used a set of parameters defined by Goodchild (1998). Goodchild's geolibrary includes a browser (or specialized software application) running on the user's computer which provides access to the geolibrary through a network connection, and a basemap or geographic frame of reference for the browser's queries. A basemap provides an image of an area corresponding to the geographical extent of the geolibrary collection. The size of the basemap depends on the scale of the search, ranging from a large geographic area (such as a state) to a smaller location (such as a city block). In addition, the geolibrary has a gazetteer (or index) linking place names to a map and a large numbers of collection catalogs on distributed computer servers. Through basic server-client architectures, users access servers over a network via their browser. Ideally, a geolibrary would provide open access to many types of information with geographic referenced queries regardless of the storage media (Jankowska & Jankowski, 2000).

The development of the geolibrary's browser, using Microsoft Visual Basic 5.0 and ESRI MapObjects technology, was a key aspect of the IGDC. The browser interface consists of three panels, resembling the Microsoft Outlook user interface. From the first or map panel, a user explores the geographic coverage of the geolibrary and selects an area of interest. The second panel in the interface indicates where the query is performed. The final panel displays the query results for analysis and options to download the spatial data (Jankowska & Jankowski, 2000).

Cornell University Geospatial Information Repository (CUGIR)

The concept of an Internet-based geospatial data distribution system was the underlying theme in establishing the Cornell University Geospatial Information Repository (CUGIR) at the Albert R. Mann Library. In 1997, the Mann Library received a grant from the Federal Geographic Data Committee's Cooperative Agreements Program (CCAP) to build a clearinghouse node as part of the National Spatial Data Infrastructure (NSDI) Federal Geospatial Clearinghouse (Herold, Gale and Turner, 1999). CUGIR contains geospatial data and metadata related to the state of New York.

Standardization was a significant theme in organizing the library's existing collection of digital geospatial data. The library first converted original file formats of its TIGER/Line files and DLG files into shapefile formats. Additional data covered a variety of socio-economic and physical features for each of the 62 counties in the state of New York. Since the accessibility of this information from remote users would depend on metadata and information retrieval standards, the Mann Library chose the content standard of the Federal Geographic Data Committee (FGDC).

CREATION OF THE USF GIS RESEARCH AND DATA CENTER

After reviewing the structures and practices of these three digital geospatial data centers, the USF Task Force identified eight specific tasks for its emerging Center: to provide and maintain a Web-based GIS interface to view spatial data and perform basic data manipulations; to provide virtual and on-site access to spatial data collections and GIS information; to serve as a point of data receipt from federal, state, and local sources; to describe and organize (i.e., catalog) existing and future spatial data collections in accordance with established metadata standards; to acquire and maintain spatial data collections; to provide a spatial data "interlibrary loan" service; and to catalog and disseminate information about USF GIS research initiatives and activities. The final task was to provide additional services including establishing a referral database; providing support for grant writers and instructors; acting as a liaison between university and public/private-sector GIS users; and securing access to ESRI software applications (Reader et al., 2000).

Identified as the first task, the proposed Website would enable different search modes for the Center's holdings, including subject, keyword, and geographic-based searches. The site would also include an extensive and categorized listing of digital spatial data links, including links to agencies and organizations that contributed data. Finally, the site would function as the main information and advertising gateway for the Center (Reader et al., 2000).

Implementation

Beginning in July 2000 under the direction of a GIS Librarian, the Center began assembling the necessary computer hardware. Two network servers and a number of Dell workstations (with enough memory and processing speed to handle GIS data transactions) were procured and loaded with a suite of ESRI GIS products. A Hewlett Packard plotter and printers were used for the production of paper maps and other output. Library support staff attended workshops to acquire basic knowledge of spatial skills and to operate and apply the GIS software to databases.

With an emphasis on acquiring data holdings pertinent to the USF service area, the center staff began to acquire digital spatial data. The first information layers acquired were of the USF service area. Subsequently, the Center acquired spatial data from a number of other federal agencies, state and local governments, and public and private organizations that produced spatially referenced data.

The initial data holdings were built from local governmental agency data (such as the Planning Commission and Property Appraiser's Office of Hillsborough County and the City of Tampa). The information, acquired in *ArcView* shapefile format, was easily imported. The shapefiles contained a variety of physical, political, and socioeconomic layers of information. The GIS coverages were built by adding extensive local attribute information to public domain data, such as United States Census TIGER/LINE Files. Information for surrounding counties and cities were provided by their respective agencies. Additional digital spatial data was provided by state agencies. For example, the Southwest Florida Water Management District provided shapefiles that described a diversified array of data from environmental assessments that mapped to the Department of Revenue's Florida County fiscal reports. Different types of imagery, such as satellite imagery and aerial photography, were also acquired in shapefile format. Once acquired, all digital spatial information had to be catalogued using commonly employed techniques in bibliographic description.

DESCRIPTION DOCUMENTATION AND GEOSPATIAL INFORMATION

Most digital spatial data is distributed in CD-ROM form and comes in a variety of GIS data formats, including thematic vector information on a particular location or raster files of a unique area satellite image. Other digital spatial data may be disseminated as a computer file in a specialized GIS software format via FTP (file transfer protocol) or by an e-mail attachment. (Larsgaard, 1999). All this data is accompanied by a file on its attributes, commonly known as metadata.

Metadata

Simply defined, metadata is data about data. One definition of metadata for spatial information is "...the data that describes the content, data definition and structural representation, extent (both geographic and temporal), spatial reference, quality, availability, status and administration of a geographic dataset" (Smits, 1999, p.305). Metadata can be interpreted as the equivalent of the recto and verso of the title page of a book, where catalogers search first for data when creating a bibliographic description for an item (Welch & Williams, 1999).

The producer of the geospatial data creates most metadata. With digital media, metadata may be supplied by an accompanying printed document, a CD-ROM or diskette file (named metadata), or as a "readme" text file attachment. Sometimes the cataloger may have to contact the producer of the geospatial data for further information. Most digital geospatial data generally adhere to Federal Geographic Data Committee (FGDC) Data Content Standards.

Federal Geographic Data Committee Data Content Standard

All federal data producers are required to produce metadata for their geospatial data using the FGDC data content standard. Many state data producers, who contribute to state spatial data clearinghouses, also follow the FGDC standard (Welch & Williams, 1999). Digital geospatial data acquired from local government agencies often lack the level of encoding performed by state or federal data producers. Commercially available GIS software and data from private developers usually contain comprehensive metadata describing items, such as data source and scale.

Developed from the user's perspective, the FGDC content standard is based on four factors: what information is necessary to determine the availability of a set of geospatial data; the fitness of the set of geospatial data for an intended use; the means of accessing the set of data, and what is needed for the successful transfer of the data. The FGDC (2001) has established names, definitions, and values for the data and compound elements. The FGDC Manual, which includes a glossary, outlines all of the items to be included in a metadata description. There are seven basic types of information found in the standard: identification information, data quality information, spatial data organization; spatial reference information, entity and attribute information, distribution information, and metadata reference information (Herold et al., 1999).

A second feature of the standard is the definition of mandatory fields. Only information about the production of metadata is mandatory for all records. All other sections of the standard are mandatory if applicable. Then, within each section are subfields that can be defined as mandatory, mandatory if applicable, or optional. The flexibility of description allows metadata creators to determine the level of detail that they can provide or the level of support based on perceived user needs. Finally, the FGDC content standard only defines the content of the record; it does not define how to organize the information or how data should be displayed.

The FGDC uses Standard Generalized Mark-up Language (SGML) for document type definition, which makes metadata records easy to index and to share. The server software uses a Z39.50 protocol, which enables seamless searching of collections. By using the FGDC content standard, SGML, and the Z39.50 protocol, digital geospatial data can be easily utilized by remote users (Herold et al., 1999). The next step is how best to incorporate the metadata of the geospatial data into the metadata of the MARC (Machine Readable Cataloging) bibliographic record, in order to provide full access to geospatial data through a library's online catalog.

The MARC Format And Digital Cartographic Data

The MARC bibliographic record is an industry-wide standard for cataloging bibliographic information, used extensively by libraries, database vendors, and library services companies across the United States. The MARC record contains descriptive information of an item including author(s), titles and variants of titles, subject headings, a classification (or call) number, as well as other bibliographic data elements based upon the format of the item (Furrie, 2000).

Recently, the academic library community has begun to address how to describe digital geospatial information using the MARC format (Welch & Williams, 1999). In 1998, several offices of the Library of Congress (the Cataloging Policy and Support Office, Network Development and MARC Standards Office, and the Geography and Map Division) issued standards for identifying materials to be catalogued as a map format and as a computer (formerly machine-readable data file) format (Larsgaard, 1999). More recently, the Joint Steering Committee for the Revision of the AACR2 (Anglo-American Cataloging Rules 2nd edition) discussed changes in the rules. Chapter 3 of the AACR2r deals with the graphic representation of information concerning digital cartographic materials. Chapter 9 outlines the description of computer files and data, though the focus of the chapter appears to be on numeric databases rather than geospatial data. By interpreting information about the spatial data provided by the producer of the geospatial dataset, a cataloger can create a more detailed bibliographic description (Larsgaard, 1999).

In describing the primary nature of an item, especially its intellectual and physical form, Larsgaard (1999) offers several MARC examples for geospatial data on CD-ROM. For example, if the 007 field, which describes most cartographic materials, is used to describe an electronic atlas, it would display as:

007 |a a{GMD: map} |b d {SMD; atlas} |c {do not use this subfield} |d c {multicolor}
|e e {physical medium: synthetic} |f n {type of reproduction:not applicable} |g z
{production/reproduction details: other} |h n {positive/negative aspect:not applicable}
(Larsgaard, 1999, p. 366).

After the 007 field, the 008 field is intended for coding primary characteristics of the material. Values for the 008 field are often given in the mnemonic beginning line of a record. Larsgaard (1999) notes that each 008 field begins with the same 00-17 positions and ends with the same 35-39 positions. These positions have to do with dates (Date), language (Lang), when the record was modified (Mrec), and cataloging source (Srce). The remaining fields are Relief, Projection, Type of cartographic material, Government publication, Index, and Special format characteristics (Larsgaard, 1999, p. 367).

In the 245 field (General Material Designation), the Anglo-American Cataloging Committee for Cartographic Materials is considering using the term *electronic resource* in the 245 field, as a substitute for *computer file,* to better reflect digital geospatial data. For example, 245 |h {cartographic material {electronic resource}} (Larsgaard, 1999, p. 367).

Welch and Williams (1999) also note several concerns with cataloging digital data within the Mathematical Data Area, including the 256 field on file characteristics, the 352 field on digital graphic representation, and the 342 and 343 fields on geospatial reference data area. For example, classifying *scale* for geospatial objects is difficult. Since the user can zoom in and out of different scales within a GIS interface, the phrase "scale not given" is used for descriptive purposes. Another aspect of scale is that of the *input scale*. When a digital cartographic item has been digitized from a paper map, certain elements are included in the electronic version selected on basis of scale. The input scale would then affect both the content of the item and the extent to which the data can be used for other purposes.

Used in recording *projection*, the 342 field uses additional subfields to add information on the longitude of central meridians and latitude of projection centers. In effect, the 342 field records information about the vertical and horizontal coordinate systems of a data set (projection or grid) and may be repeated (Welch & Williams, 1999). The 255 field also contains the *geographic extent* (coordinates) of the geospatial dataset in a subfield of c.

The information described above is derived from the metadata description when the metadata producer has followed FGDC standards. Describing digital geospatial data can be difficult because it utilizes a specialized nomenclature that is often unfamiliar to non-map catalogers. The availability and comprehensiveness of metadata and local library cataloging policies determine the amount of information entered in the Digital Graphic Representation Fields (352) and Geospatial Reference Data fields (342 and 343) (Welch & Williams, 1999; Larsgaard, 1999). For example, the standard adopted by the USF GIS Research and Data Center includes basic descriptive bibliographic and cartographic elements of the GIS item, including data source, title, spatial display characteristics, and software requirements for viewing. The 352 and 342 fields are used when a need arises for records that are more comprehensive.

When the cataloger cannot adequately describe the geospatial data using the mathematical data fields, additional information can be included in the MARC note fields. The 514 field (data quality note) contains information about the accuracy and completeness of the data. The 551 field (entity attribute) allows the cataloger to add attribute information to the record. The 538 field (systems requirements) would include notes on the type of GIS software processing abilities needed to properly display the digital spatial data. (Welch & Williams, 1999).

When classifying geospatial data (050 field), the Library of Congress treats digital cartographic material as a form subdivision in its G classification schedule. The cataloger classifies geospatial data by map or atlas number without regard to style, and uses a format indicator to indicate the location of the CD-ROM or diskette. When creating subject headings for this data, the Library of Congress uses the 653 field form, which allows the construction of an index term added entry that is not constructed by standard subject heading/thesaurus-building conventions (e.g., Maps—Digital—Raster or Maps—Digital—Vector). Use of this form division can also be used after other materials designations such as Remote-Sensed Images-Digital-Raster (Welch & Williams, 1999; Larsgaard, 1999).

The amount of bibliographic information for geospatial data can become quite lengthy. If there is good metadata and original documentation available, the cataloger can create detailed MARC records for the data. Another strategy to enable access to information is to mount the geospatial metadata on a separate webpage, and then supply the URL for the user through the MARC record via either the 500 field (general note) or the preferred 856 field (electronic location and access) (Welch & Williams, 1999).

CONCLUSIONS

Using ESRI's *ArcIMS* software, the USF Library System established a beta-site on which initial coverages of various aspects of socioeconomic data pertaining to Hillsborough County were mounted. In using standards, such as Chapters 3 and 9 from the ACCR2 and with additional classification information from the FGDC metadata standards, it is easy to catalog geospatial items using the MARC format. The MARC format enables the tagging of important descriptive data elements of the bibliographic record for information retrieval purposes.

For the next phase of the USF GIS Research and Data Center, staff will be actively involved in the creation of a search interface, using fields, coordinates, and free text keywords about geospatial data. The building of a Web-based interface will create an efficient and flexible means to distribute and collect digital geospatial data.

FUTURE ISSUES

The use of GIS technology in the online environment of the Virtual Library will continue to evolve as an important resource for academic communities across the nation. The GIS Research and Data Center initially functioned solely in a data storage capacity, acquiring and archiving significant digital geospatial data.

Academic GIS Centers have a number of important roles in their communities. First, GIS centers play a vital role in community development, both as a data storage center and in data analysis for local and state agencies. Second, the use of GIS as a teaching resource is expanding, as faculty, staff, and students receive instruction in the proper use of GIS software. This will require academic institutions to address issues of accessibility and site licensing issues. In addition, feedback from the community of GIS users will assist in evaluating computer hardware and software needs and shaping collection development policies.

REFERENCES

Decker, D. (2001). *GIS Data Sources*. New York: John Wiley & Sons.

Federal Geographic Data Committee (2001). *Content Standard for Digital Geospatial Metadata*. Retrieved November 12, 2001 from Federal Geographic Data Committee Website: *http://www.fgdc.gov/metadata/contstan.html*

Frank, S. (1994). Cataloging Digital Geographic Data In the Information Infrastructure: A Literature and Technology Review. *Information Processing & Management*, 30(5): 587-606.

Furrie, B. (2000). *Understanding MARC Bibliographic Machine Readable Cataloging*. Washington, D.C.: Library of Congress.

Goodchild, M.F. (1998). What is a GeoLibrary? White Paper for the Distributed GeoLibraries Workshop, 15-16 June 1998, Washington, D.C., hosted by National Research Council Distributed GeoLibraries Panel. Retrieved November 12, 2001 from http://www4.nationalacademies.org/cger/besr.nsf/.

Herold, P., Gale, T. D., & Turner T. P. (1999, winter). Optimizing Web Access to Geospatial Data: The Cornell University Geospatial Information Repository (CUGIR). *Issues in Science and Technology Librarianship*. Retrieved November 11, 2001 from the World Wide Web: Available: http://www.library.ucsb.edu/istl/previous.html.

Hill, L. L., Janee, G., Dolin, R., Frew, J., Larsgaard, M.. (1999). Collection Metadata Solutions for Digital Library Applications. *Journal of the American Society for Information Science*, 50(13):1169-1181.

Hill, L. L., Carver, L., Larsgaard, M., Dolin, R. Smith, T.R., Frew, J., & Rae, M-A. (2000). Alexandria Digital Library: User Evaluation Studies and System Design. *Journal of the American Society for Information Science*, 51 (3):246-259.

Jankowska, M. A. & Jankowski, Piotr. (2000). Is this a Geolibrary? A case of the Idaho Geospatial Data Center. *Information Technology and Libraries*. 19(1):4-10.

Joint Steering Committee for Revision of Anglo-American Cataloguing Rules (2001) *News & Announcements: Outcomes of the Meeting of the Joint Steering Committee Held in Washington, DC USA, 2-4 April 2001* Retrieved November 10, 2001 from World Wide Web: *http://www.nlc-bnc.ca/jsc/0104out.html*.

Korte, G. B. (2001). *The GIS Book*. Albany: OnWord Press.

Larsgaard, M. L. (1999). Cataloging Cartographic Materials on CD-ROMs. *Cataloging & Classification Quarterly*, 27(3/4): 363-374.

McGlamery, T. P. (2000). *Issues of Authenticity of Spatial Data. IFLA Council And General Conference: Conference Proceedings*. Retrieved ERIC database (ERIC Reproduction Service. Microfiche. No ED 450 779).

McGlamery, T. P. (1995). Identifying Issues and Concerns: The University Of Connecticuts's MAGIC-A Case Study. *Information Technology and Libraries*, 14(2): 116-122.

Reader, S., Chavez, T., Abresch, J. (2000). *Report to the Council of Deans. GIS Research and Data Center Task Force*. Unpublished manuscript, University of South Florida, Tampa.

Rigaux, P., Scholl, M., & Voisard, A. (2002). *Spatial Databases: With Application to GIS*. New York: Morgan Kaufmann.

Smith, L. C. & Gluck, M. (Eds.) (1996). *Geographic Information Systems and Libraries: Patrons, Maps, and Spatial Information.* Urbana: Graduate School of Library and Information Science, University of Illinois.

Smits, J. (1999). Metadata: An Introduction. *Cataloging and Classification Quarterly*, 27(3/4): 303-319.

Teng, A.T. (1991). Building geographic databases with input from federal digital data Files. *Technical Papers ACSM/ASPRS annual convention,* Baltimore. Bethesda: American Society for Photogrammetry and Remote Sensing and American Congress on Surveying and Mapping, pp.208-216.

U.S. Census Bureau. (2001) *TIGER Overview.* Retrieved November 11, 2001 from   World Wide Web: *http://www.census.gov/geo/www/tiger/overview.html.*

U.S. Geological Survey. (2001) *USGS Digital Line Graph Data.* Retrieved November 10, 2001 from World Wide Web: *http://edcwww.cr.usgs.gov/glis/hyper/guide/usgs_dlg.*

Welch, G. D. and Williams, F. (1999). Cataloguing Digital Cartographic Materials. *Cataloging & Classification Quarterly,* 27(3/4):343-362.

PART II:

SERVICES
&
FUNCTIONS

Chapter V

Access Services in the 21st Century

Merilyn Burke

Tampa Library at the University of South Florida-Tampa, USA

Information technologies have transformed libraries in ways that most academic librarians could not have imagined twenty years ago. Traditional services, such as interlibrary loan and document delivery, have changed dramatically with the advent of technology and new telecommunications protocols. Electronic access to a myriad of databases, the proliferation of Internet sites, and patron expectations of speedy service have forced academic libraries to re-examine how they function. Higher education is no longer campus bound. Where librarians once served as the gatekeepers to information, that role is less important, as patrons now find information without the use of an intermediary.

Thus, the questions for those librarians working in access services areas become those of service and resource provision. This chapter will examine interlibrary loan, electronic reserves, licenses and contracts, and the impact of distance learning on access to electronic resources and services.

INTERLIBRARY LOAN

"Libraries have always recognized that their users will want materials they do not own, …and as a result, someone will have to pay for un-owned materials…" (Martin & Murray, 1998, p.3). Budget cuts, along with spiraling journal and materials costs have caused many libraries to re-examine collection and service philosophies. Previously, libraries collected materials with a 'just-in-case' mentality; now they have shifted to an 'as-needed' basis (Martin & Murray, 1998). The cost of acquiring plus the cost of storage is a major issue. Ownership has now given way to access (Martin & Murray, 1998), with far-reaching implications. Ownership requires specific types of investment, for example, staff for shelving, processing, and repairing the materials, and valuable physical space within the library to ensure access. However, access does not require extensive physical space, nor does it entail the same labor-intensive workflow. In addition, remote users (i.e., those outside of the library building) can access electronic materials on their own. However, the costs associated with this new type of activity include training staff and users to retrieve the materials. More important is the realization that the library has no permanent files in its possession, relying upon the stability of the companies that supply these databases.

Brief History of Interlibrary Loan

Libraries, for decades, have been participating in resource sharing. The premise of interlibrary loan (ILL) was that "no library can be completely self-sufficient in meeting the needs of its patrons" (Boucher, 1984). However, in most libraries, the Interlibrary Loan office was part of reference or circulation, and services were considered slow at best, with turn-around times being measured in weeks. Patrons would submit requests for materials to librarians who would verify the information in standard resources, then would fill out the four-part American Library Association paper form that was mailed to the library that contained the requested material. The lending library would then receive the request and hopefully find and send the material to the requesting (borrowing) library. This slow and tedious process gave way to technological advances.

Automating the Process

With the introduction of the Web, many libraries simply copied their traditional ILL paper forms and placed these forms on their websites. The forms would be sent to the interlibrary loan department, which would print them out, and then process the requests as if they had been the traditional paper forms. This process allowed staff to better read the requests, and allowed patrons to request materials from their computers; it was a small step in the right direction but more was possible. In addition, the online availability of a national union catalog, OCLC, which listed the holdings of the member libraries, allowed for expeditious identification of sources.

The next two significant changes were, first, patrons were able to input their requests online, track their requests with ease, and review their borrowing history, an important benefit when working with the collection development departments within their library. Second, ILL staff were able to respond to these mediated requests in an automated manner, eliminating many repetitive processes, and requiring fewer staff to process the same number of requests.

The new library management systems now allow patrons to request an article or book that they came across while conducting an online search, sending their requests directly to their Interlibrary Loan department. The opportunities for distribution of articles now include desktop delivery or faxes to the requestors. Although a researcher still checks out books at the local library, the researcher has less need to leave his home or office.

A possible future direction is unmediated interlibrary loan, where the patron sends a request directly to the lending library. Unmediated interlibrary loans are usually available within consortia that have borrowing agreements that allow direct requests by patrons or with commercial document delivery companies. Studies on unmediated document delivery demonstrate that library fears about patrons bankrupting library budgets are unfounded. With patron education and training, a prerequisite when initiating unmediated services, nuisance requests are minimal.

The Impact of Standardization

Re-keying requests into national automated interlibrary loan systems, such as OCLC or DOCLINE, is simply not an efficient way to utilize staff or take advantage of technological innovations. In the last decade, there has been an increasing development in new interlibrary loan software and systems by library vendors.

The International Organization for Standardization (ISO) ILL Protocol has radically changed interlibrary loan. ISO ILL is a systems-based replication of the older paper-based work forms and workflows. In addition to automated messaging between systems, there are other Application Protocol Data Units (APDUs) that include status or error reports. The goal of ISO ILL is to allow ILL staff to easily conduct ILL with other ISO ILL compliant systems easily, making lending and borrowing a seamless operation even though multiple library systems are involved. Some commercial vendors have begun to incorporate the ISO ILL Protocol into their programs, while others offer ILL programs that support patron-initiated ordering, or sell products that manage statistics or keep track of copyright use in order to avoid violations in copying.

It is important to realize that there is a range of libraries with different needs based on size, location, type of patrons served, and volume of materials borrowed and requested. With a lower ILL volume, smaller libraries do not need a complex statistical program. However, the lack of such a component would cripple large institutions. There are packages designed for consortial libraries while other programs support singular or specific functions. Any librarian visiting the vendors at a major convention might think that such companies have the solution to his or her interlibrary loan problems in a box.

Library management systems can offer an online interlibrary loan system as part of their package. Those that do range from simple statistical packages to programs that are more complex. Such programs can allow patron initiated interlibrary loans to connect with the databases located in the systems' online public access catalog (OPAC), statistical packages, and notification systems. However, there are no simple solutions and an out-of-the-box program may not answer all of the questions or solve all of the problems.

Independent systems, such as *ILLiad* from OCLC/ Virginia Technical Institute (Kriz, Glover, & Ford, 1998), Pigasus Software's *Wings*, and *Clio* are just a few of the commercially available systems. Jackson (1997, 2000) reviews the strengths and weaknesses of the selected systems. She examines each product for its ability to archive records, customize to the client's needs, interface with other systems, price, use mediated or unmediated systems produce, a reports and statistical package, support of standards (ISO-ILL or the Z39.50), system architecture, the target audience, and technical support and training. Jackson includes over twenty-eight categories in her review, and her checklist is a comprehensive guideline for determining technology needs.

There has been a new twist in the marketplace as vendors form partnerships with other vendors to develop better and more creative products. For example, The Library Corporation, which was a forerunner in using the ISO ILL protocol and the Z39.50 standards, has had parts of its ILL program incorporated into the Research Library Group's ILL Manager and the National Library of Medicine's DOCLINE program (Jackson, 2000). These combined products allow libraries to have statistical reports, a smoother workflow for the staff, and user-friendly interfaces that create less stress on both the staff and the patrons.

Sending Documents

Traditionally the lending library would send requested documents via the U.S. Postal System. When new breakthroughs in technology occurred, document delivery also changed. As the telefacsimile (fax) machine became an intricate part of the ILL department, librarians were able to send articles more quickly to requesting libraries, with same-day service. However, the poor quality of the fax transmissions diminished the clarity and readability of the document. Scientific papers were especially vulnerable to these problems. Although faxing was faster than traditional forms of delivery, it was more costly and labor-intensive.

In 1990, the Research Library Group (RLG) developed a document delivery software program, Ariel, using FTP (File Transfer Protocol), that allowed libraries to use the Internet to exchange articles. Ariel provided high-speed, cost-effective, and high-resolution document delivery, allowing the scanning and sending of articles directly from the journal or book without making that additional photocopy necessary to fax articles.

Recently, libraries using Ariel and other methods of document delivery are experimenting with delivering documents directly to their patrons (desktop delivery). Users can request that a library send a document directly to them using different methods of delivery. These methods include attachments by email or putting the article on a protected website in a PDF format and informing the patron when the document is available, minimizing staff involvement.

Financing and Budgeting Issues

User demand for information has mushroomed and interlibrary loan has grown with it, mirroring the introduction of online library catalogs, CD-ROM-based indexing and abstracting resources, and online full text journals and aggregator databases (Kelsey & Cohn, 1987; Moore, 1990; Gyeszly & Allen, 1991). Both aggregator databases and indexing and abstracting resources yield rich and tempting citations, irresistible to the researcher or academician who want the materials immediately.

These trends, such as the increase in online information, automation of interlibrary functions, the costs of journal storage, and the need to cut periodical collections due to budget constraints, require libraries to reassess their interlibrary loan departments with a focus on service.

The Cost of Interlibrary Loan

Library users often consider ILL as a free service since many locations do not charge patrons for these services. Roche (1993) reviewed the costs directly associated with interlibrary borrowing and lending for the Association of Research Libraries and the Research Libraries Group (ARL/RLG). The study included the costs for staff, networks and communications, supplies, equipment, and other factors. Roche (1993, p. iv) found that research libraries spend an average of nearly $19 to borrow a research document or to purchase a photocopy and an average of approximately $11 to lend a document to another library. Therefore, the cost for a completed ILL transaction (combining borrowing and lending components) averages approximately $29.50. While 77% of the cost of interlibrary loan operations is staff, other expenses, including computer hardware and peripherals and software, may vary dramatically. Jackson (1997) found that the costs had not changed dramatically in the ensuing years.

Libraries have a variety of methods to handle the costs of an interlibrary loan. These range from a true cost-recovery operation to a standard low fee to deter frivolous requests. Although there may be no charges for libraries within a consortium, that does not negate the cost of running an interlibrary loan department. Libraries still must budget for interlibrary loan services, document delivery, and the costs of new technologies as they emerge in the market place.

Combining Interlibrary Loan and Document Delivery

Growing pressures faced interlibrary loan departments: decrease delivery time, re-allocate resources, improve resource sharing, and cut costs. It became evident to larger academic ILL departments that resource sharing would not be enough. By combining the Interlibrary Loan department with the Document Delivery department, this new redefined functional area would embrace the new technologies, redefine staff roles and user participation, and update work processes.

Document Delivery departments had long used commercial document delivery companies as a 'resource of last resort'. No longer seen as the competition, in many cases commercial vendors could be faster and less expensive than trying to obtain a free item. After factoring the cost of staff time involved in searching, entering, and waiting for a response into the ILL process, just pressing the 'order this document' key at $15 after a quick search is less expensive than the "free" article. The benefits are many: copyright issues are negated, articles come quickly, staff is freed up to obtain more difficult articles, saving in staff costs, and increased patron satisfaction with services.

Database publisher services also allow library patrons and non-affiliated users to place orders directly. Individual users access these services, using credit cards over secured websites, acknowledging that the speed of these services outweighs the costs.

Although it appears that those services might render libraries obsolete, libraries are busier than ever in obtaining items for their patrons. The access to databases, now more readily available in many libraries, has only increased the desire to obtain information – in multiple formats. In addition, companies, such as Ingenta and the British Library, work in conjunction with libraries and individual patrons in supplying articles. Libraries may choose to offer their patrons unmediated access for document requests or mediate the user's requests before sending it to a commercial supplier. Each library should individually address the issues of mediation, reliability, speed, and cost, but such services are valuable for both the library and the patrons.

ELECTRONIC RESERVES

Reserve departments allow students better access to materials due to limited circulation periods. Reserve rooms helped both professors and students in obtaining and protecting materials necessary for their classes. Since the reserve room was an extension of the classroom, copyright issues were not a major concern. Faculty could share their own materials with students as well as materials collected by faculty from other academicians, vendors, or publishers. Videos, old tests, practice problems, and other proprietary material found a protected environment in the reserve room.

This concept worked with the traditional campus setting. However, with the advent of distance learning, urban universities, and a changing student population, the need for change became obvious. In 1993, San Diego State University Library reported on an experiment in delivering course-reading materials through a computer network located within the library (Bosseau, 1993). Although the user could only access the first page without charge, he or she could print the entire article for a fee.

Libraries have found it relatively easy to digitize materials that were on the traditional reserve shelf. Electronic reserves allow students to view materials without the traditional loss or damage, for an unlimited amount of time, and have accessibility 24 hours a day, seven days a week. This reduces staffing levels at the public reserve desk, although there is an increase in the back room work level required to scan materials.

Three factors worked in favor of creating electronic reserves. First, patrons grew sophisticated in their computer usage. Second, faculty members became increasingly more comfortable in requesting the placement of their materials on electronic reserve. Finally, the concept of online materials was becoming less of a novelty. In addition, libraries created their own electronic reserve system or purchased commercial packages. The first issue of *Transforming Libraries* listed fifteen academic institutions and five non-library organizations including vendors and copyright clearance agencies for their work in electronic reserves (ARL, 1996). By 2001, the list had grown to over 140.

Libraries are now able to place pointers or URLs (universal resource locators) directing students to articles within online databases. There is no longer the need to recopy the article, digitize it, and place it on reserves, thus eliminating the need for permission from either the publisher or the Copyright Clearance Center. The addition of course authoring software at many universities has also allowed faculty to place scanned materials within the course websites, bypassing both traditional and electronic reserves. However, there is still the issue of payment for use of these materials due to copyright compliance.

Costs of Access

Libraries are still struggling with who pays for electronic reserve royalties or copyright fees after "fair use" is exhausted. There are numerous models of payment, e.g., the library paying the entire cost, or a range of fees paid by the department of the faculty member who has the materials on electronic reserve. Some libraries simply remove the material after the period for fair use expires, refusing to pay any fees. Other libraries avoid all copyright issues by only posting materials that are in the public domain or belong to the faculty member personally, such as tests and class notes.

Staffing

While the advantages of electronic reserves are obvious, the disadvantages are sometimes harder to explain to administrators. Even "out of the box" programs require training, which drain resources from the department. Libraries rarely add new staff to support electronic reserves; existing staff has the tasks simply added to their existing workflow. Sites, such as the *Electronic Reserves Clearinghouse* [http://www.mville.edu/Administration/staff/Jeff_Rosedale/] and the *Electronic Reserves Listserv* [listproc@arl.org], reflect staff interest in this area.

LICENSES AND CONTRACTS

Interlibrary Loans

Traditional interlibrary loan copying agreements are based on the concept of fair use and that section of the copyright law, § 108 (United States Copyright Office, 1996). Libraries have a special allowance to conduct the business of lending and sending articles and books to each other. However, fair use issues have become more complex in the digital world. With the increased use of databases, which only allow access not ownership, contract law supersedes copyright and fair use. The majority of digital works are licensed and the permissions for distribution are dependent upon the language of the contract. Harper (2001) states that contractual agreements may replace specific provisions of copyright law as the immediate source of authority to archive, use, and distribute digital works. This also includes materials in library purchased databases. Therefore, it is extremely important to know what the terms are in the contracts for the databases 'housed' in one's library before using them for interlibrary loan, electronic reserves, or any other purpose that might have legal ramifications.

With the advent of electronic access, licensing and contracting issues have become more complex. Electronic subscriptions do not follow the traditional lending agreements. For example, subscribing Library A may or may not be able to lend a document found in electronic journal XYZ to borrowing Library B if Library B does not subscribe to print journal XYZ. Some vendors place no such restrictions on the use of the articles found in their journals or databases. When libraries or consortia negotiate these contracts, they should include interlibrary allowances. To do otherwise makes these contracts problematic in the context of a library's interlibrary loan use.

It is difficult for library staff to keep current with licensing restrictions. Vendors drop and add titles with little or no notice. The fluidity of these licensing changes can present challenges to any interlibrary loan department trying to remain compliant with contractual restrictions. Therefore, maintaining current contacts with vendors and those individuals who negotiate the contracts is crucial to keep updates and changes current.

Electronic Reserves

There is still much debate over the intellectual property issues and the concept of fair use in electronic reserves. The Electronic Reserves Drafting Sub-group of participants in the Conference on Fair Use (CONFU) established fair use guidelines for electronic reserve systems in 1994. However, publishers are still concerned about indiscriminant dissemination of materials. With the turmoil that surrounded the Napster case (Kemp, 2000), both publishers and librarians have become even more sensitive to the issues of copyright and intellectual property, particularly in the use of non-print formats.

With the passage of the Digital Millennium Copyright Act (DMCA) in 1998, there were major changes in the copyright law, taking copyright issues into the digital age. The DCMA was a complicated law with major impact on the library community (Lutzker, 1999). It crippled the use of electronic reserves in distance education, since it forbade the transmission of digitized materials.

However, Senate Bill 487, "The Technology, Education, and Copyright Harmonization Act" to amend Chapter 1 of Title 17, U.S. Code, relates to the exemption of certain performances or displays for educational purposes. Protecting digitized copyrighted works from infringement is only part of the problem. The major issue is how to best protect the transmitted materials. One proposed methodology encompasses the digital watermark, fingerprint, or digital signatures, which provide copyright protection (Shaw, 1999). Until the passage of such legislation, electronic reserves for non-print materials cannot be readily available off-campus, and distance learning suffers.

DISTANCE LEARNING

Shea & Boser (2001) stated that, at the turn of the century, approximately 70 percent of American universities had offered at least one course online. They predict that by 2005, nearly all the universities in America will offer an online course.

Although educational institutions create courses and programs for distance learners, they often forget the support component that students and faculty consider critical. Students involved in distance education courses are unlikely to walk into the sponsoring institution's library for instruction on how to use the resources or how to use electronic reserves and interlibrary loan. To properly support distance education students, remote access to the library is essential.

The virtual classroom needs not only a virtual library but also access to the paper resources. The library must be able to deliver materials to students, assist them in finding alternate sources for physical resources, and authenticate and verify student information. This is especially important for accessing databases that are limited to currently enrolled students that often come under the auspices of the library. Students, whether distance learners or local, need to communicate with the library to make sure that they have computer access. Help desks, chat rooms, email programs, live reference, and enhanced online catalogs, all contribute to the support of the distance learning programs. In addition, many programs request reciprocal borrowing privileges for their students located far from the originating campus. Libraries are establishing mail services to their distance learning students, and when that is not possible, direct students to local libraries to take advantage of the interlibrary loan system. For a more in-depth discussion on distance learning, see Chapter 10 in this volume.

CONCLUSION

Libraries must provide the services to their patrons while balancing budgets, space, and user needs. The virtual and the physical library have become one, and it is important that the library make the combination of these two units seamless. The future of electronic reserves and interlibrary loan is still entangled with copyright and intellectual property issues. Copyright notices are standard fare on all electronic materials stating access restrictions. Further, if payments are necessary to access specific resources, it is incumbent upon the library to ensure that policies are in place to ensure payments.

FUTURE TRENDS

Two critical issues remain unresolved in access services in this new century. First, with spiraling subscription and increasing material costs, how will academic libraries create a more effective method of providing information to their faculties and researchers? A closer relationship between collection development librarians and the Interlibrary Loan department is essential. Collection development decisions that affect the information needs of researchers require ILL to supply the missing resources quickly. Armed with usage studies from interlibrary loan and electronic reserve software applications and input from other departments, collection management can be more precise in obtaining important resources with dwindling funds.

The second challenge focuses on accountability for library support for students in the era of distance learning. For example, when a student is enrolled in a distance learning course, which library is responsible for providing library services - the geographically closest library or the one affiliated with the educational institution offering the distance learning course? It is important to take these factors into account when developing service policies for those distance learners who are far from their 'home' institutions but still require services.

REFERENCES

Association of Research Libraries (1996). *Transforming Libraries, Issue 1: Electronic reserves.* Washington, D.C.: Association of Research Libraries.

Bosseau, D. L. (1993). Anatomy of a small step forward: the electronic reserve book room at San Diego State University. *The Journal of Academic Librarianship,* 18(1):366-8.

Boucher, V. (1984). *Interlibrary loan practices handbook.* Chicago, IL: American Library Association, p.2.

Gyeszly, S. D. & Allen, G. (1991). Effects of online periodical indexes on interlibrary loan services and collection development. *Journal of Interlibrary Loan & Information Supply,* 1(3):39-48.

Harper, G. (2002). *Copyright in the library.* The University of Texas System. [Electronic Resource]. Retrieved 10/09/2001 from http://www3.utsystem.edu/ogc/intellectualproperty/.

Jackson, M. E. (1997). *Measuring the performance of interlibrary loan and document delivery services: Bimonthly Report on Research Library Issues and Actions.* Washington, D.C.: Association of Research Libraries.

Jackson, M. (2000). *Interlibrary loan and resource sharing products: An overview of current features and functionality.* Chicago: IL: American Library Association. [Also available in *Library Technology Reports,* 36(6) : Special issue on Interlibrary Loan Products].

Kelsey, A. L. & John M. Cohn, J.M. (1987). The impact of automation on interlibrary loan: one college library's experience. *Journal of Academic Librarianship,* 13(7):163-166.

Kemp, T. (2000). When Does Copying Become Illegal Use?—Napster copyright battle may impact text, video, software protection at other content sites. *Internetweek,* 284:16.

Kriz, H. M., Glover, M. J., & Ford, K. C. (1998). ILLiad: customer-focused interlibrary loan automation. *Journal of Interlibrary Loan, Document Delivery & Information Supply,* 8(4): 31-47.

Lutzker, A. (1999). *Primer on the digital millennium.* [Electronic Resource]. Retrieved 10/09/2001 from http://www.arl.org/info/frn/copy/primer.html

Martin, M. & Wolf, M. (1998). *Budgeting for information access,* Chicago, IL: American Library Association, p.3.

Moore, M. M. (1990). Compact disk indexing and its effects on activities in an academic library. Journal of Academic Librarianship, 16(5): 291-295.

Roche, M. M. (1993). *ARL/RLG interlibrary loan cost study.* Washington, D.C.: Association of Research Libraries.

Shaw, S. (1999). Overview of watermarks, fingerprints and digital signatures. [Electronic Resource]. Retrieved 10/09/2001 from http://www.jtap.ac.uk/reports/htm/jtap-034.html.

Shea, R. H. & Boser, U. (2001). So where's the beef?(limits of online learning at college level). *U.S. News & World Report,* 131(15):44.

United States Copyright Office (1996). *Copyright Law of the United States of America and related laws contained in title 17 of the United States Code: Circular 92.* Washington, D.C.: The Office.

Chapter VI

Cataloging and Metadata Issues for Electronic Resources

Susan Jane Heron and Charles L. Gordon
University of South Florida Library System-Tampa, USA

The environment in which cataloging principles and standards operate has changed dramatically. The development of automated systems for the creation and processing of bibliographic data, the growth of large-scale shared cataloging programs, and emerging technologies have created new opportunities to provide access to national and international academic library collections. However, economic pressures have also prompted libraries to try to simplify the cataloging process, using "minimal level" cataloging records in order to keep pace with the continued growth of publishing. Cataloging librarians have identified two significant needs: 1) to adapt existing [cataloging] codes and practices to accommodate change resulting from new forms of electronic publishing and the advent of networked access to information resources, and 2) to respond more effectively to an increasingly broad range of user expectations and needs. München (1998) wonders how catalogers will guarantee the quality and relevance of bibliographic access within the exploding world of online materials. If so, what kind of bibliographic records will be required to meet the different uses and user needs? Finally, how should these bibliographic data be organized and structured for intellectual and physical access to the documents?

This chapter will provide an overview of current cataloging principles, issues in handling evolving formats, and challenges for academic catalogs. It will include a brief examination of a model created by a large multi-campus urban university in determining best practice in the creation of records for shared, online academic environments. Finally, the chapter will look at the development of alternative frameworks for describing online resources.

THE EVOLUTION OF CATALOGING IN ACADEMIC LIBRARIES

In 1876, Charles Ammi Cutter originally promulgated his *Rules for a Printed Dictionary Catalogue* (Cutter, 1904). This code is remarkable since it covered not only the objectives (Objects) but also the methods (Means) of creating catalog entries to provide access library materials. Cutter's *Objects* were to 1) enable a person to find a book of which either the author, title, or subject is known; 2) show what the library has by a given author, on a given subject, or in a given kind of literature, and 3) assist in the choice of a book, as to its edition (bibliographically) or to its character (literary or topical). His *Means*, or method of doing so, provides author-entry with the necessary references; title-entry or title-reference; subject-entry, cross-references, and classed subject-table; form-entry; edition and imprint, with notes when necessary. These principles are still the foundation of best cataloging practice, including the notion of specificity, the consideration of the user as the principal basis for subject-heading decisions, the practice of standardizing terminology, the use of cross-references to show preferred terms and hierarchical relationships, and solving the problem of the order of elements. To bring the terminology of the 19th century into the 21st century, replace book with resources, prefix it with any number of adjectives (e.g., print, digital), and filter it through the lens of the user of today's academic library system.

Transitioning into Virtual Cataloging

Cataloging and classifying remote-access publications and databases puts these resources into the context of the entire academic library collection. One envisions a faculty member, in his or her office on campus, doing routine research on the online catalog. He or she can identify and then search the databases needed, call up records for cited journals in the databases, and either gain access to recent journal issues online or instantly submit a delivery order, all in one seamless process starting from the library's catalog.

A virtual library has tremendous impact on the cataloging departments of academic libraries. As Zyroff (1996, p. 50) asserts "...skills that assure consistency, predictability, and repeatability of access are as needed as ever...There is a precision of approach that cataloging uniquely provides with regard to the inner workings of catalogs, databases, and indexes. This and not the amount of the budget, the architecture of the building, or size of the CD-ROM tower...is the touchstone of good libraries." Six years later, this is still true.

Computer-readable items require descriptive cataloging just as print materials do. Changes from the current descriptive cataloging rules include the description of items in digital terms and, with the inception of web-based catalogs, the use of SGML (Standard Generalized Markup Language) to add "hot" links to items on the online catalog. Access terms and additional indexing of large full-text files are essential components for access to documents and files. Authority files with references to related, broader, and narrower terms allow the use of concept mapping across disparate databases.

As virtual libraries become a reality in academic settings, adequate staffing in technical services is essential. Not only must staff know how to operate computers and related equipment effectively, they must also utilize specialized online tools to run acquisitions and bibliographic and/or authority control.

HANDLING EVOLVING FORMATS

One of the major challenges for academic catalogs is the cataloging of constantly changing Internet resources with those of commercial databases. Cline (2000) raises two critical concerns of librarians when she asks first if libraries are creating sustainable *systems* of access and second if libraries are building reliable databases and durable objects. She emphasizes that it is important that libraries, in their enthusiasm for access, not overlook important issues of reliability, redundancy, and the ability to replicate results, which are important elements for continuity for scholars.

Related to improved discovery of digital resources, there is a need for mechanisms to promote greater efficiency in sharing authority data for those elements used as access points (i.e., persons, corporate bodies, and geographic places). Fostering effective use of authority records at an international level would benefit access to library materials. Tillett (2001) emphasizes that authority control enables precision and recall, which are lacking in today's Web searches. The international aspect of the web complicates this endeavor. For example, linguistic characteristics of the entity names and a lack of agreement among national codes as to the treatment of forms of headings are only two problems facing international authority control.

Finally, it is difficult, if not impossible to link individually those multiple resources residing at an Internet site, particularly within a dynamic site. The content and organization of many of these sites are not stable enough or do not reside high enough up in the site architecture to capture databases reliably in catalog records. For example, users may not have direct access to a specific database in a large databank, requiring the user to enter through the main menu, then select the database, and search. The question becomes one of how to use the records within the online catalog to best inform the user.

History of the MARC Format

The method used in most online library catalogs is the MARC (Machine Readable Cataloging) format. The use of electronic bibliographic records began in the 1960s. The Library of Congress (LC) developed a communications format (MARC) to represent its bibliographic records in computer stable form. Originally designed for the printing of catalog card sets, LC also made this data available for purchase. Large academic libraries, such as Stanford, University of Chicago, Northwestern, and University of Toronto, chose to purchase this data and created their own databases for acquisitions and cataloging purposes. Other groups, such as the Ohio College Library Center and the Washington Library Network, created a single database, which allowed libraries to share and contribute records. The eventual result was that machine-readable records became available to all but the smallest of institutions. LC still distributes MARC records to institutions, commercial vendors, and the two major online shared cataloging utilities, OCLC (now Online Computer Library Center) and RLIN (Research Libraries Information Network). The MARC format has grown to encompass all formats of library materials (books, media, serials, electronic resources, scores, maps) as well as holdings and authority records.

There were three major benefits to libraries with the development of the MARC format. First, libraries were able to reduce dramatically their amount of original cataloging as they began to share records with each other. Second, it created a uniform standard of data sharing for libraries. Vendors could create online catalogs, since most libraries used MARC in a relatively equivalent way. Third, with the development of the Z39.50 standard for the electronic sharing of data, users could search web-based library catalogs from a variety of libraries located throughout the world.

The MARC format is a combination of fixed and variable length fields. Fixed fields contain excerpted information in predetermined length strings to allow ease in searching the datasets. For example, sample fixed fields include date and place of publication, language of the material, type of material (book, serial, sound recording, etc.), type of illustration, and target audience (adult or juvenile). Variable fields have no predetermined lengths, can contain extensive amounts of information, and are of variable length because the amount of information differs for each item.

All information is entered into defined fields, that designate the type of data, and is then further subdivided into discrete pieces. For example, an author can be one of three types of data: a person, an entity, or a conference. Depending upon its type, the data is entered into its three-character field. The field is subdivided by additional information. For example, if a person's name is used as the author, the type of name is indicated, such as forename (Henry VIII) or surname. Within the field, a title (King of England) or birth date are considered subfields of the name and given separate delimiters.

100:0 : |a Henry |b VIII, |c King of England, |d 1491-1547

The person entering the information can choose how fully he or she would like to use the format.

National standards exist for core (minimal) and full coding. If materials are permanent parts of a collection, full coding provides the maximum amount of information to the user of the online catalog. However, the institution is the ultimate decision maker on this issue.

Enter the Internet

Since the inception of the MARC record, librarians have created an amazing number of records in a relatively brief period. However, with the immediacy of the Web, patrons expect instantaneous cataloging of electronic resources and Websites. There is the widespread perception that robots automatically index Websites with the speed of light, but studies show that some search engines take more than three weeks to visit a site and it may take up to six weeks or longer to have a site actually indexed by a search engine vendor (Brewington & Cybenko, 2000).

Multimedia websites are not radically different from traditional documents. Librarians have substantial experience in cataloging pictures, sound recordings, and even electronic files. Websites, often considered unlike traditional documents because their content may change, are actually no different from the variant forms of print that scholars have dealt with for centuries. Before the era of movable type, people copied manuscripts by hand. The human factor introduced errors, but there were other sources of variation between copies of a work. Similarly, frequently revised and restructured Websites are comparable to printed serials. Librarians track the new issues and deal with title changes, mergers, and splits of journals. Changing the location of Websites is similar to the reclassification of a book in a library. Librarians know how to control all the references to a call number in a catalog, and revise them when the number changes. The disappearance of a Website is comparable to the removal of a book from a library. Librarians make a decision to retain the catalog record for lost or stolen books, which is analogous to recording Web sites that no longer exist. In summary, librarians continuously update classification schemes, subject heading lists, and thesauri to reflect literary warrant, i.e., the actual documents that require content analysis. This experience can be applied to the indexing of the ever-changing Web.

CHALLENGES FOR ACADEMIC CATALOGS

There are eight major challenges for academic catalogs. These challenges include using single or multiple records, reaching consensus with academic libraries sharing a union catalog, authority control within an online catalog, making decisions concerning partial full text databases and aggregators, the unpredictability of Internet resources, variability of vendor product, whether to classify web items, and personnel issues.

Single Or Multiple Records

Most e-resources have some relationship to a print item. A major problem in cataloging an e-resource is how to identify its relationship (if any) to its corresponding print item. Each has unique characteristics based on its format and is of value to the patron when deciding if the resource is what he or she wants. Is the library patron better served by using one record that indicates both forms or separate records which allow the cataloger to tailor the description to the specific form?

This is further complicated when a resource is available from several vendors, each vendor having a different file format (e.g., pdf, ASCII, image) as well as varying amounts or types of coverage. Using one record is usually more efficient for the cataloger, but creating a cogent description of the library's holdings for a non-cataloger can present difficulties. This difficulty is further exacerbated by the fact that an item record is used for a variety of purposes by both library patrons and by library staff.

The MARC record is reformatted for public display. The original intent of the MARC format was to replicate the catalog card, but the careful tagging and subfielding of the information allows a catalog designer to easily index, rearrange, suppress, or express a field in whatever manner is most appropriate for the target audience. Since the basic record remains unchanged, libraries can periodically revisit these design decisions. The display of MARC data has implications in the decision to use single or multiple records for an e-resource.

In the case of multiple records, a patron searching a catalog may be unhappy when confronted with an index screen listing many records for the same title. Some of the multiple listings may be for the same work in a different format or with different

Figure 1: Electronic Resource Record (One record for each form of the journal)

USF Library Catalog   WebLuis
Search: tj=journal of   **Title Results List**
accounting and public policy
Hit Count: 3 Records: 1 to
3

JOURNAL OF ACCOUNTING AND PUBLIC POLICY

❑ **1 Journal of accounting and public policy**
    Amsterdam :; [serial]; 19uu
    <http://www.sciencedirect.com/science/journal/02784254>
    USF electronic resource   No call number available -- Library Has
    ScienceDirect
    Online access restricted to USF students, faculty & staff
    Commercial ISP? see: www.lib.usf.edu/virtual/help/proxy.html
    THIS TITLE ALSO AVAILABLE IN OTHER FORMATS--SEE RESULTS
    LIST

❑ **2 Journal of accounting and public policy**
    New York, NY :; [serial]; 1982
    <http://www.sciencedirect.com/science/journal/02784254>
    TAMPA periodicals (Non-Circulating) H97 .J66 -- Library Has
    Current Issues in Storage. Ask at Periodicals Info Desk
    Library has discontinued its subscription to print version
    THIS TITLE ALSO AVAILABLE IN AN ONLINE VERSION--SEE LINKS
    Online access restricted to USF students, faculty & staff
    Commercial ISP? see: www.lib.usf.edu/virtual/help/proxy.html

❑ 3 Journal of accounting and public policy
    Amsterdam :; [serial]; 19uu
    <http://www.sciencedirect.com/science/journal/02784254>
    USF electronic resource   No call number available -- Library Has
    ScienceDirect

coverage. The searcher may be required to examine most, or all, of the listed records in order to complete a successful search.

The single record approach may be no less frustrating to the user. Although there may be fewer records to view, the variations in holdings or accessibility may be difficult to discern by the user. For example, the library may hold all volumes in print of a given title but have access limited to select volumes via the Internet. This can be a major disappointment for a remote user with expectations of full access.

Figure 2: Electronic Resource Record (One Record for all Forms of the Journal)

WebLuis   **University of Florida (UF)**

Search: tj=journal of   **UF Electronic Resources**
accounting and public policy

Title:
 Journal of accounting and public policy.
Published:
 New York, N.Y. North Holland, c1982 – frequency quarterly.
Publishing history:
 Vol. 1, no. 1 (fall 1982)-
Indexed by: Accountants' index. Supplement 0748-7975.
  ABI/INFORM Spring 1983-
  Public Affairs Information bulletin 0033-3409
Notes:
 Title from cover.
ISSN: 0278-4254
Subjects, general:
  Policy sciences--Periodicals.
  Accounting--Periodicals.
  Policy sciences--Accounting—Periodicals.
LINKS:
 Full Text of Recent Years
 .<http://www.sciencedirect.com/science/journal/02784254>
 Full text licensed only for UF students, faculty, and staff
Holdings: back [to previous screen]
LOCATION:
  LIBRARY WEST, Periodicals
CALL NUMBER:
  H97.J66
CURRENT ISSUES:
  v.20:no.1-4/5 2001 Spring-Winter
LIBRARY HAS:
  v.9-19 1990-2000

---

  back [to previous screen]
LOCATION: See LINKS to Connect
CALL NUMBER: No call number available
STATUS: Circ. info not available
LIBRARY HAS: 1997-

Figure 3: Multiple Record Display in SUS Union Catalog

WebLuis

SUS Libraries Union Catalog
Title Results List

Search: tj=JOURNAL OF ACCOUNTING AND PUBLIC POLICY **Hit Count:** 12

❑ **1 Journal of accounting and public policy**
   Amsterdam :; [serial]; 19uu
   Online version; connect to ScienceDirect. (Access restricted to FAMU students, faculty & staff)
   <http://www.sciencedirect.com/science/journal/02784254>
   Florida A&M University
   Electronic access No call number available -- Library Has In Elsevier ScienceDirect: See LINKS above

❑ **2 Journal of accounting and public policy**
   Amsterdam :; [serial]; 19uu
   Link to selected fulltext (ScienceDirect)
   <http://www.sciencedirect.com/science/journal/02784254>
   University of North Florida
   ONLINE: use link above H97 .J66 elec.ver. -- Library Has

❑ **3 Journal of accounting and public policy**
   Amsterdam :; [serial]; 19uu
   Link to selected fulltext (ScienceDirect)
   <http://www.sciencedirect.com/science/journal/02784254>
   University of South Florida
   USF Electronic Resources
   USF electronic resource No call number available -- Library Has ScienceDirect
   Online access restricted to USF students, faculty & staff
   Commercial ISP? see: www.lib.usf.edu/virtual/help/proxy.html
   THIS TITLE ALSO AVAILABLE IN OTHER FORMATS--SEE RESULTS LIST

   ❑ **4   Journal of accounting and public policy**
   ❑ **........**
   ❑ **11 Journal of accounting and public policy**

A study by Chaudhry and Periasamy (2001) found there to be no clear answers on the issue of single versus multiple records. Of the 19 libraries studied, four used the single record approach, five used separate records, and ten used both single records and multiple records with specific criteria for making the choice. Most libraries in the study preferred full records, but some cataloged e-journals using a brief record to identify and locate the resource.

Reaching Consensus for a Union Catalog

An online union catalog represents the collections of a number of individual libraries. This allows users to either easily search the comprehensive union catalog or limit their queries to a single library. Union catalogs are quite common, particularly with the increased growth of local and regional library cooperatives. Libraries that have the luxury of participating in a network that shares a common automation system gain a great technical infrastructure for sharing materials, performing cooperative cataloging, and employing strategic collection development (Breeding, 2000). While the growth of union catalogs is a good thing, the major difficulty for users of the catalog is that there is no consensus among libraries in general on how to handle records for electronic materials.

Authority Control Within an Online Catalog

As a further challenge to improved access to networked resources, librarians need to pursue efforts to achieve semantic interoperability of controlled subject terminology and classification data, also known as authority control. Chan (2001) has noted that experimentation conducted on subject access systems in WebPACs and metadata processed systems demonstrates the potential benefit of structured approaches to the description and organization of Web resources. This would involve the use of established subject heading schemes and thesauri at a general level, recognizing that more local or specific schemes may also be necessary to provide more detailed indexing. However, the success of this endeavor will depend on trained catalogers for their proper application according to current (and often complex) policies and procedures, the cost of maintenance, and their incompatibility with most tools now used on the Web (Chan, 2001).

Decisions Regarding Aggregated Databases

Electronic databases come in a variety of formats. However, aggregator databases present a particular problem. An aggregator database is a compilation of resources from a number of publishers that are gathered together by a vendor based upon a specific subject area, a multidisciplinary focus, or the type of library (e.g., academic, public, school, special). These 'selective resources' (i.e., not all journal articles from all volumes from all publishers in the database are available) mean that there is not complete coverage of a title, either through index terms, abstracts, or as full-text. This causes problems for academic libraries since one can purchase the same title in a number of different aggregated databases from different vendors, each with varying coverage and cost implications. It is critical that libraries address decisions on the value of cataloging these e-resources at the collection or analytical level (for a more thorough discussion on electronic collections, see Chapter 2 in this volume).

Variability of Vendor Product

Resources that are available from multiple vendors bring additional challenges. The user will base his or her choice of a resource on the information gleaned from the catalog record. Hardware, software, or network requirements to access the item affect a user's choice of format (e.g., image vs. text). In addition, vendors interpret full text differently. Some vendors may interpret 'full text' as only the words of a work and omit illustrative data (e.g., charts, graphs, tables, maps, plans, or photographs). Other vendors may omit only color illustrations or change them to monochrome illustrations in the electronic version. Accurately interpreted illustrative material is critical for those individuals doing research in the visual arts, engineering, and medical sciences. In addition, full text online may actually be a condensed version of the print article. Therefore, an accurate description of "full-text" is important to the user.

Depth and breadth of coverage is another issue, even with an excellent electronic resource such as JSTOR (http://www.jstor.org/), a scholarly journal archive. With the transition to remote online searching, users want comprehensive search results of those items available immediately online without having to reconstruct a search to discover and obtain a print source. Therefore, scope of holdings (breadth and depth of coverage) is an essential piece of information.

Finally, vendor stability has become a critical issue in the cataloging of electronic resources. A number of electronic resource vendors are no longer in business or are new subsidiaries of existing vendors. In addition, when vendors acquire a "new" resource, they add and drop material with little or no notice, causing problems with online access for the patron as well as the currency of the online catalog.

Unpredictability of Internet Resources

Internet resources can, and often do, disappear in an instant. They may change in coverage and scope of topic, in visual presentation, or in sponsorship, while retaining the same Internet address. Evaluation of Internet resources, most notably free sites, is important before cataloging. Pitschmann (2001) lists a number of critical issues when evaluating Internet websites, such as the authority of site's sponsor (e.g., the American Medical Association vs. a personal homepage); the relevance to the academic needs of the library user; the number of similar sites on a topic area; currency of the information; format and delivery of information; stability of the site; depth and/or breadth of content coverage; and 'added value' services such as current awareness services or discussion lists. Additionally, libraries must monitor Internet sites for change and stability once they become a part of the catalog.

Classification

Classification traditionally has been used to group like items together; a user can browse the call number physically on the shelves or online to find related materials. Since electronic resources are intangible resources, they seem unlikely candidates for a "call number". This simplistic view overlooks the actual advantages of using classification, which include traditional access (e.g., logical grouping of related materials in bibliographies and catalogs, shelf order browsability), as an access point to metadata records, as well as a tool for retrieval on the Web (i.e., subject browsing and navigation). The Association for Library Collections & Technical Services (ALCTS) (1999a) identified seven functions of classification: location, browsing, hierarchical movement, retrieval, identification, limiting/partitioning, and profiling. Class numbers, such as Dewey and LCC, also address the multilingual challenge of subject analysis as mapping devices among subject vocabularies in different languages (Landry, 2000). Therefore, the inclusion of classification data (i.e., class numbers) in metadata records is a serious consideration for libraries developing policy to catalog online resources (ALCTS, 1999b).

Personnel Planning and Costs

The library budget limits the quantity of material a library may purchase and encourages selectors to be careful of the quality of the items bought. Electronic resources are often bundled together, which the library cannot alter to suit specific needs or eliminate duplication. One purchase order can result in thousands of titles in a single collection to process, which the reference staff and patrons expect to be available immediately. A similar issue exists for free sites: selectors are not hindered by budget considerations, therefore they are enthused about adding cataloging records for their favorite sites with no consideration of the financial implications for the cataloging staff.

With print resources it was possible in the past to estimate the amount of staff necessary to keep up with the processing; the Internet has complicated this dramatically. Maintenance has also increased. As with print serials, many e-resources require repeated updating of their records. Sites relocate, coverage changes, subject matter evolves, and titles are added, dropped, merged, split, or mutated. With this in mind, Calhoun (2001) argues that the highly centralized model for cataloging library materials so characteristic of most libraries needs to give way to a new model that values a team-based work organization, bringing together selectors, public services librarians, and catalogers into the record creation process.

THE UNIVERSITY OF SOUTH FLORIDA MODEL

In 1994, the University of South Florida Libraries Cataloging Policies Committee (CPC), with multi-campus and departmental representation, broached the first e-resource discussions. Cataloging electronic resources became a critical issue with the joint purchase of aggregator databases by the State University System (SUS) libraries to replace CD-ROM products. The organization of the USF Libraries further complicated this decision; its five libraries shared a union catalog, which was a subset of the larger SUS union catalog. The CPC decided to simplify cataloging efforts for the USF union catalog by providing a single shared bibliographic record for each online resource that would display both the USF and the SUS union catalogs. Although this was a choice for a single shared bibliographic record, it was in effect, a decision to use the multiple record approach, i.e., separate records for online and print versions of the same resource. However, many of the other SUS libraries used the single record format to expedite the cataloging of these resources.

The Virtual Library Project (VL), established in 1996, had no formal Technical Services representatives. Eventually, a VL committee, the Metadata/Cataloging Project Group, was created to address the following issues: determine the feasibility of enhancing electronic collections by adding metadata to the online catalog; decide how to catalog current electronic collections journal titles and holdings and Internet links; establish minimum standards for records used by the USF Libraries; determine how SGML will work within the NOTIS environment; and create a cataloging standards manual for the USF Libraries.

Meeting weekly, the Metadata/Cataloging Project Group began to set local standards. Since national cataloging standards for electronic resources were still evolving, the Group adopted the earlier CPC Subcommittee recommendation for using a single shared record for each electronic resource.

The scope of online materials continued to broaden. The focus on aggregators narrowed as groups of journals containing complete issues and volumes became available. While somewhat more stable than the aggregators, they presented additional descriptive cataloging challenges. Compatibility with national and state standards was deemed critical. At a national level, CONSER (the Cooperative Online Serials Group) was working to define the standards for the cataloging of electronic resources. In Florida, the Chair of the USF Metadata/Cataloging Project Group joined the Cataloging & Access Guidelines for Electronic Resources (CAGER) Committee of the SUS Libraries to help develop statewide standards for digital resources. Although the Metadata/Cataloging Project Group had been working with electronic resources for several years, having a formal body of other catalogers was seen as useful, particularly when reviewing concepts embodied in the Draft Library of Congress Rule Interpretations for seriality.

Cataloging the online resources required a level of expertise held by few in the profession. After discussing specific policies and procedures, the team approved and put into practice the *Guidelines for Cataloging USF Electronic Resources* (1999). In addition, the team requested and received two new positions, an e-resources cataloger and a technical assistant, for the Cataloging Department.

For other academic libraries considering a virtual library, the USF model offers a concrete review of some of the issues that needed discussion within a multi-library consortia within a statewide consortia of state university libraries.

CONCLUSION

Traditionally, research libraries have held significant roles in research and education. By constructing intellectual and physical systems of access through its online catalogs, academic libraries add value by organizing and classifying information into collections (author, subject, and genre). The ubiquitous Internet is a controversial resource confronting those who organize academic virtual libraries or virtual collections – the catalogers. Demands for the organization of and access to these new forms of information confront today's catalogers or "metadata creators". Although the focus is the future, it is from the past that libraries derive fundamental principles of access and organization. Today's academic libraries must create sustainable systems of access to enduring scholarly resources so that students, faculty, and researchers can rely on them with confidence, or as Cline (2000, p. 22) questions "While we work to incorporate vast amounts of digital information into our libraries, schools, universities, and colleges, how much should we concern ourselves with 'virtual continuity'?"

FUTURE TRENDS

Two major trends for cataloging electronic materials focus on the increased need for access and bibliographic control. First, the migration away from standard data elements with established descriptions to the free-floating formats established by a variety of work groups overlooks important issues of reliability, redundancy, and the ability to replicate results. For example, a comparison of the MARC format to the Dublin Core (DC) elements demonstrates that MARC is, and has been, a national and international standard for over three decades for a number of reasons. In addition to being clearly defined and regularly updated by a national organization, a large pool of professionals and paraprofessionals are proficient in MARC and have access to print and online resources. However, possibly the two most important reasons for the continued use of MARC are that 1) Librarian A can predict how Librarian B will use a particular field, and 2) cross-database searching is facilitated through the use of authority records to create inter-record/database linkages. MARC's major disadvantage is that it does require skill and time to effectively use the MARC format and its descriptive 'bibles': the Anglo-American Cataloguing Rules, specialized thesauri, and specific criteria for specialized formats, such as archival or visual resource materials.

The Dublin Core record, by comparison, is very 'creator' driven, and, as such, is as good as the level of its creator. The person filling in the data fields in the record defines DC fields. The creator also limits the level of complication. The DC's major advantage is that it is viewed as an embeddable element in an electronic resource. Three major disadvantages are: 1) the lack of predictability of a field, i.e., Field A may be defined "this way" by Librarian A and "that way" by Librarian B; 2) the lack of national and international standards; and 3) no current parallel system to facilitate cross-database searching. It is critical that librarians establish crosswalks to access the data held across a variety of data structures to ensure that academicians, researchers, and students can find the requisite resources needed for their work. How this will be done is still in its formative stages.

The second major challenge for catalogers or metadata creators is that access to materials and greater precision and relevance in searching for those materials are still the major impetuses for describing what libraries own or access. Cutter's principles accrue importance and validity with every expansion of the Internet. Byrum (2001) believes a first step in encouraging the metadata community to give greater attention to content standardization is to develop and disseminate a statement of basic principles to explain clearly and convincingly why there is cost-benefit from the work that catalogers do.

REFERENCES

ALCTS/CCS/SAC/Subcommittee on Metadata and Classification. (1999a). *Final report.* [Electronic Resource]. Retrieved 09/23/2001 from http://www.ala.org/alcts/organization/ccs/sac/metaclassfinal.pdf.

ALCTS/CCS/SAC/Subcommittee on Metadata and Subject Analysis (1999b). *Subject data in the metadata record: Recommendations and rationale.* [Electronic Resource]. Retrieved 09/23/2001 from http://www.ala.org/alcts/organization/ccs/sac/metarept2.html.

Breeding, M. (2000). Technologies for Sharing Library Resources. *Information Today,* 17(9):60-61.

Brewington, B. E. & Cybenko, G. (2000). Keeping up with the changing web. *Computer,* 33,(5): 52-59.

Byrum, J.D. (2001). Challenges of Electronic Resources: State of the Art and Unresolved Issues. *International Conference on Electronic Resources: Definition, Selection, and Cataloguing.* [Electronic Resource]. Retrieved 09/23/2001 from http://w3.uniroma1.it/ssab/er/relazioni/byrum_eng.pdf.

Calhoun, K. (2001). Redesign of Library Workflows: Experimental Model for Electronic Resource Description. In Sandberg-Fox, A. M., *Proceedings of the Bicentennial Conference on Bibliographic Control for the New Millennium: Confronting the Challenges of Networked Resources and the Web.* Washington, D. C.: Library of Congress. [Electronic Resource]. Retrieved 09/23/2001 from http://lcweb.loc.gov/catdir/bibcontrol/calhoun_paper.html.

Chan, L. M. (2001). Exploiting LCSH, LCC, and DDC to retrieve networked resources: Issues and challenges. In Sandberg-Fox, A. M., *Proceedings of the Bicentennial Conference on Bibliographic Control for the New Millennium: Confronting the Challenges of Networked Resources and the Web.* Washington, D. C.: Library of Congress. [Electronic Resource]. Retrieved 09/23/2001 from http://lcweb.loc.gov/catdir/bibcontrol/chan_paper.html.

Chaudhry, A. S., & Periasamy, M. (2001.). A study of current practices of selected libraries in cataloguing electronic journals. *Library Review,* 50(9):434-443.

Cline, N. M. (2000). Virtual continuity: The challenge for research libraries today. *EDUCAUSE Review,* 35(5/6):22-28. [Electronic Resource]. Retrieved 09/23/2001 from http://www.educause.edu/ir/library/pdf/ERM0032.pdf

Cutter, C. A. (1904). *Rules for a dictionary catalog.* (4th ed.). Washington: U.S. Government Printing Office.

Landry, P. (2000). The MACS project: Multilingual access to subjects (LCSH, RAMEAU, SWD). *International Cataloguing and Bibliographic Control,* 30(3):46-49.

München, Saur (1998). *Functional Requirements for Bibliographic Records: Final Report: IFLA Study Group on the Functional Requirements for Bibliographic Records.* Deutsche Bibliothek: Frankfurt am Main. [Electronic Resource]. Retrieved 09/23/2001 from http://www.ifla.org/VII/s13/frbr/frbr.pdf

Pitschmann, L. A. (2001). *Building Sustainable Collections of Free Third-Party Web Resources.* Washington, DC: Digital Library Federation. [Electronic Resource]. Retrieved 09/23/2001 from http://www.clir.org/pubs/reports/pub98/pub98.pdf.

Tillett, B. B. (2001). Authority Control on the Web. In Sandberg-Fox, A. M., *Proceedings of the Bicentennial Conference on Bibliographic Control for the New Millennium: Confronting the Challenges of Networked Resources and the Web*. Washington, D. C. [Electronic Resource]. Retrieved 09/23/2001 from http://lcweb.loc.gov/catdir/bibcontrol/tillett.html.

USF Virtual Library Metadata/Cataloging Team (1999). *Guidelines for cataloging USF electronic resources*. Tampa, FL: University of South Florida Libraries. [Electronic Resource]. Retrieved 09/23/2001 from http://www.lib.usf.edu/~jmichael/metadata-team.html.

Zyroff, E. (1996). Cataloging is a Prime Number. *American Libraries,* 27(5): 47-50.

BIBLIOGRAPHY

Joint Steering Committee of the Anglo-American Cataloguing Rules. Available: *http://www.nlc-bnc.ca/jsc/*.

Library of Congress. MARC Standards Office. Available: *http://lcweb.loc.gov/marc/index.html*.

Program for Cooperative Cataloging. Available: *http://www.loc.gov/catdir/pcc*.

Chapter VII

E-Reference

Amy Tracy Wells
Belman-Wells, Michigan, USA

Ardis Hanson
The Louis de la Parte Florida Mental Health Institute at the
University of South Florida-Tampa, USA

The "information literacy competency" taxonomy in Table 3 is provided with the permission of the Journal of Information Technology Education. First published as Vitolo, T.M. & Coulston, C. (2002). Taxonomy of Information Literacy Competencies. Journal of Information Technology Education, 1(1):43-51. [Electronic Resource] Retrieved 01/12/02 from http://jite.org/documents/Vol1/v1n1p043-052.pdf.

Lipnow (1997) talks about traditional reference as a mediated, one-on-one service that intervenes at the information seeker's point of need. Further, she suggests that this point of need is part of the universal predicament of an information seeker – someone who wants to move forward (cognitively) but is unable to progress until he or she finds that missing piece of information. Research clearly shows that information seekers want and need that gap filled with as little interruption as possible, so they can continue where they left off (Dervin, 1998, 1989). From a library perspective, the two questions emanating from that need are first, how to ensure that clients who use a reference service get up-to-date assistance that integrates paper and electronic resources, and second, how to reach the user who has a question but no obvious place to ask it. Technology may have simultaneously ameliorated and exacerbated these questions.

There are numerous local, national, and international initiatives for the provision of e-reference. These include efforts within centralized library environments, between libraries under different management structures within the same institution, libraries within the same region, as well as larger initiatives such as the IPL (Internet Public Library) Reference Center, AgNIC's (Agricultural Network Information Center) distributed service, VRD (Virtual Reference Desk), or the Library of Congress' CDRS (Collaborative Digital Reference Service), which attempt to serve any user, any where.

E-Reference means many things to many people such as asynchronous or, conversely, synchronous communication, software tools such as email or an off-the-shelf CRM (Customer Relations Management) package or even an in-house tool built in Perl, to policy and management goals, to cooperative and non-cooperative ventures. However, there are some trends as defined by market-share development. This chapter begins with a brief definition of e-reference and places it within the continuum of services provided by an academic virtual library. The authors then examine the functional requirements of systems, real world issues including policy and standards, market growth and issues in information literacy. Finally, they discuss future issues for e-reference services.

EVOLUTION OF E-REFERENCE

The definition of reference services in the electronic environment has evolved from the traditional definition which stresses that the central reference service within libraries is answering patrons' questions (Moore, 1996; Ferguson, 1997). In the networked environment, traditional reference services are evolving into more user-driven "self-services". For example, Owen (1996) has redefined reference services in a networked environment into personal assistance, help/support, subject guides, and instruction. He has ranked these services by the importance of supporting the users in *their use of information* instead of *their seeking of information*, i.e., what the user intends to do with the information once found (report, chart, graph), rather than simply looking for items with keywords that might be useful.

Within an historical perspective, electronic reference has only recently become a standard. Academic libraries began offering basic e-mail reference services in the late 1980s (Bushallow-Wilber, Devinney, & Whitcomb, 1996). By the early 1990s, "Ask A Librarian" services were common. By the mid 1990s, at least 75 of 122 ARL (Association of Research Libraries) member libraries and 45% of academic libraries offered digital reference service via electronic mail or a web-form (Goetsch, Sowers, & Todd, 1999; Janes, Carter, & Memmott, 1999). By the end of the 1990s, 99% of 70 academic libraries offered e-mail reference and 29% offered real-time reference service (Tenopir, 2001). The latter part of 1999 brought the advent of live reference in academic libraries with the use of "chat" or commercial call center software (i.e., synchronous) to communicate with users in real time. The year 2000 brought the advent of live reference in academic libraries with the use of "chat" or commercial call center software to communicate with users in real time. The vendor, Library Sytems and Services, Inc. (LSSI), caused a stir at the 2000 Annual Conference of the American Library Association by unveiling the first commercial adaptation of call center software (Oder, 2001). Collaboration has kept pace with technology with the implementation of regional and international reference services. For example, the Library of Congress began its Collaborative Digital Reference Service project to test the provision of professional library-quality reference service to users any time anywhere (24 hours per day, 7 days per week), through an international digital network of libraries.

Underpinning much of the discussion on virtual libraries is an assumption that "disintermediation," that is unmediated access to information, provides a total solution for the Internet user community (Missingham, 2000). However, the service model for libraries took a new direction with the recognition that the print and electronic environments exist in parallel, creating a "hybrid library". The hybrid library concept acknowledges that academic reference departments would continue to utilize print resources as well as electronic resources in their provision of services. The issue, though, of *how* an academic reference department would provide reference in this hybrid environment requires a definition of electronic reference in terms of its mechanisms, services, staffing, policies, and expected outcomes.

In conjunction with this evolving service model is an evolving definition of what constitutes a "remote" patron. Initially, this population was conceptualized as perhaps faculty who were on sabbatical or distance education students. Increasingly, however, the "remote" patron is the student on campus in their dorm room or even one in another part of the physical library connecting from their laptop.

How do new developments in technology, education (e.g., distance learning), architecture, publishing, and so on affect the responsibilities and subsequently skills of reference librarians today? Domains such as human-computer interaction (HCI), computer-mediated communication (CMC), and systems architecture, are also germane to library environments. Are these domains and skills subordinate to or complementary to understanding the reference process? That is, are these in-house skills and/or out-sourced issues?

DEFINTION OF E-REFERENCE

E-reference can mean many things. However, it is essentially divided into two "time-based" camps. There is the asynchronous view that involves the use of FAQs (frequently asked questions); e-resources, which are comprised of subject guides, lists, journals, and other content; and e-mail, which may be forms-based or address-based. FAQs and e-resources tend to be passive services, i.e., the patron reads and evaluates. E-mail reference service is problematic. E-mail has an immediacy problem, with an average turnaround time of twenty-four hours, leaving it within the asynchronous camp (O'Neill, 1999). There is also an acknowledged, inherent difficulty in conducting a "formal" reference interview over e-mail (McGlamery and Coffman, 2000).

Much of the computer-mediated communication (CMC) literature discusses two items that are considered crucial to create a successful online interaction. The first, social presence, is the degree to which a medium is perceived to convey the actual presence of communicating participants (Short, Williams, & Christie, 1976; Mason, 1994; Gunawardena, 1995; Gunawardena & Zittle, 1997; Tu, 2000). The second, media richness, is concerned with determining the most appropriate communication medium for dealing with uncertainty and equivocality (Daft & Lengel, 1984, 1986; Daft, Lengel & Trevino, 1987). Although earlier media richness studies accounted for differences in the way individuals choose among traditional media and between traditional and new media, current studies are focused on communication mode and filing/retrieval capabilities, on the basis of their communication role (as senders or recipients of messages) and other personal, task, social or organizational factors (El-Shinawy & Markus, 1997). Therefore, some academic libraries have turned to synchronous, real-time technologies to recreate the immediacy found in traditional face-to-face reference interactions.

With synchronous, real-time technologies, typically using text, patrons click a button on a web page to exchange messages with a librarian in real time. CRM software has emerged as one of the newest technologies for the virtual library; with some products designed for use in library settings (such as Docutek's Virtual Reference Librarian) and other commercial products (such as Virtual Reference Software and 24/7 Reference which use eGain and QuestionPoint developed by Convey Systems) have been adapted for use in library settings (eGain, 2002).

These software offer a number of features, including user queuing; the ability to push text, images, files, and web pages; the ability to standardize responses; escorting and co-browsing; application sharing; routable messages; call escalation; and voice-over-IP. (Explanations of these and other functionalities are provided in the following section.) In addition, real-time virtual reference services have many advantages to library users, who can get immediate help without having to leave the computer or disconnect the modem line to make a phone call.

Ehrlich (1987) introduces the concept of "critical mass" as an important factor to the acceptance of an information system or service and advises targeting groups that may be able to make the most effective use of the electronic reference service.

Although librarians may be enthusiastic over the introduction of a new service, Sloan (1998) suggests that faculty members and students conversant with using e-mail and at a distance from the library on a regular basis might be a primary target group. Vander Meer, Poole, and Van Valey (1997) address the issue of those faculty who are infrequent or non-users of library services. By not informing this faculty of new services or enquiring about specific faculty needs, a library may unintentionally indicate that it does not care about the information needs of this faculty. In this era of dwindling funds and growing competition for campus resources, academic libraries cannot afford to disregard any of its constituents.

The choice of software for coordinating the operation of a digital reference service is critical to the success of such a service. From a library perspective, questions one might ask should focus on functionality, communication, and evaluative processes (Wells, 2001). For example, the software should provide the functionality necessary to enable staff to carry out assigned tasks in accordance with established e-reference procedures. In addition, the software must provide efficient channels for communication between the patron and the librarian as well as the librarians providing e-reference. Finally, one should determine how useful the statistics are in evaluating the performance of a service, particularly in the area of improving service.

FUNCTIONAL REQUIREMENTS

According to Shelly, Cashman and Rosenblatt (1998, pp. 1.4-1.6), the fundamental units of information systems are hardware (physical components of a system), software (instruction sequences for a system), data (static representations of system content), procedures (tasks and activities to be performed by people in conjunction with a system), and finally people (stakeholders of a system). Wells (2001) reviews functional requirements within the context of mission statement, personnel (providers & administrators), policy, platform (hardware and software), and evaluation. Both perspectives are useful when deciding upon minimal functional requirements.

Minimum functional requirements focus on a number of parameters. For the purposes of this chapter, only a few of the requirements were chosen out of a larger list of front end and back end requirements (see Table 1 and Table 2). The first discussion point concerns *access*. Librarians must determine which services they wish to provide, whether they want to provide basic or in-depth service, and how they wish to offer the service. If the goal in this area is to offer the same level of reference service that a user might expect were he or she physically in the library, librarians can then decide what is realistic and what does not readily lend itself to the provision of remote services. The next crucial decision is whether the system is synchronous (real time) or asynchronous (time-delayed).

The next functional requirement concerns *affiliation*. Although college and university libraries have their faculty, students, and staff as their primary constituencies, most academic libraries have special arrangements for local residents, alumni, and persons interested in the institution itself to use the library and its resources. A guideline for this might be whether the primary clientele of the electronic service mirror the primary clientele of the physical reference desk (in terms of categories of users). *Validating* affiliation is typically handled in one of two ways — by authenticating users based on their (campus assigned) IP(s) and then sometimes requiring a corresponding user ID or by permitting anyone to submit the query while soliciting self-disclosed membership information, i.e., student, faculty, alumni, or other formal or informal affiliation (e.g., by requiring an email address). This latter approach has the advantage of permitting an individual who is not formally related to the institution to ask questions about the institution, its services, or its resources. The approach to accessing licensed e-reference content is handled in much the same way. Affiliates gain access via their IP or use a proxy server to self-identify and authenticate.

A *customizable interface* — both graphical and text — includes basic features such as the ability to include logos, text, and/or re-arrange or completely (re)design the interface from the main page throughout the system as a whole.

Text-based chat interfaces such as one-to-one chatting or MOOs or even chat rooms are common components of the Web. For a library patron trying to navigate an online database, it is far easier to connect to a reference service with chat than to perhaps go offline and pick up a telephone. Chat interfaces also allow the easy transfer of clickable URLs and blocks of instruction.

Some text-based chat interfaces are outsourced applications. Advantages of outsourced applications include: no hardware or software installation, no dedicated library servers, no plug-ins for patrons to install, and no special setup or maintenance. HTML links are simply placed on the web site pages that will be linked to the application. As with all things, there are advantages and disadvantages with outsourced applications.

Page pushing allows the librarian to "push" a page over to the client and the patron to "push" a page to the librarian. Using this feature, a librarian can demonstrate a search strategy for a patron or provide a web page for the patron to consult, without the patron having to go through all the steps.

Librarians should evaluate the use of *plug-ins* when deciding upon a CRM. Depending upon a "guesstimate" of the average user's skills, workstation, and bandwidth, one can choose a system where the plug-ins are hosted on the vendor's site, locally hosted by the library, or must be loaded on the user's PC.

Predefined or standardized responses are useful for certain types of reference interactions. For example, simple questions such as those concerning hours can be written once, but sent many times. Alternatively, very complex or ambiguous questions may be answered by a pre-formatted, response asking/ requesting that the patron contact the library staff by phone or by email with more details.

E-mail default is an option that provides the patron with the option of sending email rather than waiting for librarian when no one is available.

System stallers are phrases that are sent automatically to patrons when they are 'on hold' waiting for a librarian. Messages such as "Just a moment please" and "Thank you for waiting. I'll be with you momentarily" are sent automatically to reassure the user that someone is still at the other end of the chat. Alternatively, some systems provide patrons with an option to "leave a message" and have the librarian call back via phone or email.

Queue information can permit the librarian to know how many patrons are waiting for assistance, their respective order "in line," and how long each patron has been on-hold.

Routable queries permit librarians to forward patrons to another librarian. So, for example, if a question requires the need for a subject-specialist, the patron is directed the appropriate person. In addition, *call escalation* can permit a patron's call to be rerouted after a period of time during which their call is not answered. So, during a peak period, another librarian would automatically receive calls to reduce wait times.

Patron information includes specifics attributes for a given individual from relationship to the institution to questions previously asked to actual transcripts of past interactions.

Co-browsing or *escorting* permits the librarian to see what the patron is seeing and vice versa, by permitting the librarian to push content (e.g., a webpage, scroll to a certain part of the item), and, by means of a secondary pointer, to direct the patron's eyes to specific text, for example, rather than the site as a whole which would then require the librarian to communicate a series of steps in order to share specifics.

User feedback is another nice feature to have with this type of software. Often the CRM software will allow the librarian to create a quality of service questionnaire to rate the service and to generate demographics. General demographic and frequency questions include user affiliation, whether they are repeat users, and how they rate this service. The better CRM programs have built-in statistical packages that can tabulate frequency of response by category and graph the results.

The definition (and examples) of *knowledge bases* is growing. One definition that is more inclusive might be

"…a(n)…engine that allows us to keyword-search the full text of our entire electronic reference collection regardless of which publisher created the source. Plus…librarians should be able to bookmark or annotate the sources to help others find the answers to difficult questions more easily, and we should also be able to refer others from a source to supplemental material…So when somebody listed in one of our biographical dictionaries dies, for example, we should be able to annotate the entry with their obituary plus references to the spate of articles that typically appear after their demise. If we could incorporate some of these ideas, our reference collections would…be living and breathing things which would develop and improve as we worked with them." (Coffman, 2001)

An additional component might be the ability to add locally scanned print to this electronic wonder. A unitary system for *resource integration* might include information such as library hours, a bibliography of the Dalai Lama's correspondence from 1949 on to session transcripts from a reference interview (whether the original session was conducted in text or voice). It would not only allow users (patrons or librarians) to query this singular source, it would allow librarians to desist from developing and maintaining separate resource lists and FAQs. There are many complementary issues including the role of metadata, rights and record management, quality control, etc. that can be learned from cataloging.

Record format is ongoing as well. In a collaborative model whether within a singular library or involving any number of disparate institutions, the issue of a reference record format or encoding structure for exchange, storage, reporting and harvesting is moving slowly toward standardization.

Returning though to a more basic function is the need to generate and maintain statistics, i.e., *reports,* to capture such basic information as how many calls are logged during any timeframe, peak times, wait times, question topics, affiliation of patron, response time, librarian involved, any need for follow-up, etc.

Table 1: Front-end issues

Access - synchronous or asynchronous or both	Call back option
Authentication and/or ID requirements	Routable queries
Customizable graphical and/or text interface	Call escalation
Plug-ins	Co-browsing or escorting
E-mail options	User feedback

Table 2: Back end issues

Remote or local hosting	Contact list and profiles
Plug-in requirements	Knowledge bases
Customizable interface	Print captures
Reporting	Privacy
Authentication i.e. resources	Maintenance
Security	Backups
Resource lists	System stallers
Session transcripts – text and voice	Queue information
Reference record format	Reports

An issue that can be linked with privacy concerns or conversely as a resource saving measure is *local vs. remote hosting* wherein the e-reference software (and hardware) is administered and maintained on campus or in another part of the country altogether.

The point of this definitional analysis is that, while resource issues may determine staffing levels, purchasing timeframes, etc., any discussion must include basic service expectations and, ultimately, functional requirements.

REAL WORLD ISSUES

Software, Hardware, and Those Associated Costs

Electronic reference services should not be planned without first understanding the campus technical infrastructure. If there is insufficient campus bandwidth or peripherals (e.g., camera, microphone) to support running software or if there is no guarantee that the user on the other side of the "pipe" will have a powerful enough workstation, bandwidth, or those same peripherals, there is little point offering a high-end electronic reference software package. In addition, there is the added complication of parity across applications within a university as well as across university systems. For example, if a reference librarian sends a patron an e-mail message encoded in HTML and containing attached files and the latter's system cannot natively interpret and display it, the patron may experience a high level of frustration.

To a certain extent, electronic reference services can be done economically. Existing reference personnel can handle questions generated electronically. The service can be "piggybacked" using existing workstations, software (e.g., e-mail), and, when necessary, servers and network capacity. Because this can be done, the temptation exists to run electronic reference services "on the cheap." In the end, this has the tendency to trivialize electronic reference services and make them a marginal or peripheral activity. If an electronic reference service is to achieve any measure of continuity or success, the service needs to be formally integrated into an institution's administrative structure. Nothing makes a service formal like having a budget. Not every library, or course, needs a formal budget line for electronic reference services; it all depends on how extensive the service is (or how extensive it is planned to be). However, any budget for electronic reference services should include lines for personnel, equipment (including equipment upgrades and, if appropriate, maintenance), software, and supplies.

Personnel Commitments

Another issue to consider is personnel. Sloan (1998) suggests that personnel issues can be a complicating factor. Electronic reference work should not be assigned only to a staff member who enjoys it. Electronic reference work needs to be distributed among all professional staff, with responsibilities formally stated.

When planning facilities, administrators should remember that electronic reference services are not the same as electronic resources. Traditional resources can and do play a role in the electronic reference process. Bushallow-Wilber, Devinney, and Whitcomb (1996) demonstrated that nearly three-fourths of the reference questions submitted via e-mail were answered using standard reference tools. Since most traditional reference tools and many esoteric tools are not yet available online, it is crucial that librarians handling electronic reference services be situated near the reference collection. Sloan (1998) stated that the "virtual reference librarian still needs to be tethered to the physical reference collection."

Policy Development

Policies need to be implemented to ensure the ability of the reference staff to provide quality service to all members of their constituency. Mission definition and prioritization is essential. According to MacAdam and Gray (2000), problems occur when large organizations try to turn fundamental values into operational strategies. Any goal of a digital reference service must be consistent with the overarching mission of its library since allotted resources and staff will be diverted from other areas within the library.

The cooperative and collaborative services tend to focus on service population issues: who, what, where, and when, not policy issues. The corporate world, however, may provide models that can be applied to the library environment, as many of the pioneering studies in virtual teams have an international perspective (Baker et al., 1997; Rocket et al., 1998). Although virtual teams have been well defined as a concept, only a few studies have contributed to the understanding of the processes of assembling and maintaining effective inter-organisational teams enabled by new modes of communication (Ratcheva & Vyakarnam, 2001). These new collaborations more closely resemble Galbraith's (1995) definition of a virtual team: electronic networks or teams of individuals who are not real teams but individually linked together electronically to behave as they are. Haywood (1998, p.66-67) stresses the importance of having compatible hardware and software for communication and exchange of information and equal ability to access shared resources and communication information to the team. Finally, a major concern for collaborative e-reference services will be the impact of cross-cultural differences on virtual team formation as academic libraries move toward international partner-ships.

Reporting Commitments

Sloan (1998) suggests administrative and management issues need to be treated on a number of levels. The first level is the Library Division/Department. The commitment and support for a remote reference services program need to be strong at the reference and public services departmental level. However, commitment to a service ideal is not enough. Department managers must make sure that such services are incorporated into the formal departmental administrative structure. Often new services are initiated by individuals with an interest in, and an aptitude for, providing such services. However, there may not be a formal revision of the employee's job description to include this new service or a distributed service model incorporated into the department. This needs to be initiated at the department or division level. Library administration is the next level that requires accountability. As with any new service, upper administrative support is critical to ensure resources for training, hardware/software, and other fiscal support. Campus administration support is also critical. All virtual resources and services are highly dependent on infrastructure at the campus level and collaboration with campus computing and networking facilities is essential. For example, at the University of South Florida, campus-computing facilities offer help desk support and work with the USF libraries' systems departments to more effectively mount and run new applications. Finally, the support of academic administrators is a key factor, especially when the service is used largely by individuals in their academic offices and it may be difficult or impossible to tally foot traffic (Sloan, 1998).

Standards

Standards are designed to facilitate the dissemination, communication, and use of information by multiple producers and users. Although standards foster openness, successful standards have to solve both technical and social problems to succeed (Libicki, Schneider, Frelinger and Slomovic, 2000). For e-reference, there are several groups working on standards for reference service and for data structure and transfer.

The National Information Standards Organization (NISO) Invitational Workshop On Networked Reference Services (NISO, 2001) identified several objectives, including the aspects of digital reference that can benefit from standardization, the major stakeholders, existing work that could be used as a foundation, a time frame for research and development of the standard(s), and the next steps for standards development. From these objectives came the following three key issues: identify relevant standards and issues (such as intellectual property rights, privacy, and language issues), articulate basic aspects of reference work and how they are carried out in the digital environment, and identify international aspects of reference work.

A proposed standard is the Question Interchange Profile (QuIP). Created as a research initiative of the Virtual Reference Desk (a project of the ERIC Clearinghouse on Information & Technology) and the National Library of Education, with support from the Office of Science and Technology Policy, QuIP is a threaded data format. This format relies on metadata to maintain, track, and store questions and answers in a consistent file format, which then aids in the development of a shared knowledge base of question and answer sets (Lankes, 1999). This type of threaded data format allows users to search and retrieve a variety of Internet-based materials, such as e-mail, HTML, Z39.50, and FTP (file transfer protocol) (McClennan, 2000). QuIP will be written in XML (Extensible Markup Language), which is fast becoming its own standard in library data sharing applications. Two components that fuel XML's popularity is that XML does not assume the existence of middleware or even that external users will employ common practices and models. For example, XML has started to replace CORBA (Common Object Request Broker Architecture) as a syntactic layer for Simple Digital Library Interoperability Protocol [SDLIP], the Dublin Core, and PubMed (Libicki, Schneider, Frelinger, et al., 2000). As new standards are developed for interactivity among applications and metadata formats, librarians will need to become conversant with the implications for their own use as well as those of their users.

MARKET GROWTH

CRM has seen an astounding growth in the marketplace with a diverse range of players. Industry consultants predict a market growth from $4 billion in 2000 to $11 billion by 2003 (Magic Software Enterprises, 2000). For libraries, the market may not have grown as spectacularly, however, the use of e-reference software is steadily increasing.

Many academic libraries provide e-reference using this feature through a variety of providers. Georgia Tech, for example, has used AOL's Instant Messenger chat software as an e-reference tool since 1999 (Henson & Tomajko, 2000). Cornell University uses *LivePerson Chat*. The University of South Florida Libraries use *RightNow Live* (see Appendix A for useful websites for identifying e-reference products and listservs).

Snapshot of E-Reference Growth: May – September 2001

In May 2001, slightly over 51 information providers reported use of e-reference software beyond that of e-mail (McKiernan, 2001; Kerns, 2001). By September, over 77 information providers were reporting use of e-reference software — an increase of over 50% (McKiernan, 2001; Kerns, 2001; Wells, 2001). One month later, in October, there was a large spike in the use of 24/7 Reference.

However, since the definition of "information provider" is also broadening (e.g., IPL, VRD, CDRS, etc.), there may be an under-reporting of non-traditional models and institutions. Specifically, these academic surveys may under-report their activities since the surveys do not specifically include special libraries, K-12 providers, government providers, and non-brick and mortar entities. For example, mailing lists for MLA (Medical Library Association), AALL (American Association of Law Libraries), SLA (Special Library Association), IFLA, AASL (American Association of School Libraries), etc., were not explicitly polled. Additionally, though specific international academic institutions were assessed, as a group, they were not polled such as through DIGLIB or IFLA-L.

Patterns

Based upon the snapshot (see Appendix B), there appears to be many solutions chosen by libraries for e-reference. One interesting trend is that within a large library or library system, more than one software application may be chosen. Another interesting trend is that there is little change in services between May and September as far as self-identifying with a particular software application. For example, if an institution was using LivePerson then, it appears to be using it now.

Costs

The costs of the respective services are dynamic. This combined with the number of users, affiliates, and type of institution suggests that an enumeration of costs rather than conditional-sensitive figures would be most helpful. Aside from salary issues (reference librarians, staff, managers, systems, and/or catalogers), at a minimum, the other considerations include: physical space (i.e., will the service be provided at the reference desk or elsewhere), software (client and server including backup, proxy, third party reporting, etc.), hardware (again, client and server), peripheral devices (such as a scanner), licensing issues, hosting (specific to the e-reference solution chosen), seat (number of users permitted to access the system at any given time), training and/or travel costs.

Emerging Technologies

Video reference services are the newest electronic reference option. Compared to "Ask-A-Librarian" and chat services, video reference most closely emulates face-to-face reference services. In 1996, the University of Michigan and the "See You See a Librarian" project tested video-conferencing software to provide electronic reference service (Morgan, 1996). Efforts that are more recent have included the use of Webline chat software (the same software that Land's End uses) at the University of California/Irvine and Santa Monica Public Library (Henson and Tomajko, 2000). Although the client side is generally easy to interpret and use, video reference doesn't appear to be readily feasible because it requires considerable technology expense for the library and the patron as well as a steep learning curve and extensive training for librarians (Morgan, 1996; Henson and Tomajko, 2000).

From the services satisfaction perspective, further research is necessary to explore the need for a variety of possible video applications, particularly how design decisions, allocation of bandwidth to different sorts of video data, could be made to maximize user satisfaction (Anderson, et al. 2000) (for more discussion on video, see the chapter by Kearns in Section 1).

MOOs (MUD (Multiple User Dimension), Object Oriented) are text-based, virtual reality sites that allow people to connect to the same place at the same time. They are completely unlike conventional chat rooms in that they allow live communication as well as manipulation and interaction with cyber-objects. Although the MUD was originally designed as a social role-playing game environment, many universities around the world have been working to use this text-based "virtual reality" to build tools for distance collaboration, education and conferencing. MOOs are widely used public domain programs and are stable, mature environments. One advantage of MOOs in e-reference is that the subject of study can be represented as text. For example, a librarian and a group of students can share information quite easily because they are "talking" using text. Another advantage to the text-based chat is that the users are simultaneously generating study notes. Reference interviews can be clarified easily and bibliographic instruction proceeds at a more interactive pace with clarification and input from all parties online. It might be noted that this contrasts with video, which emulates traditional face-to-face in that both are difficult to record and "replay."

Although forms-based e-mail reference have been given a less than glowing reputation, for many libraries, this is a relatively low-cost win-win approach to asynchronous electronic reference. The structured format of a Web form can be beneficial to both the library and the user by beginning a preliminary or conducting *en toto* a reference interview and gathering pertinent information, such as level of request, scope and depth of request, and topical areas. Most forms require an e-mail address, which permits the librarian to contact the patron to clarify the question or schedule an appointment for in-person assistance. Haines and Grodzinski (1999) emphasise other benefits of web-based forms, such as statistical gathering, quality of service issues, and marketing, for a library.

At the University of South Florida Libraries, the use of auto-responders, based on key words in the email, have been effective in responding to patron requests after-hours or during the day. Each auto-responder includes a contact person, phone number and email, and hours of "in-person" operation as well as a request to follow-up again with the library if the information in the e-mail does not solve the problem. The system uses filters to detect and provide answers to common questions and directs complex enquiries to library staff.

OPAL (Online Personal Academic Librarian), an eighteen month research project based at the Open University (OU) in the United Kingdom (Open University Library), is exploring the development of a fully automated online 24/7 reference service for distance students. With approximately 200,000 distance students based in the UK and across the world, the OU library is developing an agent based architecture to create a generic "artificial librarian" capable of answering more complex questions about library resources. It will be integrated with university student authentication systems, enabling user profiling and the delivery of user specific answers.

The most familiar instant messenger (IM) is desktop-to-desktop instant text messaging. IM applications run from a client program that connects to a server on a network. Since the servers are interconnected and pass messages from user to user over a network, a single server can be connected to several other servers and up to hundreds of clients. Instant messaging systems, such as ICQ ("I Seek You) and IRC (Internet Relay Chat), are heavily used by students and by libraries. Both ICQ and IRC may be downloaded from the Internet as freeware.

ICQ is provided by a number of commercial vendors (e.g., AOL and Microsoft) and shareware applications. With ICQ, the user can chat as well as send messages, files and URLs. It supports a variety of popular Internet applications and serves as a universal platform from which the user can launch various peer-to-peer applications such as ICQPhone. Groups can conduct conferences using the multiple-user mode. Since the program runs in the background, it takes up minimal memory and internet resources. (For more information, the reader is referred to the latest version (5) of the ICQ protocol http://www.algonet.se/~henisak/icq/icqv5.html.

IRC is a multi-user, multi-channel chat system, where people meet on "channels" (rooms, virtual places, usually subject/topic based) to talk in privately or in groups. There is no restriction to the number of people that can participate in a given discussion, or the number of channels that can be formed on IRC. (Although there are no formal protocols for IRC, the reader is referred to this site for more information, http://corridors.sourceforge.net/.)

With additional technology, IM could be extended to the wireless realm. Orubeondo (2001) suggests that by working with mobile devices (such as digital cellular phones and PDAs), chatting could occur via voice or video. Further, if IP telephony is mixed in, users could instantly communicate with any colleague at anytime, even without Internet access. However, a major disadvantage of the IM applications is that this technology lacks full interoperability among the various vendors' clients. Until a single protocol becomes standard, this technology will fall short of its full potential.

EVALUATION METHODS

Evaluations of reference services on library web sites demonstrate the need to improve the quality of the majority of services, which appears to be insufficient and an impediment to promotion of libraries as competitors with commercial information web sites. Hummelshoj (2000) offers a model for the development of reference services based on public web sites from The European Commission. Her model, grounded within the question *"we really want to serve our users"* has been the basis for evaluations of both public and research libraries' websites.

Domas White (2001) presents a framework for analyzing and evaluating digital reference services (DRSs). Using systems analysis, her framework consists of approximately 100 questions related to 18 categories in four broad areas (mission and purpose, structure and responsibilities to client, core functions, and quality control). Using a selective sample of 20 DRSs, her analysis focused on a number of factors (including public archives, content, selectivity, privacy, access, browsability and searchability, and knowledge management). Her framework can help to develop descriptive models of DRS functions, assist in identifying best practices, reveal gaps in coverage or implementation, and support comparisons across individual services.

In addition to evaluating the why and the how of how libraries serve their users, the choice of tools is also important. Major streams of evaluation prevalent in computer-mediated communications include those studies evaluating why individuals choose a medium to convey a message and those studies that review the impact of an elected medium on communication. A review of how AskA services have worked in the k-12 environment might offer solid suggestions for improvement of the academic and university services (Lankes, 1999b; Kasowitz, Bennett, & Lankes, 2000). According to Barcellos (2000), these areas provide insight into factors related to the medium that may affect its use for a particular task and the impact of using a communication medium that may also influence an individual's use of it.

INFORMATION LITERACY

Adding to the discussion of e-reference is the overlay of the American Library Association's requirements for information literacy, which focuses on the user's ability to recognize when information is needed; the ability to locate the needed information; the ability to evaluate the suitability of retrieved information, and the ability to use the needed information effectively and appropriately. However, with the multiplicity of online systems and interfaces, Vitolo and Coulston (2002) postulate that information professionals must go one step further and consider the use of analytical and model-based reasoning when reviewing the implementation of new systems from the naïve and professional user perspective. Both forms of reasoning consider the understanding of relationships among objects, the application of ordering principles to the objects, and the use of basic computational tasks/operations relevant to the relationships and ordering (Educational Testing Service, 2000; Russell and Norvig, 1995, p. 209).

Information literacy is similar to these forms of reasoning since all begin with the ability to gather data about an environment to an ability to understand cause and effect relationships and end with the ability to do deductive reasoning within an environment (Vitolo & Coulston, 2002). Vitolo and Coulston (p. 47) map the six levels of the educational objectives of Bloom's Taxonomy to the five fundamental units of information systems (Shelly et al., 1998, pp. 1.4-1.6) to yield an information literacy competency taxonomy (see Table 3). This taxonomy provides an expanded way of thinking about not only the skills but also how one may assists a user to acquire and hone those skills. Bloom's Taxonomy was devised to express educational objectives—"intended behaviors which the student shall display at the end of some period of education" (Bloom, 1956, p. 16), these educational objectives are relevant to larger information literacy competencies, "e.g. intended behaviors *in the context of information literacy* which the student shall display at the end of some period of education." (Vitolo & Coulston, p. 46). As e-reference and other e-services continue to evolve, this taxonomy may be useful in the development of policies, procedures, and applications.

Table 3: The "information literacy competency" taxonomy (Vitolo & Coulston, 2002).

	Knowledge	Compre-hension	Appli-cation	Analysis	Synthesis	Evaluation
Hardware	What are the hardware components of a system?	What do the components of a hardware system do?	When would the hardware suit my needs?	How does this piece of hardware work?	How would I build this hardware?	What improves hardware design?
Software	What are the software components of a system?	What is the role of software is in a system?	When would the software fit the situation?	How does this software work?	How would I build this software?	What conditions produce quality software?
Data	Where can I get data?	What does this data mean?	When would I use this data?	How is this data interpreted?	How would I appropriately gather the data?	What factors increase the value and reliability of data?
Procedure	What actions can be taken?	What is the purpose of an action?	When would an action occur?	What are the steps of the action?	How would I define the steps of the action?	Which aspects of an action are necessary and which are sufficient?
People	Who are the stakeholders?	What are the roles and relationships of individuals in a situation?	When should an individual become involved?	How is the person responding?	How can the individuals have their responses changed?	What significance does an individual have to the progress of a system?

As librarians become more involved in the support of distance education within the academic setting, the selection of tools for their use and use by their patrons becomes paramount. Librarians will need to see the larger picture of how tools drive procedures for instruction, instruction is driven by intended outcomes for students, outcomes are driven by institutional mission, and mission is driven by stakeholders and accountability to larger educational systems.

SUMMARY

The nature of academic reference work and the environment of reference departments have changed profoundly in the last few years. Gapen (1993) suggests that virtual libraries provide "the effect of a library which is a synergy created by bringing together technologically the resources of many, many libraries and information services." More sources, more options for sources, higher patron expectations, and, of course, more reliance on new technologies creates a constantly changing environment.

The definition of reference services in the electronic environment has evolved from the traditional definition that stresses that the central reference service within libraries is answering patron's questions (Moore, 1996; Ferguson & Bunge, 1997). In the networked environment, traditional reference services are evolving into more user-driven "self-services". The early reference services that began as "Ask A Librarian" services carry a positive, helpful appeal and "Ask A" remains the most common name used for the spectrum of these services.

Though dozens of academic libraries now offer real-time reference (see Appendix A), few have tremendous volume of interactions (Sears, 2001). The choice of software for coordinating the operation of a digital reference service is critical to the success of such a service. The more interactive electronic reference services such as "chat" or "real-time reference" have begun in only the last two to three years. Video reference services are the newest electronic reference option.

In addition, Domegan (1996) sees the advent of new software applications enhancing customer service in three ways: clerical effectiveness via automating basic functions; operational efficiency of the department and individual; and strategic effectiveness based on the information generated by the software and transaction logs. She also states that there is a direct positive correlation between the exploitation of information technology in customer service and the degree of information orientation, certainly a bonus for academic libraries and their patrons. This is in keeping with the idea that, as knowledge-bases mature and resources are integrated, the concept of time-based camps will blur into another technological hybrid.

Remote reference services programs need commitment from all levels within an academic setting, from campus and library administration as well as at the reference and public services departmental levels. Electronic reference services should not be planned without first understanding and formalizing goals, the service models, staffing patterns, functional needs, and the campus technical infrastructure at a minimum. The hybrid library concept acknowledges that as hi-tech as some of the e-library components are, academic reference departments will continue to utilize print resources in its provision of services.

FUTURE ISSUES

Although patrons expect academic libraries to offer "one-stop shopping," they recognize that different resources and reference services are provided depending upon the nature of each library. From the user's perspective, the time required to retrain and reorient for each library's services and resources is seen as a significant impediment to effective research. Although, from a research perspective, e-reference can be seen as more of a collaboration between librarian and researcher, the question becomes one of exactly how transparent can a service become so that the patron "sees" no difference between their library(ies) resources and services.

Questions of collaborative e-reference efforts center around how much service to provide to a patron (undergraduate vs. senior research faculty), turnaround time, and issues of a service that goes beyond institutional mission, access to restricted content, training, administrative commitment, and acknowledgment. However, collaboration appears to be the key for effective use of mediated and unmediated information services. Future evaluations of the effectiveness of these collaborative services will certainly include consideration if smaller projects are amalgamated into larger combined services.

Another future issue will certainly center on the roles of national bibliographic databases as combined metadata repositories and knowledge management systems. Rather than to continue to create additional frameworks for "cataloging" content in external metadata repositories, librarians should look to expansion of current modules that allow efficient information (and cognitive) processing. Information processing has always been an expression of an individual's interaction with his or her environment. As our environment has become more complex and more international, the need to handle information in an appropriate, efficient, and verifiable manner has grown. Ercegovac (2001) suggests that the functional requirements for the bibliographic record (FRBR) entity relationship model for works, expressions, manifestations, and items be examined from the perspective of both the reference provider and the consumer. The literature clearly demonstrates that library patrons will be using libraries more as remote users rather than as in-house users. Further, these remote patrons have high expectations from other 24/7 real-time services (e.g., banking, automated gas stations, et al.) and expect those expectations to be matched by libraries offering similar real-time services.

Reference and cataloguing will need to establish better relationships as new library technologies emerge. For example, what are optimal (good enough) display elements and relationships between the different entity groups? Questions as to how well the display elements are on a page or how fully the MARC record might convey the "substance" of an item take on additional consideration as librarians "push" OPAC pages to users who may or may not be conversant with the existing screen display. Quality assurance issues, such as authenticity, provenance, permanency, reliability, and validity, take on new meaning as librarians interact with remote patrons who expect a level of integrity in the material they are receiving.

Another area that will be equally important to consider is the capability to use seamless languages by the reference provider and the library patron (Ercegovac, 2001). Search languages will need to ensure consistency, accuracy, precision, and negotiation power between the remote parties as well as to accommodate whatever communication languages will be needed for disadvantaged users if the Library of Congress' CDRS becomes the standard for 24/7 international e-reference (Abels, 1996; Dervin & Dewdney, 1986). This becomes even more important as reference librarians across national boundaries will be relying upon their library-based bibliographic systems as well as commercial and general Internet reference tools to provide reference and research assistance to their patrons.

Finally, further research on the information needs and patterns of use of electronic reference will provide the basis for future developments. Text-based chat service is seen as an interim technology. With the advance of broadband communications and users that are more sophisticated, a real-time audio/video exchange seems inevitable in a few years. For reference librarians, the challenges in virtual services are just beginning, requiring exploration beyond traditional library walls.

REFERENCES

Abels, E. G. (1996). The email reference interview. *RQ, 35*(3):345-358.

Anderson, A. H., Smallwood, L., Macdonald, R. Mullin, J., Fleming, A.M. & O' Malley, C. (2000). Video data and video links in mediated communication: what do users value? *International Journal of Human-Computer Studies, 52*:165-187.

Baker, M., Barker, M., Thorne, J. & Dutnell, M. (1997). Leveraging human capital. *Journal of Knowledge Management, 1* (1):63-74.

Barcellos, S. (2000). Understanding Intermediation in a Digital Environment: An Exploratory Study. In Kasowitz, A. S. & Stahl, J. (Eds.), *The Facets of Digital Reference. Proceedings of the Virtual Reference Desk Annual Digital Reference Conference* (2nd, Seattle, Washington, October 16-17, 2000). [ERIC Document ED457861].

Bloom, B. S. (Ed.) (1984, 1956). *Taxonomy of Educational Objectives. Handbook 1; Cognitive Domain.* New York: Longman.

Bushallow-Wilber, L., Devinney, G. & Whitcomb, F. (1996). Electronic mail reference service: a study. *RQ, 35* (Spring): 359-366.

Coffman, Steve (2001) We'll take it from here: developments we'd like to see in virtual reference software. *Information Technology and Libraries, 20*(3):149-53.

Daft, R. L. & Lengel, R. H. (1984). Information richness: A new approach to managerial behavior and organization design. In Staw, B. M. & Cummings, L. L. (Eds). *Research in Organizational Behavior*. Greenwich: JAI Press.

Daft, R. L. & Lengel, R. H. (1986). Organizational information requirements, media richness and structural design. *Management Science, 32*, 554–571.

Daft, R. L., Lengel, R. H. & Trevino, L. K. (1987). Message equivocality, media selection, and manager performance: implications for information support systems. *MIS Quarterly, 11,* 355–366.

Dervin, B. (1989). Users as research inventions: how research categories perpetuate inequities. *Journal of Communication, 39* (2): 216-32.

Dervin, B. (1998). Sense-making theory and practice: an overview of user interests in knowledge seeking and use. *Journal of Knowledge Management, 2*(2):36-46.

Dervin, B. & Dewdney, P. (1986) Neutral questioning: A new approach to the reference interview. *RQ*, 25(Summer): 506-513.

Domas White, M. (2001). Digital reference services: Framework for analysis and evaluation. *Library & Information Science Research, 23*(3): 211-231

Domegan, C.T. (1996). The adoption of information technology in customer service. *European Journal of Marketing, 30*(6):52-69.

Education Testing Service. (2000). *GRE Analytical Reasoning Questions*. Princeton, NJ: Author. [Electronic Resource] Retrieved 07/26/01 from http://www.gre.org/practice_test/takear.html.

eGain (2002, March 18). Library Systems and Services, Inc. Selects eGain to Power Virtual Reference Desks. [Electronic Resource] Retrieved 03/18/01 from http://www.egain.com/pages/Level2.asp?sectionID=6&pageID=936.

Ehrlich, S.F. (1987). Strategies for encouraging successful adoption of office communication systems. *ACM Transactions on Office Information Systems, 5*: 340-357.

Ercegovac, Z. (2001). Collaborative e-reference: a research agenda. 67th IFLA Council and General Conference, August 16-25, 2001. [Electronic Resource] Retrieved 01/12/02 from http://www.ifla.org/IV/ifla67/papers/058-98e.pdf.

Ferguson, Chris D. and Charles A. Bunge (1997) - The shape of services to come: value-based reference services for the digital library. *College and Research Libraries, 58*(3):252-265.

Galbraith, J.R. (1995). *Designing Organisations: An Executive Briefing on Strategy, Structure, and Process*. Jossey-Bass, San Francisco, CA.

Gapen, K. D. The virtual library, society, and the librarian. In Saunders, L.M. (ed.) *The Virtual Library: Visions and Realities*. Westport, CT: Meckler, 1993.

Goetsch, L..; Sowers, L., & Todd, C. (October 1999). *SPEC kit 251: Electronic reference service: executive summary*. [Electronic Resource] Retrieved 01/10/02 from http://www.arl.org/spec/251sum.html.

Gunawardena, C.N. (1995). Social presence theory and implications for interaction collaborative learning in computer conferences. *International Journal of Educational Telecommunications*, 1(2/3):147–166.

Gunawardena, C.N. & Zittle, F. J. (1997). Social presence as a predictor of satisfaction within a computer-mediated conferencing environment. *The American Journal of Distance Education*, 11(3): 8–26.

Haines, A. & Grodzinski, A. (1999). Web forms: Improving, expanding, and promoting remote reference services. *College & Research Libraries News*, 60(4):271-2.

Haywood, M. (1998). *Managing Virtual Teams: Practical Techniques for High-technology Project*. Norwood, MA: Managers, Artech House.

Henson, B. & Tomajko, K. G.(2000). Electronic reference services: opportunities and challenges *Journal of Educational Media & Library Sciences* 38(2):113-21.

Hummelshoj, M. (2000, May 16). Do we really serve our users ? A model for evaluation and development of reference services on the Internet. IFLANET Reference Work Discussion Group (102). [Electronic Resource] Retrieved 01/12/02 from http://www.ifla.org/VII/dg/dgrw/dgrw5.htm.

Janes, J., Carter, D. S., & Memmott, P. (1999). Digital reference services in academic libraries. *Reference & User Services Quarterly*, 39(2):145-150.

Kasowitz, A. S. (2001). Trends and Issues in Digital Reference Services. ERIC DIGEST [EDO-IR-2001-07]. [Electronic Resource] Retrieved 02/08/02 from http://www.ericit.org/digests/EDO-IR-2001-07.shtml.

Kerns, K. Live Reference. [Electronic Resource] Retrieved 02/08/02 from http://www-sul.stanford.edu/staff/infocenter/liveref.html.

Lankes, R.D. (1999). The Virtual Reference Desk: Question Interchange Profile White Paper Version 1.01d May 13, 1999. [Electronic Resource] Retrieved 02/08/02 from http://www.vrd.org/Tech/QuIP/1.01/QuIP1.01d.PDF.

Lankes, R.D. (1999b). AskA's lesson learned from K-12 digital reference services. *Reference & User Services Quarterly*, 38(1): 63-71.

Levin, R. (2000). A Services Suite to Replace Internet Relay Chat. [Electronic Resource] Retrieved 03/08/02 from http://corridors.sourceforge.net/.

Libicki, M., Schneider, J., Frelinger, D.R., & Slomovic, A. (2000). *Scaffolding the New Web: Standards and Standards Policy for the Digital Economy*. Arlington, VA: RAND Science and Technology Policy Institute.

Lipow, A.G. (1997). Thinking out loud: Who will give reference service in the digital environment? *Reference & User Services Quarterly*, 37(2):125-129.

MacAdam, B. & Gray, S. (2000). A management model for digital reference services in large institutions. In Kasowitz, A. S. & Stahl, J. (Eds.). *The Facets of Digital Reference. Proceedings of the Virtual Reference Desk Annual Digital Reference Conference* (2nd, Seattle, Washington, October 16-17, 2000). [ERIC Document ED457861]

Mackenzie Owen, J.S. & Wiercx, A. (1996) - Knowledge models for networked library Services. Final report. NBBI -Project Bureau for Information Management, Hague. [Electronic Resource] Retrieved 01/12/02 from http:www.nbbi.nl/kms/kmspage.html.

Magic Software Enterprises (2000). *White Paper: The CRM Phenomenon.* Irvine, CA: Magic Software Enterprises.

Mason, R.(1994). *Using Communications Media in Open and Flexible Learning.* London: Kogan Page.

McClennon, M. (2000). Draft proposal for QuIP standard (Ann Arbor version).[Electronic Resource] Retrieved 01/12/02 from http://www.ipl.org:2000/papers/QuIP-aa-1.pdf

McIsaac, M. S. & Gunawardena, C. N. (1996). Distance Education. In Jonassen, D. H. (ed.) *Handbook of Research for Educational Communications and Technology.* New York: Macmillan Library Reference, 403–437.

Missingham, Roxanne (2000, November 11). Virtual services for virtual readers: reference reborn in the E-library. *ALIA 2000 Conference Proceedings.* [Electronic Resource] Retrieved 01/12/02 from http://www.alia.org.au/conferences/alia2000/authors/roxanne.missingham.html

Moore, Audrey D. (1996). Reference librarianship: "It was the best of times, it was...", *Reference Librarian,* no. 54, p. 3-10.

Morgan, E.L. (1996). *See You See a Librarian Final Report.* December 10, 1996. [Electronic Resource] Retrieved 01/12/02 from available at http://sunsite.berkeley.edu/~emorgan/see-a-librarian.

NISO (2001). *National Information Standards Organization (NISO) Invitational Workshop On Networked Reference Services.* [Electronic Resource] Retrieved 03/06/02 from http://www.niso.org/news/events_workshops/netref.html#key%20issues.

Oder, N. (2001). The shape of e-reference. *Library Journal,* 126(2):46-49.

Orubeondo, A. (2001). Business getting the instant message - As vendors begin expanding tools with collaborative features, IM is slowly being elevated from toy status.(Buyers Guide). *InfoWorld,* 23 (August 20):34, 36

Ratcheva, V. & Vyakarnam S. (2001). Exploring team formation processes in virtual partnerships. *Integrated Manufacturing Systems,* 12(7):512-523.

Rockett, L., Valor, J., Miller, P., & Naude, P. (1998). Technology and virtual teams: using globally distributed groups in MBA learning. *Campus-Wide Information Systems,* 15(5):174-182.

Russell, Stuart J. & Norvig, Peter. (1995). *Artificial Intelligence: A Modern Approach.* Upper Saddle River, NJ: Prentice Hall.

Sears, J. (2001). *Chat Reference Service: An Analysis of one Semester's Data. Issues in Science and Technology Librarianship* [Electronic Resource] Retrieved 02/06/02 from http://www.istl.org/istl/01-fall/article2.html#2

Shelly, G. B., Cashman, T. J., & Rosenblatt, H. J. (1998). *Systems Analysis and Design* (3rd ed.). Cambridge, MA: Course Technology.

El-Shinnawy, M. & Markus, M. L. (1997) The poverty of media richness theory: explaining people's choice of electronic mail vs. voice mail. *International Journal of Human-Computer Studies,* 46, 443-467.

Short, J., Williams, E., & Christie, B. (1976). *The social psychology of telecommunications.* London: John Wiley.

Sloan, B. (1998). Electronic reference services: some suggested guidelines. *Reference & User Services Quarterly,* 38(1):77-81.

Tenopir, C. (2001). Virtual reference services in a real world. *Library Journal,* 126(11):38-40.

Topolinski, Thomas. Shifting dynamics in the CRM software market. *Strategy & Tactics/Trends & Direction* (29 March 2001). [Electronic Resource] Retrieved 10/06/01 from http://www.gartnergroup.com/.

Tu, Chih-Hsiung (2000). Critical examination of factors affecting interaction on CMC. *Journal of Network and Computer Applications,* 23(1):39-58.

Vander Meer, P.F., Poole, H. & Van Valey, T. (1997). Are library users also computer users? A survey of faculty and implications for services. *The Public-Access Computer Systems Review:* 8(1):6-31. [Electronic Resource] Retrieved 01/12/02 from http://info.lib.uh.edu/pr/v8/n1/vand8n1.html.

Ware, S. (2000). Communication Theory and the Design of Live Online Reference Services. In Kasowitz, A. S. & Stahl, J. (Eds.). The Facets of Digital Reference. *Proceedings of the Virtual Reference Desk Annual Digital Reference Conference* (2nd, Seattle, Washington, October 16-17, 2000). [ERIC Document ED457861]

Wells, A.T. (2001). E-Reference Round-up. Invited presentation at the From Research to Policy: Informing Mental Health in the New Millennium annual conference of the Association of Mental Health Librarians, Tampa, Florida October 11-13.

Vitolo, T.M. & Coulston, C. (2002). Taxonomy of Information Literacy Competencies. *Journal of Information Technology Education,* 1(1):43-51. [Electronic Resource] Retrieved 01/12/02 from http://jite.org/documents/Vol1/v1n1p043-052.pdf.

APPENDIX A

List of useful web sites for identifying library chat services, products, and listservs (All current as of April 7, 2002):

1.   Francoeur, S. Digital Reference <http://pages.prodigy.net/tabo1/digref.htm>
2.   Kerns, K. Live Reference, <http://www-sul.stanford.edu/staff/infocenter/liveref.html>
3.   Lindell, A. Pappas, M.; Ronan, J., & Seale, C. Shall We Chat? Extending Traditional Reference Services with Internet Technology. <http://web.uflib.ufl.edu/hss/ref/chat/cc3.html>
4.   McKiernan, G. LiveRef(sm): A Registry of Digital Reference Services <http://www.public.iastate.edu/~CYBERSTACKS/LiveRef.htm>

APPENDIX B: MARKET SHARE : SNAPSHOT OCTOBER 2001

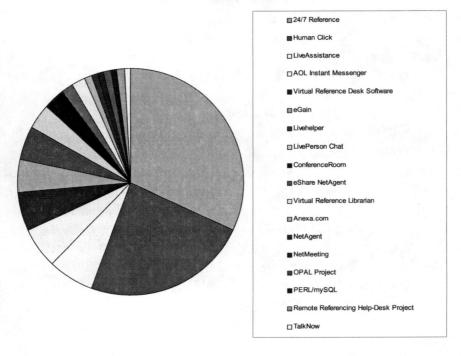

- 24/7 Reference
- Human Click
- LiveAssistance
- AOL Instant Messenger
- Virtual Reference Desk Software
- eGain
- Livehelper
- LivePerson Chat
- ConferenceRoom
- eShare NetAgent
- Virtual Reference Librarian
- Anexa.com
- NetAgent
- NetMeeting
- OPAL Project
- PERL/mySQL
- Remote Referencing Help-Desk Project
- TalkNow

Chapter VIII

Website Development Issues

Beverly Caggiano
University of South Florida Library System-Tampa, USA

Since 1995, university academic libraries have seen increased computer demand and use by faculty, staff, and students; widespread use of bibliographic databases to identify the existence and content of local and remote information; the emergence of full-text electronic resources; and a plethora of network databases, protocols, and applications growing piecemeal throughout the academic setting. To provide on-line access to these resources, libraries created web 'gateways' using new browser-based technology.

When any new technology develops, there is a tendency to discard the traditional way of doing things and start again. However, rather than arguing which approach is better, it is more constructive to examine and combine the strengths of each approach to provide a better service for the end-user. This is particularly applicable in the case of web sites, since the creation of a web site has become a relatively easy task. This chapter reviews the best practices gleaned from various disciplines, sprinkled with real-life examples, and tempered by experience. The goal of the chapter is to provide the framework for a viable library web project.

THE DESIGN PROCESS

The interface ("look" of a website) is a bridge between the developer's interpretation of the "real world" and the user's expectation (Jorna & Van Huesdsen, 1996). Without understanding who will be using the site and why they are there, the presentation may not demonstrate clear and appropriate choices. A site identity needs to convey a key message that is "succinct and repeatable" (Barrett, Levinson & Lisent, 2001).

Mission Statement and Project Objectives

The basic purpose of a website should be reflected in its mission statement. An example from an academic library might be: "Our online mission is to provide library users with access to electronic resources and research tools." After establishing the mission statement, the project objectives should be defined. Lewis (1997) described the "essential qualities" of objectives as SMART (Specific, Measurable, Attainable, Realistic, Time-Limited). Objectives are more specific than mission statements and define achievable results. They provide an avenue to monitor project progress and are a critical step in the development process. Without objectives, there is no way to measure success or failure. To continue with the academic library example, one objective would be: "To provide a web-based tutorial for the online catalog before Fall semester."

Describe Your Audience

User requirements can be gathered from market research, focus groups, surveys, and scenario building (Fuccella, Pizzolatus & Franks, 1999). After determining user requirements, the next step is to develop "personas". A persona is a "precise description of our user and what he wishes to accomplish" (Cooper, 1999). During the design process, the persona is consistently and continuously referenced. Through an iterative process, personas are defined by their goals, have specific skill levels, given names and, believe it or not, a face. A persona prevents the designer from using his or her own likes and dislikes during the implementation process, thereby ending feature debates. Frequently, primary personas end up with their own interface. In a 'web site by committee' situation, personas need to be strongly implemented to keep the design on task.

Tasks

A task is the route taken to accomplish a goal. The major difference between a *task* and a *goal* is that tasks tend to change with technology while goals tend to stay the same. A designer's responsibility is to get the user safely to the goal without confusion or embarrassment, by implementing his or her tasks in an efficient and reasonable manner. For example, the designer's task of creating a user-friendly navigation system allows easy access to information by the user. The instant gratification of having achieved his or her goal will keep the user coming back.

Identify Content and Define Scope

From the mission statement, there are objectives. From the personas, there are goals and the associated tasks. The next step is to identify and categorize the web content, remembering to include scope. Allowed to expand uncontrollably, scope will drive projects late and over budget. The scope needs to fit with the mission statement, staffing issues, programming limits and fall within time constraints.

At this point, the designer needs to determine whether "static" pages, "dynamic" pages, or a mix of the two better fits his or her objectives. Static pages do not change unless a person edits or replaces the contents of the file. Dynamic pages use a relational database to store content, headers, and footers. They are created 'on the fly' when the user clicks on a link. Dynamic pages generally are easier to maintain. Newsletter archives of a newsletter, which do not change, best fit the static page model, while library hours, which change throughout the academic year, could come from dynamic pages.

Build in Accessibility

An electronic library presence, like a library building, needs to be accessible to all. With that in mind, the World Wide Web Consortium (W3C) started and maintains the Web Accessibility Initiative (WAI) web site (W3C WAI, 2001). The WAI site is the definitive accessibility site and contains links to guidelines, checklists, techniques, alternate browsers, repair tools, and evaluators. Some common guidelines include advising against use of color to communicate a message and advocating the use of text-equivalents for every non-text element ("alt" and "longdesc" tags), redundant text links on image maps, and relatively sized fonts.

Designers often receive a rude awakening when running an accessibility evaluation. Sites should be tested using a text-only browser, a speaking browser (make sure the monitor is turned off), magnification software, and standard browsers. Standard browsers should turn off the graphics, JavaScript, and font changes. If web accessibility was never considered an issue before, it will be a priority after experimenting with alternate browsers and special adaptive technology.

One benefit of designing for accessibility issues can lead to less time spent in maintenance mode. The Web is the ultimate cross-platform system with hundreds of types of browsers used internationally. Since content is presented on such a variety of devices, the WAI (2001) recommends that pages should specify the meaning of the information and leave presentation details to a merger (or "cascade") of site-specified style sheets and the user's preferences, i.e., the separation of presentation and content.

For example, the use of style sheets handles many of the accessibility issues dealing with fonts, tables, and frames while minimizing the amount of time needed to code HTML (Hypertext Markup Language).

Usability

Usability is defined as: ease of learning, efficiency of use, memorability, error frequency, and subjective satisfaction (National Cancer Institute, 2001). Couple this definition with recent research to visualize how web pages are actually used for information. According to Cockburn and McKenzie (2001), users spend a very short period of time at most pages and rapid navigation calls for quickly loading pages and clearly presented links. Dyson and Haselgrove (2001) states that the optimum number of characters per line for effective reading at fast and normal speeds is fifty-five characters. These two behavioral characteristics should guide design initiatives.

The goal of a page is to quickly deliver information to the user via navigational aids. Navigational aids should be kept consistent, new and used links should show clearly and have descriptive text. A user should be able to drop into a site at any point and know where they are. Remember, results from search engines frequently leave a user in the 'middle' of a site.

A site index, like a book index, serves as a supplemental navigation system and is not constrained by the site's hierarchy. It is especially useful when the main organization system does not anticipate all possible uses of the site. A sitemap reflects the organization system and is useful when browsing. A search engine for the site is often touted as a major navigational aid. However, it is important to bear in mind that "typical web searchers use approximately two terms in a query, do not use complex query syntax, view no more than ten documents from results and have a session length of one query" (Jansen & Spink, 2000). Search engines should also correct for misspellings and offer relevancy ranking and limits. Search engines are useful when they respect robot rules and metadata tags giving the site the power to determine which information should be included/excluded.

In addition, a site must display efficiently when using slower connection speeds and allow for some form of feedback mechanism, e.g., email, forum, or chat. Web server error messages should be informative, not merely a string of numbers or obscure language.

Organizational Structure

Web directories should be created with names that make sense (e.g., ejournals, databases, newsletters.). The goal is to limit movement of pages and ease confusion during updates and maintenance. For example, when archiving newsletters, policies, or other documents, using the date as part of the directory structure makes sense. If a site includes "staff only" areas, the easiest maintenance route would be to include them all under one directory. The actual segregation depends on the content. Related files should be grouped together and common files should live in a top directory. Names should not include punctuation, non-alphanumerics, or spaces.

Prototyping and Testing

With personas and content considered, it is time to prototype the site. The prototyping/testing cycle should turnaround quickly. Nothing is to be cast in stone during prototyping. If one is implementing dynamic pages, test with a subset of entries as the database schema may change after testing. The National Institute of Standards and Technology (NIST) Web Metrics site [NIST] offers a set of tools to "explore the feasibility of a range of tools and techniques that support rapid, remote and automated testing and evaluating of website usability".

Remember, prototyping is an iterative process. First, the designer develops the prototype. Next, he or she watches what people do with the prototype and identifies the problems based upon user feedback. Then, the designer fixes the problem(s) and retests. Testing is usually done a few people at a time. A good rule is to let users try the prototypes from their own computers, since people tend to blame unfamiliar computers for failure (Moon & Nass, 1998). Anyone who wants to observe the testing should be invited. Sessions should not be longer than one hour and come in two flavors: *get it* and *key tasking*. 'Get it' is when users are shown the site and asked if they understand the purpose of the site. Key tasking is asking users to do something, then watching how well they perform (Krug, 2000). Test results should be reviewed immediately. During review, Krug recommends ignoring "kayak problems", i.e., when users go astray momentarily, and then get back on track.

MANAGING THE CONTENT

The site has been prototyped, tested, and is now up. Who is responsible for the content? If the responsibility lies with more than one person, how does one ensure everyone is using the same HTML tags, or table size or links to library hours? How does one decide which links are best - relative or absolute? Setting up a site style guide is a way to establish "textual coherence and a standardized appearance" (Sauers, 2001). Style guides can include templates, colors, fonts, metadata, and anything else that may appear in a web page on a site. Because the HTML generated by website tools frequently differs, all staff should use the same product. Ideally, there are a number of advantages of keeping content separate from presentation. Individuals can update content without having to 'know' HTML or cascading style sheets. A webmaster can define the appearance of a document separately from its content, making it much easier to script changes to that document. Accessibility increases. In addition, as voice browsers become more sophisticated, separate stylesheets that describe voice inflection can be created and served for those browsers, but the content remains the same.

Content management software can provide uniformity to a site by automating many of the tasks involved in website maintenance, e.g., creating, publishing, and updating website content. Points to consider include the amount of content that needs to be kept current and the frequency of updates required to keep it current, the number of content contributors, costs and time required for staff training, whether content approval is required before upload, the cost and return on investment, scalability, the placement of software (client or vendor site), the need for single or multiple locations or servers, whether software is non-proprietary or platform independent, and which operating system servers and hosts are affected. Although proprietary content management software is expensive, there are several content management options available in the Open Source Software domain (http://www.opensource.org/).

Adding Value

Interoperability adds value to a site and its associated resources. The goal of the Open Archives Initiative [OAI] is to increase access to scholarly publications by creating interoperable libraries. Supported by the Digital Library Federation, the OAI developed a framework for sharing digital objects on the web, which is accomplished by the harvesting of metadata. Metadata harvesting enables the extraction of descriptive surrogates for documents (Bowman, Danzig, Hardy, Manberg & Schwartz, 1995). Interoperability is based on three factors: the definition of a set of simple metadata elements, the Open Archives Metadata Set (OAMS); the use of a common syntax, extensible mark-up language or XML, for representing and transporting both the OAMS and archive-specific metadata sets; and the definition of a common protocol to enable extraction of OAMS and archive-specific metadata from participating archives.

Archival Information

To keep archival information accessible to commonly used browsers, avoid the use of non-proprietary formats or plug-ins. The simpler the data, the easier it is to preserve. Archives benefit from descriptive access tools, e.g., inventories, register, index, or guide. Encoded archival description (EAD) is one method of creating finding aids. For more information, see volume 60, nos. 3 and 4 of the *American Archivist.*

Persistent Access

Persistent access to documents can be maintained through "resolver" systems. A resolver system works by sending a redirect to a requestor. In 1995 OCLC created, and still maintains, the free PURL (persistent uniform resource locator) system. The Digital Object Identification (DOI) System is a commercial resolver used by many publishers, although it is available to anyone who pays for this service. The DOI system is more complex than PURL and gives publishers tight control over how they share information. If the location of a commercial document is changed and that document has an associated PURL or DOI, it needs to be changed in it the handler.

Writing and Linking

Text for the web needs to be scannable by users with "highlighted keywords, meaningful subheadings, bulleted lists, one idea per paragraph … written in inverted pyramid style with news and conclusions presented first, then details and background information" (Morkes & Nielsen, 1997). If the site is in the public domain, *Linking Policies for Public Web Sites* (Kennedy, 2001) is required reading. Kennedy recommends developing a "linking policy" to avoid use of links that do not serve the purpose of the site and cites several litigation cases regarding linking.

MANAGING THE SERVER

Security

When managing a server, one must be aware of security issues. An excellent article on the legal liability of hacked e-business Web sites is found in "Distributed Denial of Service Attacks: Who Pays?" (Radin, Scott & Scott, 2001). At this writing, no legislation is in place that will hold e-businesses liable for customer's harm. However, Radin et al. recommend adoption of industry-wide best practice policies as a way to defend oneself should a court appearance suddenly appear on one's calendar.

The best practice policies begin with monitoring and following the security alerts issued by CERT and The SANS Institute. If a system administrator has never heard of CERT or SANS, he or she needs to be informed about these security alerts or be replaced with a new person who does place a priority on security. If there is not a local systems administrator, someone needs to visit the CERT site, read the "security practices and evaluations" area, and ensure that the server has been patched. Firewalls should not give a sense of complacency to any systems person; they are not impenetrable. Since both SANS and CERT issue alerts via email, there is no excuse for not subscribing to them. In addition, SANS publishes free security e-newsletters that function as additional reminders.

Backups and Software Updates

Backups are another frequently overlooked critical aspect of server management. They must be performed, verified and stored offsite (or at least in a fireproof cabinet). One does not appreciate the value of reliable backups until staff been through a crisis and then it is too late. To prevent problems, software updates should be done on a regular basis. Most vendors post updates on their sites and some notify by email.

General Health

To run a local server, it is critical that staff dedicate the time and effort to maintain it. Without proper maintenance, the server could become a target for hackers, lose valuable data, and devalue the institution's credibility. If the staff is unable to care for a server, shop around for a web-hosting site.

Authentication and Remote Access

Libraries now find the provision of access to networked information services a major part of their daily duties. Managing this access is increasingly difficult as the number of services and products grows and users become more sophisticated. Lynch (1998) summarizes these problems as a symbiotic "user-system". For example, one of the most frustrating user issues is that users remember and manage a large number of different user identifications (IDs) and passwords issued by different publishers and different service providers. If libraries issued each user a single ID and password for all licensed external network resources, then transmitted them to each service provider, administrative costs would be phenomenally high and security would be a high-risk proposition. The example: IDs and passwords for 38,000 users to 892 vendors times the number of work-hours and staff, and percent of staff salary to send, store, and authenticate each one.

The most commonly used method at present is the user's source IP network address that serves as a substitute for demonstrating proof of "university" membership. However, the IP solution is inadequate. It allows no granularity in terms of service provision and fails to deal with user populations that rely on commercial Internet service providers (ISPs) for remote access. A way around this is through the use of proxy.

There are many ways to authenticate users: NT domain passwords, UNIX passwords, .htaccess passwords, IP, LDAP, user-created passwords, cookies, etc. How a system administrator authenticates depends on the intention. If the staff needs authentication, they will probably use the same passwords used on their staff PCs. However, if patrons needs authentication, Lightweight Directory Access Protocol (LDAP) is a good solution.

The LDAP is a protocol for accessing online directory services. Directories can hold and manage a range of functional requirements including: logon and related services; programs/content; people/roles/groups; security/credentials; devices and services; mobility and usage costs; documents and Web pages; database transition and integration (McLean, 1999).

The primary advantages of adopting a directory services strategy are consistent information applied collectively, but managed individually; protected operational contexts, and applications are managed in a flexible, distributed and scaleable manner. It runs directly over TCP, and can be used to access a standalone LDAP directory service or to access a directory service that is back-ended by X.500. X.500 is an overall model for Directory Services in the OSI world. The model encompasses the overall namespace and the protocol for querying and updating it. X.500 also defines a global directory structure. It is essentially a directory web in much the same way that *http* and *html* are used to define and implement the global hypertext web. Anyone with an X.500 or LDAP client may peruse the global directory just as he or she can use a web browser to peruse the global Web.

Therefore LDAP is a network protocol for accessing information in the directory, an information model defining the form and character of the information, a namespace defining how information is referenced and organized, and an emerging distributed operation model defining how data may be distributed and referenced. Both the protocol itself and the information model are extensible. Some campuses provide one-stop authentication. Individuals new to authentication should read "Remote User Authentication in Libraries" (RUAL).

Once a system is convinced the user is 'who' he or she says, the user needs to be passed to the resource. This can be done by scripting the appropriate username and logon via a proxy server or by using a commercial solution like EZProxy. EZProxy rewrites URLs to make them appear as if the URL is coming from the local server. Although it does not require browser configuration, it does require that cookies are enabled. A proxy server requires the user to configure his or her browser. Either way, there is maintenance involved. The solution chosen will depend on where one decides to place one's resources.

Monitoring Usage

All access to a web server is recorded in a logfile, the format of which is configurable. Logfile analyzers are used to generate various statistics. There are many flavors of analyzers ranging in price from free to several thousand dollars. They can run on a server or on a desktop—it is all a matter of configuration and what fits one's needs (and pocketbook). It is important to understand how the analyzers segregate data and perform calculations to avoid embarrassing misinterpretations (for an expanded review of the use of statistics, please see Chapter 13 in this volume).

CONCLUSION

There are a number of issues to consider when developing an interface for an academic library website. To recap, complying with information-related standards provides for compatibility and interoperability among systems, increases the usability of organizational knowledge, and improves the ease of maintaining and distributing it—three key factors in effective knowledge management. Measurable information applications and services that provide access and services should be scalable, efficient, and interoperable. Finally, the most important component of any website is the time and attention given to the planning, development, and maintenance of the site.

FUTURE ISSUES

Until very recently, new technologies have been employed simply to automate existing library functions. These new applications and services have enormous potential for a fundamental reconfiguration of the entire process of scholarly communication and for libraries' emerging role in that process. (Cummings, Witte, Bowen, Lazarus & Ekman, 1992). Technology can drive the evolution of traditional library functions. The question now becomes of how librarians will help to drive and shape technology to assist in their academic missions.

REFERENCES

Barrett, E., Levinson, D.A. & Lisanti (2001). *The MIT guide to teaching web site design*. Cambridge, MA: The MIT Press, 24.

Bowman, C.M., et al. (1995). The Harvest information discovery and access system. *Computer Networks and ISDN Systems*, 28(1&2):119-125.

CERT. *Cert Coordination Center*. [Electronic Resource]. Retrieved 09/14/2001 from http://www.cert.org/security-improvement/.

Cockburn, A. & McKenzie, B. (2001). What do web users do? An empirical analysis of web use. *International Journal Human-Computer Studies,* 54:903-922.

Cooper, A. (1999). *The inmates are running the asylum: Why high-tech products drive us crazy and how to restore the sanity.* Indianapolis, IN: SAMS, p. 124-130.

Cummings, A.M., Witte, M.L., Bowen, W.G., Lazarus, L.O., & Ekman, R.H. (1992). *University libraries and scholarly communication.* Washington, DC: The Association of Research Libraries.

Dyson, M.C. & Haselgrove, M. (2001). The influence of reading speed and line length on the effectiveness of reading from the screen. *International Journal Human-Computer Studies,* 54(4):585-612.

EZProxy. EZProxy homepage. Available: http://www.usefulutilities.com.

Fuccella, J., Pizzolatus, J. & Franks, J. (1999). Finding out what users want from your web site: Techniques for gathering requirements and tasks. *IBM DeveloperWorks.* Available: http://www-106.ibm.com/developerworks/library/moderator-guide/requirements.html.

Jansen, B.J. & Spink, A. (2000). Methodological approach in discovery user search patterns through web log analysis. *Bulletin of the American for Information Science,* 27(1):15-17.

Jorna, R. & Van Heusden, B (1996). Semiotics of the user interface. *Semiotica,* 109(3/4):237-250.

Kennedy, S. (2001). Linking policies for public web sites. [Electronic Resource]. Retrieved 09/02/2001 from http://www.llrx.com/features/internetwaves.htm.

Krug, S. (2000). *Don't make me think: A common sense approach to web usability.* Indianapolis, IN: Que.

Lewis, James P. (1997). *Fundamentals of Project Management: A WorkSmart Guide.* New York, NY: American Management Association, 33.

Lynch, C. (1998). *A white paper on authentication and access management issues in cross-organizational use of networked information resources.* Coalition for Networked Information (Revised Discussion Draft of April 14, 1998). [Electronic Resource]. Retrieved 09/01/2001 from http://www.cni.org/projects/authentication/authentication-wp.html.

McLean, N. (1999). *Matching people and information resources: Authentication, authorisation and access management.* [Electronic Resource]. Retrieved 09/24/2001 from http://www-text.lib.mq.edu.au/conference/mclean/matching/.

Moon, Y. & Nass, C. (1998). Are computers scapegoats? Attributions of responsibility in human-computer interaction. *International Journal Human-Computer Studies,* 49(1):79-94.

Morkes, J. and Nielsen, J. (1997). *Concise, SCANNABLE, and objective: How to write for the web.* [Electronic Resource]. Retrieved 09/10/2001 from http://www.useit.com/papers/webwriting/writing.html.

National Cancer Institute (2001). Usability Basics. [Electronic Resource]. Retrieved 09/04/2001 from http://www.usability.gov.

NIST. *National Institute of Standards and Technology: Web Metrics.* Available: http://zing.ncsl.nist.gov/WebTools.

OAI. *Open Archives Initiative.* [Electronic Resource]. Retrieved 09/14/2001 from http://www.openarchives.org.

Radin, M.J., Scott, W. B., & Scott, L.M. *Distributed Denial of Service Attacks: Who Pays?* [Electronic Resource]. Retrieved 09/23/2001 from http://www.mazunetworks.com/radin-print.html.

RUAL. *Remote User Authentication in Libraries.* [Electronic Resource]. Retrieved 09/14/2001 from http://library.smc.edu/rpa.htm.

SANS. *The SANS Institute.* [Electronic Resource]. Retrieved 09/14/2001 from http://www.sans.org.

Sauers, M. (2001). Style guidance. *Webtechniques*, 6(5):35-36.

W3C WAI. *Web Accessibility Initiative.* [Electronic Resource]. Retrieved 09/14/2001 from http://www.w3.org/WAI.

Chapter IX

Marketing the
Virtual Library

Kim Grohs, Caroline Reed, and Nancy Allen
Jane Bancroft Cook Library at the
University of South Florida-Sarasota/Manatee, USA

During the last decade, there have been significant changes in higher education, particularly in the emergence of distance education and the 24/7-access mantra (24 hours a day, seven days a week). This, in turn, has had a continuing impact upon efforts to reconceptualize what an academic library is and what it does. Not surprisingly, academic libraries face a number of critical issues, including increased costs of resources, expansion of traditional services, increased competition from other information vendors, and the impact of new technologies. Although these issues appear as threats, they are opportunities for libraries to design their own future (Denham, 1995).

In the near future, academic libraries will remain a vital resource for faculty, students, and staff. While it is easy for academic libraries to become complacent about their status within a university since there is no competition on campus, successful marketing programs can enhance visibility, create understanding about the value of the library, and shape public perception of the scope of its resources and services (Gómez, 2001). This chapter will briefly look at marketing issues in academic libraries, how those issues were dealt with in marketing the Virtual Library, and where marketing for academic libraries may be going in the future as the physical and virtual worlds shift, meld, and merge.

THE DEVELOPMENT OF MARKETING FOR ACADEMIC LIBRARIES

Historical Perspective

During the 1960s, libraries began to explore new information technologies such as microfilm and microfiche, tapes, and sound recordings. The 1970s brought full-text databases, such as LEXIS and WESTLAW. The 1980s brought about significant changes with the emergence of electronic card catalogs in many academic, public, and special libraries. Libraries initiated cooperative efforts and resource sharing became the norm. Electronic databases, containing subject specific information, helped libraries to expand what they could offer their patrons beyond their own physical collections. The concept of "libraries without walls" began to take hold in the field of librarianship.

During this period, many academic libraries felt little need to market their services and resources. Although libraries had continually expanding print collections and a captive audience, new technologies were changing the manner in which patrons viewed libraries. With the gradual emergence of materials available via dial-up services (such as Dialog and BRS) and later the Internet, a common misperception grew among students, faculty, and administrators that libraries themselves were becoming superfluous. However, librarians knew that this was inaccurate and thus explored ways to convince these groups that libraries still provided the essential sources for their patrons' academic needs. Librarians began to market their resources in an effort to reeducate faculty and students of the importance and availability of both traditional and electronic resources. Furthermore, librarians needed to also reeducate university administrators regarding the political importance of maintaining their financial commitment to both the traditional and virtual library, in terms of personnel, services, and resources. First, academic libraries provide cost-effective information services and products to resident communities of scholars (Wolpert, 1998). Second, every university needs a respectable library collection to ensure accreditation of individual programs as well as the university itself (Block, 2001). Third, over time and after numerous interactions, students and scholars recognize the quality of the resources and services of the library, and become comfortable with it, much as people become comfortable with a particular type of service. They then expect it to maintain or increase the level of quality they have come to expect (Wolpert, 1998).

Emergence of Virtual Libraries

The literature began to reference virtual libraries, not as a replacement for traditional libraries but as an enhancement to their offerings. With the increase in electronic materials and on-line services, such as e-mail reference, reference chat, end-user initiated interlibrary loan, and electronic reserves, it has become essential that students and faculty become aware of not only what is available in virtual libraries but also how to access the materials they need. To add to the confusion, electronic resources come in various formats, needing explanation to the users of academic libraries.

Marketing is intrinsic to the success of modern libraries (Brunsdale, 2000). Over a very short period of time, articles and books appeared that shared marketing techniques specifically geared towards librarians promoting the services and resources of these new virtual libraries (Marshall, 2001). Librarians have taken on a new role of publicizing or marketing the services and materials that exist in their virtual libraries. It is imperative to remind users that library services and collections are constantly changing. Libraries must become a visible entity, both as a physical structure as well as virtually.

The image of a library is an important component to the usage of its resources (Heckart, 1999). Just building a service or product does not insure that students and faculty will use it. Merely providing access to content is not going to meet the information needs of library patrons. If the marketing is successful, a virtual library will be the first place patrons search for information, rather than considered a poor substitute for the Internet. During the 21st century, librarians must learn how marketing techniques help to bring vision to the libraries' overall operation (Harrington & Li, 2001).

Basic Tenets of Marketing for Libraries

The four "Ps"–*product, price, place,* and *promotion*–form the basis of marketing principles (McCarthy, 1978). In today's virtual library, these translate into knowing who one's patrons are, targeting and reaching those patrons, explaining what resources are available, evaluating the success of the marketing efforts, and insuring that funds are available to continue marketing efforts (Hart, 1999).

Marketing should assist in changing the perception of libraries and librarians. The stereotype of the librarian as a middle-aged, bun-wearing woman who is constantly trying to quiet her patrons is as outdated as the concept that the library is only a physical container of knowledge. More important than the self-image of the librarian is the realization that students and faculty use a virtual library for many reasons. Satisfied users are educated users; therefore, marketing is part of the education process for users to learn about available resources and services. When developing a marketing plan, it is essential that patrons hear, see, and remember the library's message. The message itself must be simple, personal, relevant, and consistent, and most importantly, repeated frequently. Successful marketing creates a positive perception among library users, i.e., that a virtual library is reliable and is the first stop in accessing information. Furthermore, from an administrative perspective, the more satisfied users there are, the easier it is to gather support for additional resources and services.

At the University of South Florida (USF), the marketing process has been an ongoing event. The following section reviews the process of marketing the USF Virtual Library during its inception and what plans are in place for the future.

CASE STUDY: THE DEVELOPMENT AND MARKETING OF THE USF LIBRARIES

The Planning Stages

Until 1995, the five USF Libraries interacted with one another only at the most basic levels necessary: cooperative functions such as reciprocal borrowing privileges and book exchange, and at administrative levels to deal with policy and budget issues. With the concept of creating a Virtual Library at the University of South Florida, the seven-member Planning Committee quickly realized that the Libraries would be working together more closely than in the past. A first step was to set up communication tools in the form of a website, e-mail distribution lists, and weekly conference calls. The Planning Committee also educated itself on all facets of designing and implementing a Virtual Library, spending over a year carrying out literature searches, surveying peer institutions, and attending conferences. One of the initial marketing tasks for the Committee was to identify potential users and identify their needs, a critical aspect considering the demographics of this multi-campus, urban university.

The First Marketing Project – Soliciting Participants for a Focus Group

Dugdale (1997) points out the difficulties facing a project team when it has to generate enthusiasm for a new service, create interest in its potential, and explain how it could meet a need. The Committee convened eight main USF focus groups, including: library staff and faculty; teaching and research faculty and staff; graduate and undergraduate students; New College faculty and students; Marine Science faculty and students; Florida Mental Health Institute faculty, staff and graduate assistants; the university Academic Computing Committee; and the university Systems Administrators Group. The purpose of the focus group methodology was to develop an impression of the use of electronic resources at USF and the perceived electronic needs and desires within these user groups. Local electronic bulletin boards, printed flyers, and word of mouth advertised the dates and times of the focus groups (Metz-Wiseman et al., 1996).

The Planning Committee's final document, *The USF Libraries Virtual Library Project: a Blueprint for Development*, distilled information from the focus groups, the literature reviews, and the institutional survey. After approval by the USF Library Directors, the Planning Committee became the Implementation Team. Each member of the Implementation Team became a Team Leader of one of the newly created eight virtual library teams, one of which was the Marketing, Training and Staff Development Team.

Marketing the Virtual Library Project to the Librarians and Staff of the USF Libraries

The staff of the USF Libraries was the target of the second major marketing project. The literature clearly notes that staff buy-in is critical for major organizational projects requiring significant change. Mitchell (2002) believes that libraries need to market to staff when the library is experiencing a fundamental challenge or change, times when employees are seeking direction, and are relatively receptive to new initiatives. Senge, Ross and Smith (1994) state that by encouraging individuals to expand their personal capacity, to share a common vision, and to develop collective thinking skills as a team, individuals are more willing to expand their horizons by tackling difficult or challenging tasks. Marketing the Virtual Library successfully to its own staff and faculty would ensure that there would be sufficient labor to carry out the enormous volume of work.

Each library hosted a meeting to discuss the design of the Virtual Library Project, its organizational structure, how it would enhance services to patrons, and the work required to bring it to reality. Staff could ask questions and express concerns. The project was an opportunity to step outside of each individual's daily work routine and to become involved in creating the Virtual Library.

The Marketing Team Begins to Function

In May of 1997, the Marketing, Training and Staff Development Team was one of the first teams convened. Since it was clearly apparent that the team had two distinct functions that needed to be carried out by two distinct groups with significantly different skills sets, the team was reconstructed with two team leaders and its 15 members were subdivided into two groups. Marketing became a discrete group from Training and Staff Development. While the functions were different, the two teams needed to work in close collaboration. Effective communication within and between the groups was crucial. A website was set up that contained the team's charge, a regularly updated checklist of projects, each meeting's agenda and minutes, templates and forms, a bibliography of resources, and links to appropriate websites. The two groups held weekly meetings via conference call discussing progress on projects and assigning tasks to members. In addition to telephone calls, members set up e-mail and distribution lists, and communicated regularly via electronic mail. The two Team Leaders each took responsibility for one group, but met with both groups, providing continuity between them.

The benchmarks established for the Marketing Team enabled its members to begin to carry out tasks almost immediately (see Appendix A). The three long-term actions set for Marketing were: dissemination of information via multiple formats; standardization of Virtual Library publications, logos, and layouts to make them readily identifiable; and communication with a diverse and growing user population. In order to effectively market the inauguration of the Virtual Library, the Team had to work quickly. One subgroup focused on mechanisms of internal and external communication, while a second subgroup developed a standard recognizable formula for marketing new resources and services. The team as a whole began discussion on a corporate identity (a name and logo) for the virtual library.

Dissemination of Information – Mechanisms, Point Persons, and Contact Persons

The first step was to identify external communication processes and patron groups on the five USF campuses. With a focus on their home campuses, team members reviewed e-mail, print, and phone directories to identify contact persons for various user groups, how each group communicated, and in what format (print/electronic). Campus computing staff that administered listservs and bulletin boards and posting submission processes were included in the team's efforts to identify primary communicators. The smaller USF libraries communicated directly with their respective campus communities, as in the case of the health sciences and mental health research libraries, while the larger libraries utilized specific librarians as college departmental liaisons. Once these "point persons" were identified, each provided a list of mechanisms he or she used to communicate with the user groups. Each mechanism (e.g., the campus newspaper) had detailed information. Minimum information included the appropriate contact person, publication intervals, amount of space provided, and whether a fee was involved. In addition, many point persons served as an intermediary to assist in marketing resources. Identifying contact persons, for both print and electronic formats, turned out to be a formidable task as a number of publications, particularly electronic, were fluid, with changes in access point and names.

The first subgroup also concentrated on developing methods of internal communication. One successful effort of the Marketing Team was the development of a Virtual Library electronic distribution list for all library staff. This provided a resource to keep everyone up-to-date on progress made toward the creation of the

Virtual Library. Another successful strategy was the development of a combined web-based directory of library staff from all five libraries to provide easy access to colleagues.

Procedures for Marketing New Resources

The second subgroup created a standardized way to disseminate information about services and resources. Using the lists compiled by the first group, patrons received information about subject specific resources. In addition, the development of a procedure checklist ensured consistent marketing services for all new databases (see Appendix B). The checklist identified the appropriate point persons, user groups, and communication mechanisms. For example, the Marketing Team initiated several methods to help market newly acquired databases. The first was to ask the Electronic Collections Team (ECT) to amend its initial vendor evaluation form with a check box to request vendor-supplied promotional items, such as mouse pads, pencils, pens, signs, and brochures. The use of vendor marketing materials to highlight library resources is effective and saves a library time and money (Kendall & Massarella, 2001). A second mechanism was the identification of the appropriate library point persons who would provide information to the ECT about potential user groups. These point persons reviewed each database, identified each user group and its communication patterns, and then notified faculty by e-mail or by a letter if accompanied by vendor promotions. Third, the Marketing Team, with support from the Implementation Team, also determined that all library staff should receive information about all databases as a current awareness tool. Fourth, staff gave demonstrations to small groups and short presentations at university and administrative meetings and committees. As Webber (1997, p. 34) points out, there is a danger in giving people more information than they want at the time. It is best to concentrate on short, intriguing items and provide information on how to find out more about the topic.

Creating a Virtual Identity

Cheney and Christensen (1999) observe that identity is a pressing issue for many institutions and that the question of what the organisation is or stands for cuts across and unifies many different organizational goals and concerns. The design of a corporate identity can help unify an organisation but also help to brand diverse operations, services, and resources into a single recognizable entity when marketing combined services to a large service group (Wolpert, 1999). The Interface Design Project Group, another virtual library team, designed a logo during its creation of a "face" or gateway to the Virtual Library's resources and services. Utilized heavily in the marketing process, the logo incorporated the elements of sun, water, palms, and limestone to define the location of specific areas of the virtual library.

Figure 1: USF Virtual Library Logo

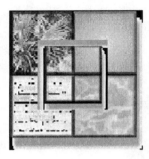

With the development of a virtual library logo, the next step was the creation of standardized publication layouts for a variety of materials. The first item created was a Virtual Library letterhead, followed by bookmarks, flyers, pens and pencils, brochures, and posters. For the actual inauguration, the team created invitations, balloons matching the colors of the logo, candy, and footprints with the logo leading to demonstration rooms. All promotional and event materials were prepared and sent to each of the USF Libraries.

Funding for Advertising

The Team decided that the more specific and tailored the budget request was, the better chance there was to receive funding for priority items. The request then went forward to the Directors, who determined the purchases and the money set aside for advertising in university publications.

Print advertising was particularly problematic. The Oracle, USF's student newspaper, charges large fees for advertising, even for a campus entity. The Team looked into prices for an insert, which had the advantage of being removable and placed on bulletin boards, and advertising within the paper. Because of the high costs, advertising in the paper was limited to the inauguration event and, after that, each month through the academic year. In addition to the main campus student paper, the Team utilized newsletters and student run publications on the regional campuses.

MARKETING THE VIRTUAL LIBRARY

Inauguration Day – November 1997

The advent of the Internet has forced libraries to shed their stodgy image and to utilize creative methods in marketing their services (Dworkin, 2001; Weingand,

1999). To publicize the inauguration, the new color logo was included whenever possible to effectively brand the USF Virtual Library in the university's mind. Using the new logo, each of the USF campuses received customized publication templates. The printed invitations, posters, and tabletop tents made extensive use of the new logo. The team also placed announcements in all identified mechanisms of communication, as well as on academic department bulletin boards and in student lounges and dining halls.

Due to the sheer size of the University of South Florida and its many campuses, the inauguration was a weeklong event with four of the five libraries hosting open houses. One member of the Implementation Team went to a library on a different campus as a volunteer, working with the Marketing Team representative for that library. There was a consistent format to the Inauguration: greeters stood at the front door and handed out candy, giveaways, and brochures; color footsteps with the Virtual Library logo printed on them led from the front door to demonstration areas; computers had balloons tied to them. Attendance was high; staff handed out all of the brochures and giveaways. A number of requests came from faculty for instruction and student orientations. All agreed that the Marketing Team succeeded in creating a highly visible profile for the Virtual Library.

The successful inauguration in turn resulted in requests from faculty to provide Virtual Library orientation sessions in classroom and library settings, which further increased visibility. The quality of resources and services available sufficiently impressed new users so that there was a ripple effect: the Virtual Library began to sell itself.

One Year Later

Not wanting patrons to "forget" the Virtual Library, the Marketing Team planned a first birthday celebration for the Virtual Library. Again, the libraries scheduled open houses, displays, and orientation sessions. Again, staff placed balloons next to computers and footprints led to orientation sessions. Since all birthdays need birthday cakes, each library found a location in or near the library to serve cakes decorated with the logo and other refreshments.

A major component of the birthday party was a display recording the use of computers within each library. Each library displayed original "dumb" terminals and old PC 8088s, with their DOS screens and abbreviated menus. Nearby, Pentium computers highlighted the graphical user interface of the Virtual Library. Posters, adjacent to each computer, described the information available in each computing evolution. A separate set of posters described the chronology (no older than five years) of changes. The older terminals and computers fascinated the students. They found it hard to believe that what they found commonplace was a relatively recent phenomenon.

KEEPING THE CAMPUS AWARE OF RAPIDLY INCREASING RESOURCES AND SERVICES

Successful marketers know that no opportunity should ever be ignored to remind potential users that the system is or will exist, what its advantages are, and what progress is being made (Dugdale, 1997). After the inauguration of the Virtual Library, it was time to start marketing the individual resources. The Team's focus turned to the procedures, revising them to market the virtual library databases. For each new database, members of the team followed the procedure checklist, communicating information about the database to members of the appropriate user groups. Attendance at training sessions and the increase in database usage statistics proved the success of the strategy. Kendall and Massarella (2001) believe that librarians should communicate their needs for promotional and informational materials to vendors and to assist in the development of new training materials. Since the Marketing Team had mapped out a communication mechanism for vendors, it was relatively easy to contact vendors on an on-going basis, usually through e-mail or a phone call, for promotional materials and assistance to augment the limited marketing budget.

Along the way, the Marketing Team found and used new communication tools. These included free student radio spots and word-of-mouth, as faculty who are sold on a particular database pass along brochures and information to colleagues and students. The Virtual Library used technology to become its own marketing tool. For example, the Team established a current awareness service, sending targeted e-mails to users when a new service or a subject specific database became available. In this way, the marketing process became standardized and routine.

A NEW ITERATION

The implementation of the Virtual Library created an environment that was able to support additional change, including the use of interlibrary, cross-functional teams; the arrival of a new Director at the Tampa Campus Library; and the installation of an interim Dean. With the successful implementation of the Virtual Library "Project", the USF Library Directors decided that it was time to formally meld the Virtual Library and the "traditional" library departments. Although this meant the dissolution of the Virtual Library Marketing Team, the directors authorized a new team with a larger focus that was more inclusive. The USF Libraries Marketing Committee now markets print and electronic resources and services as well as the libraries themselves. Convened in March 2001, the charge of the Committee was to provide leadership in marketing the services and resources of the USF Libraries. The Committee focused on the creative and content aspects of marketing. The members of this group included representation from each of the libraries, but, for the first time, stepped beyond the library system to include representation from campus public affairs offices. The committee completed its most challenging task: that of developing a marketing plan to provide direction for all of the multi-campus libraries in a quest to provide useful, immediately identifiable information to library patrons.

The Plan was broken out into four sections: audience, marketing groups, budget, and evaluation (Allen et al., 2001). The Planning Committee identified six target audiences (faculty and staff, returning students, first time in college (FTIC) and transfer students, graduate students, the community, and external library professionals) with unique needs and characteristics needing specialized marketing activities. The second section of the plan focused on the role of library staff and faculty in the marketing process. The Committee divided library staff and faculty by status (paraprofessional and administrative staff members, library faculty, the Library Directors, and the Dean) and by department (bibliographic instruction/reference, collection development, systems, and the Coordinator of Information and Publication Services for Library Development) with specific activities noted for each segment. The annual marketing budget focused on advertising, contract and professional services (e.g., photography and graphic design), production costs (printing and mailing), promotional items, and special events. Finally, the plan identified methods of evaluating the success of marketing efforts. These included increase in customary services; analysis of survey data; and increased recognition in area publications. Other measures of success included an increase in highly qualified job applicants for USF Libraries positions, increased service by library staff and faculty on external committees, and more grant and publishing opportunities for library staff (for a more thorough discussion on the use of statistics within academic libraries, see the chapter in this volume).

CONCLUSION

Although change is constant, the marketing of an academic virtual library is similar to other traditional methods of marketing. Libraries need to promote themselves internally as well as externally. This is particularly critical when the library is experiencing a fundamental challenge or change, times when employees are seeking direction and are relatively receptive to new initiatives. Internal and external marketing campaigns should be consistent; that is, library staff, patrons, and university administration should hear the same messages. The need for "brand identity" is critical. Branding campaigns should reinforce emotional connections to the library, introducing and explaining the brand messages in new and attention-grabbing ways. University administration should recognize that libraries are part of the larger picture of marketing the university. Virtual libraries and their physical complements are attractive to potential faculty and students as well as integral parts of academic accreditation. Although the USF Virtual Library is barely five years old, there has been a sea change in the knowledge base of the campus community. Initially, marketing efforts convinced students and faculty to recognize the value of a Virtual Library. Today, the Virtual Library has fully integrated into the academic lifestyle.

FUTURE ISSUES

Libraries will need to learn how to identify and target significant subsets of their user communities, their research predilections and methods, and then act on that profile by delivering services and resources. This will involve the use of marketing techniques, such as market segmentation and geodemographics. These techniques cluster potential patrons into meaningful, definable cross sections (Sumison, 2001). With the growth of distance education, information literacy becomes an increasingly needed component of virtual classrooms and virtual libraries (Wolpert, 1998). Basic elements of an effective marketing strategy for local as well as remote services must include product planning (user guides and tutorials), technical assistance (access, download, and navigation), and communication (not only learning about resources and services but also giving feedback).

REFERENCES

Allen, N., Arsenault, K., Brown, T., Cassedy, D., Leone, T., & Vastine, J. (2001). *Marketing plan*. Tampa, Florida: University of South Florida.

Block, M. (2001). The secret of library marketing: Make yourself indispensable. *American Libraries,* 32(8): 48.

Brunsdale, M. (2000). From mild to wild: Strategies for promoting academic libraries to undergraduates. *Reference and User Services Quarterly,* 39(4):331-335.

Cheney, G. & Christensen, L.T. (1999). Identity at issue: Linkages between internal and external organisational communication. In Jablin, F.M. & Putnam, L.L. (Eds.), New handbook of organisational communication. Thousand Oaks, CA.: Sage.

Denham, R. (1995). Strategic planning: Creating the future. *Feliciter*, 4(11/12): 38.

Dugdale, C. (1997). Promoting electronic services in an academic library. *Man-*

aging Information, 4(9):38-41.

Dworkin, K.D. (2001). Library marketing: eight ways to get unconventionally creative. *Online,* 25(1):52-54.

Gómez, M.J. (2001). Marketing models for libraries: A survey of effectiveness muses from far afield. *Library Administration & Management*, 15(3):169-171.

Harrington, D.L. & Li, X. (2001). Spinning an academic web community: measuring marketing effectiveness. *Journal of Academic Librarianship,* 27(3):199-207.

Hart, K. (1999). Putting marketing ideas into action. Lanham, UK: Library Association Publishing.

Heckart, R.J. (1999). Imagining the digital library in a commercialized Internet. The Journal of Academic Librarianship, 25(4):274-280.

Kendall, S. & Massarella, S. (2001). Prescription for successful marketing. *Computers in Libraries*, 21(8), 28-32.

Marshall, N. J. (2001). Public relations in academic libraries: A descriptive analysis. *The Journal of Academic Librarianship*, 27(2):116-21.

Metz-Wiseman, M., Silver, S., Hanson, A., Johnston, J., Grohs, K., Neville, T., Sanchez, E. and Gray, C. (1996). *The USF Libraries Virtual Library Project: A Blueprint for Development.* Tampa, Florida: University of South Florida. (ERIC Document Reproduction Service No. ED 418 704).

Mitchell, C. (2002). Tool kit: Selling the brand inside. *Harvard Business Review,* 80(1):99-105.

Senge, P., Ross, R., Smith, B., Roberts, C., & Kleiner, A. (1994). *The fifth discipline fieldbook.* New York, NY: Doubleday.

Sumsion, J. (2001). Library statistics for marketing. *IFLA Journal,* 27(4):221-231

Webber, S. (1997). Promoting your information service over the Internet. *Managing Information,* (4)6:33

Weingand, D.E. (1999). *Marketing/planning library and information services.* Englewood, CO: Libraries Unlimited.

Wolpert, A. (1999). Marketing strategies: Lessons for libraries from commercial brand management. *IATUL Proceedings*. [Electronic Resource]. Retrieved 12/02/2001 from http://educate2.lib.chalmers.se/IATUL/proceedcontents/chanpap/wolpert.html.

Wolpert, A. (1998). Services to remote users: Marketing the library's role. *Library Trends* 47(1):21-41.

APPENDIX A – MARKETING CHARGE, SHORT AND LONG TERM ACTION ITEMS

The real revolution in information technology is about communication, not computation. This assumption is the basic fabric of library partnership. Although technological innovation is required of all USF Libraries, the essential catalyst for change must be in how our cooperative efforts are communicated both internally and externally, electronically and in print. Currently, various marketing methods include flyers, the USF-NEWS listserv, the *Oracle, Inside USF*, word-of-mouth, departmental liaisons, Library and Information Science classes, bibliographic instruction lectures, reference desk encounters, personal contact, and the "What's New" section on library home pages.

Benchmark:

In order to measure the effectiveness of a marketing program for the Virtual Library Project, the VLPC has identified the following benchmarks:
1. The USF Libraries regularly disseminate information using a wide variety of formats, including electronic.
2. Virtual Library Project publications, logos/logotypes, and layouts are standardized so that potential users will find them instantly recognizable as Virtual Library Project materials.
3. The USF Libraries communicate effectively to a growing and diverse user population.

Short-term actions:
1. Include an "announcements" section on the Gateway to advertise new services and databases, changes in services, and instructional workshops available.
2. Include the Gateway URL on library stationery.
3. Place an electronic suggestion form on the Gateway.
4. Engage in outcome assessment to ensure that the marketing program is effectively meeting the needs of the USF user population.
5. Utilize the USF Libraries' instructional programs as a means of marketing the resources on the Gateway.

Long-term actions:
1. Expand marketing and use of the Virtual Library Project on the university campus-wide information system.
2. Promote the USF Libraries' Gateway in print publications via articles, on listservs, and via popular World Wide Web stopping points such as "Cool Site of the Day."
3. Incorporate the Gateway into university promotional films and packages.
4. Describe technical and staff achievements at conferences, fundraisers, and presentations."

Metz-Wiseman, M., Silver, S., Hanson, A., Johnston, J., Grohs, K., Neville, T., Sanchez, E. and Gray, C. (1996). *The USF Libraries Virtual Library Project: A Blueprint for Development.* Tampa, Florida: University of South Florida.

APPENDIX B - MARKETING PROCEDURE CHECKLIST

Name of Service or Resource:
Brief Description:

Step One
Does the vendor have marketing resources? Yes: list

Step Two
Identify appropriate point people from each library to assist in determining Steps 3 & 4. Provide them with deadline of:
   <name of each library and point person>

Step Three
Determine the audience based on recommendations from point persons.
   <name of each audience for each library>

Step Four
Market to all library staff, identifying whether staff development is ready with training resources.
   List methods of communication to be used:
   Date of distribution:

Step Five
List ways to distribute to the public:

a) established lines of communications (campus publications, electronic listservs, etc.)
Publication   Contact person   Distribution date

b) library initiated (postcards, web pages, posters, newsletters, etc.)
Identify format   Distribution type   Distribution date

Completion Date:

Chapter X

Distance Learning

Merilyn Burke
University of South Florida-Tampa, USA

Bruce Lubotsky Levin and Ardis Hanson
The Louis de la Parte Florida Mental Health Institute at the
University of South Florida-Tampa, USA

Gapen (1993) states that the concept of remote access to the contents and services of libraries and other information resources provides the user technology that brings access to the resources of multiple libraries and information services. With the evolution of a variety of methods involved in distance education, the role of academic libraries has broadened to provide resources and services to these invisible but very tangible students.

This chapter begins with a brief review of the history of distance education and the impact of this technology on higher education. The chapter also explores the role of libraries and librarians in providing the variety of services, resources, and technology necessary to support this steadily growing facet of academic institutions. Finally, the chapter will present a case illustration of how one university has incorporated its virtual library as a critical element in its distance learning educational initiatives.

BRIEF HISTORY OF DISTANCE LEARNING

Historically, distance learning or distance education began as little more than "correspondence courses" that promised an education in one's own home. One of the first advertisements for distance learning in the United States was in an edition of the *Boston Gazette* dated March 20, 1728. Caleb Phillipps, who was a teacher of shorthand, advertised that any "Persons in the Country desirous to Learn this Art, may by having the several lessons sent weekly to them, be as perfectly instructed as those that live in Boston" (Distance Learning, 2002). In 1900, Martha Van Rensselaer came to Cornell University to organize an extension program in home economics for New York State's rural women (Cornell University, 2001).

During the 1920s, new technology, radio and radio-based courses were offered by Pennsylvania State University and the University of Iowa. By 1926, interest in distance education had increased to the point that a National Home Study Council was formed under the cooperative leadership of the Carnegie Corporation of New York and the National Better Business Bureau, with the goal of promoting sound educational standards and ethical business practices within the distance/home-study field.

In 1933, the world's first educational television programs were broadcast from the campus of the University of Iowa, with subjects ranging from oral hygiene to identifying star constellations. Television courses became increasing popular during the 1960s and continue to be broadcast in the 21st century.

Another innovation in distance education was the use of teleconferencing that began in 1982 with the creation of the National University Teleconferencing Network, based at Oklahoma State University (Oregon Community Colleges for Distance Learning, 1997). This technology was used to provide site-to-site classroom teaching. Along with videotaped lectures or taped-for-television programs, teleconferencing added a human dimension to distance education. Students and faculty were now able to interact with each other in real time, and questions and responses were immediate, which enhanced the learning process by allowing student access to teachers, even from a distance.

APPLICATION OF DISTANCE LEARNING TO SERVICES & RESEARCH

In an era of increasing fiscal constraints, new technologic advances, and an explosion of information, technology has and will continue to revolutionize the manner in which societies function and communicate. Selected technologies, such as email, the Internet, and telecommunications, continue to evolve in both the scope and depth of their impact upon communities. This continuing technologic revolution has significant implications in terms of vastly increasing the accessibility and availability of information as well as providing increased global connectivity. These innovations also have significant applications for the provision of a variety of health and human services as well as for use in research and education.

Services Delivery

Telecommunications currently plays an increasingly important and prominent role in society, in knowledge exchange, and in commerce. However, it is within the fields of public health and behavioral health where the most remarkable opportunities, challenges, and obstacles have emerged in relation to telecommunication initiatives.

For example, telecommunication or "telehealth" has been described as the use of telecommunications technologies to provide health care in a cost efficient manner and to strive to improve health care, particularly when distance separates consumers and providers (Angaran, 1999). While telehealth technologies have included video-conferencing, telephones, computers, the Internet, e-mail, fax, radio, and television, additional technologies are increasingly being introduced and utilized to link providers and consumers to health care services. The use of telehealth strategies continues to broaden access to medical care, health education, and health services delivery, particularly for at-risk populations in rural America (Levin & Hanson in Loue & Quill, 2001). The development of computer-based patient records, personal health information systems, and unified electronic claims systems utilize various electronic communication technologies to streamline and centralize databases (National Telecommunications and Information Administration, 1998; National Rural Health Association, 1998).

The use of telecommunications also has been utilized for specialized health services delivery. For example, for over thirty years mental health professionals have been investigating the use of advanced telecommunications and information technologies to improve mental health care. For many rural areas, radio and telephone technologies have remained the critical component in the development of crisis care and community mental health programs. Unfortunately, many rural and frontier areas continue to have relatively low telephone penetration. However, Yasnoff, Corroll, Koo, Linking and Kilbourne (2000) have suggested that the application of information technology in public health has been slow to be implemented, primarily in areas of monitoring the health of communities and in guiding improvements in applying prevention strategies. This has been attributable, in part, to the absence of formal graduate educational programs, continuing professional training, and expertise in information technology and information systems for health care professionals.

Nevertheless, one of telemental health's most significant barriers remains the overwhelming costs of telecommunication. In most rural and frontier regions of the United States, telecommunication costs have been far greater than for their urban counterparts. Higher bandwidths, such as ISDN, frame relay, T-1 (not to mention tremendous geographic challenges), have been so expensive in rural regions that their costs prohibit the utilization of these industry advancements in technology. As a result, the utilization of telemedicine technology by rural and frontier mental health care providers has been limited and subsequently, places the rural mental health field at a distinct technologic disadvantage without adequate structural, service, and fiscal infrastructure for the implementation and utilization of currently available technology in twenty-first century America.

Research

In 1997, then President Clinton initiated the "next generation Internet" (NGI) project. Under the President's plan, six federal agencies (the Defense Advanced Research Projects Agency, the Energy Department, the National Science Foundation, the National Aeronautics and Space Agency, the National Institute of Standards and Technology, and the National Library of Medicine and the National Institutes of Health) would connect at least 100 sites (including universities, national laboratories, and other research organizations) at speeds that are 100 times as fast as those of the commercial Internet, allowing research to begin on both advanced network technologies and the kinds of applications that would use this type of bandwidth (Cordes, 1997). The agencies would work directly with the Internet 2 project to help tie its high-performance campus backbones into the broader federal infrastructure. In addition, the NGI program would promote a variety of powerful new applications to take advantage of the new network technologies. A potential application of particular relevance to universities include distance research, including "real-time" experiments that could involve scientific instruments and data banks at multiple sites. To help carry out its role in the effort, the National Science Foundation (NSF) relied heavily on its partnership with the Internet 2 project (the effort by 110 major universities to develop high-performance networks to be dedicated to research).

In 1998, the next-generation research network known as Abilene became available (McCollum, 1998). On university campuses, most faculty and students use the commercial Internet for calling up Web pages or sending e-mail. But overlapping the commercial backbone are faster paths that are off-limits to the average Net user. Although these high-speed research networks rely on many of the same fiber optic cables as the commercial backbone, research traffic now travels on a virtual "express lane."

Within the academic setting, the increased capacity for deliverables across the next generation Internet spurred interest in concerting this research into the classroom setting.

ACADEMIC DISTANCE LEARNING & THE VIRTUAL LIBRARY

At the beginning of the 21st century, distance learning is defined as taking courses by teleconferencing or using the Internet as a method of communication. This change, seen as the second generation of distance education, involves the use of a variety of sophisticated technologies. For example, universities often own broadcasting studios, public broadcasting radio and/or television stations, and cable and satellite facilities that are used in conjunction with computers and CD-ROMs to reach students who are at off-campus (i.e., remote) sites. Thus, access becomes one important issue with the use of technology, whether it is from campus to campus or from campus to individuals located in their own homes.

The development of course instruction, delivered through a variety of distance learning methods (e.g., including Web-based synchronous and asynchronous techniques, e-mail, and audio/video technology), has attracted major university participation (including the University of Arizona, University of Illinois, University of Missouri, University of Nevada-Las Vegas, University of North Carolina, University of South Florida, University of Pittsburgh, Virginia Commonwealth University, and many others). Factor in the ability to increase the growth of the student body while minimizing the costs of new buildings, plus the consortial efforts by some educational institutions that encourage joint enrollment in these distance courses. These electronic learning environment initiatives increase the number of courses and undergraduate/graduate degree programs being offered without increasing the need for additional facilities or faculty appointments, and potentially prevent low enrollments that might have, in the past, forced cancellation of selected courses.

The perception that increased use of technology and distance education would replace instructors has been unproven. It is the very popularity of distance education that has increased the number of instructors needed to teach these courses. It is projected that full-time college enrollment will rise by 17% while the number of adults returning to educational institutions (in an effort to increase job skills or allow career changes) will also increase by 21% (National Center for Education Statistics, 2001). According to O'Leary (2000), in 1998 approximately 5% of college and university students took distance learning courses. By 2002, this share is expected to be 15%, with dramatic increases expected in future years. Shea and Boser (2000) report that 70% of American universities have put at least one course online and predict growth to 90% by 2005.

The academic institutions view the distance learning market as a way to continue or increase revenue flow, an important factor with the static pool of traditional students, and the increase in the number of non-traditional students. In the new millennium, students often face a number of barriers to higher education, including distance, time, and work schedules. In addition, the rising costs of education have made it more difficult for many families to absorb the cost of tuition and the cost of room and board. Distance education allows access to those who might never have any access. Workers who want to increase their skills or obtain a promotion see distance or online education as the opportunity for advancement that was never open to them prior to use of the Internet. Loftus (2000) writes of students who are working full time, traveling but still able to pursue a career. One such student notes that she can be in Paris on business and still chat online with her classmates, she is able to pursue her doctoral degree despite her constant travels. Courses are as varied as the students who take them, ranging from high school level to post-graduate courses in whatever field one can imagine. The use of the Web and all the technologies have allowed interaction with the faculty and the students through "chat rooms," bulletin boards, and streaming and real-time videos. The concept of the student hunched over a computer devoid of any interaction has given way to active participation by serious, disciplined students who have the desire to succeed.

With more colleges and universities offering courses and degrees through distance education, the advancement of this method does not appear to be slowing. According to the National Center for Education Statistics (NCES) (Lewis, Snow, Farris, Levin & Greene, 1999), during the twelve-month 1997–98 academic year, an estimated 49,690 different college-level, credit-granting distance education courses were offered, with most of those (35,550) at the undergraduate level. The remaining credit-granting courses (14,140) were at the graduate/professional level. Thus, distance education has become an increasingly important component in many colleges and universities worldwide.

At the same time, how do academic libraries support these programs? Educational institutions create courses and programs for distance learners but often omit the support component that librarians consider critical. Students are unlikely to walk into the university's library for instruction on how to use the resources, from print to electronic journals, as well as services, such as electronic reserves and interlibrary loan. The elements of any successful distance program must include consideration of the instructors and the students, both of whom have needs that must be examined and served.

Function and Role of Virtual Libraries

So where do libraries fit within the emerging distance education environment? With imaginative use of technology, libraries have been able to create "chat" sessions, which allow 24/7 access to librarians who can direct students to the resources that are available online. In addition, librarians can assist faculty in placing materials on electronic reserve so that their students can access the materials as needed. Additionally, libraries have become more willing to provide mail services to their distance learning students and, when that is not possible, refer their students to local libraries to take advantage of the interlibrary loan system, if and when possible. Many academic libraries have created online tutorials to help the students learn how to use their resources, while other libraries have specific departments that assist their distance education students and faculty. The role of the library in this process is one of support, both for the students and the faculty.

Libraries, often overlooked in this process, have to be far more assertive in the distance learning process; this growing field allows librarians to re-create their roles, request monies for becoming more technologically advanced–to become as "virtual" as the classes being taught. The opportunity to become part of the new methods of education, and modifying how the libraries do business will allow them to serve their patrons successfully.

Changes in Distance Librarianship

Providing materials, having electronic resources, reciprocal borrowing, and all the other "traditional" library functions made available to the distance learner have not filled the gap of reference service. While chat lines and other 24/7 services have been made available, these services simply do not provide the distance learning (DL) student with the same quality of service that the on-campus student gets when he or she walks into the library. It is not the lack of desire to serve these students, rather the technology has been lacking. The technologies that have been developed for the classrooms (such as WebCT or Blackboard) or the wonders of videoconferencing that work well for online classes do not translate effectively into how the DL student uses a library. It would be financially impossible and a technological nightmare to install interactive video conferencing on every student's computer just in case he or she wanted to ask a reference question. WebCT and similar programs have interactive components that allow students to emulate the classroom environment. He or she can click an icon to raise his or her hand and get answers from the instructors as the class progresses–quite similar to the traditional classroom. It works well in the classroom setting but such raising of hands would not translate well into the line of students "waiting" at the desk for a reference librarian.

Web courses also have limitations: the content may be somewhat static, the faculty can present materials that have been placed on the site, but the software doesn't allow the student or the faculty to move around the Web to find other sources, such as an online reference source or database pertinent to the materials being covered. So, libraries have been limited in offering reference service by email and live chat sessions.

Recently, libraries have been looking at business models. E-commerce has become commonplace. For example, customers are more savvy and businesses have become more sophisticated in responding to the customer's needs. Coffman (2001) discusses the adaptation of business tools as customer relations management (CRM) software, such as the Virtual Reference Desk, Webline, NetAgent, and LivePerson. These programs are based on the "call center model", which can queue and route Web queries to the next available librarian. A quick visit to the LSSI website (http://www.lssi.com) allows a look into the philosophy of offering "live" real-time reference services. LSSI's "Virtual Reference Desk" allows librarians to "push" Web pages to their patron's browser, escort patrons around the web and search databases together, all the while communicating with them by chat or phone (www.lssi.com). Many of these systems provide the capability to build a "knowledge base" that could track and handle diverse range and volume of questions. These collaborative efforts, with a multitude of libraries inputting the questions asked of them and creating FAQs (frequently asked questions lists), provide another level of service for the distance learner. (For a more in-depth discussion of CRM, see the chapter on E-reference in this volume).

These systems have great potential, and while they show tremendous possibilities, they need more work to make them more functional for library use. While "chat" is useful, it is somewhat cumbersome, and sometimes phone lines are not available since the patron is using his or her phone line to connect to the computer. Possible solutions include voice over Internet protocol (VoIP), which allows the librarian and the patron to actually communicate on the same line they are using for connectivity. This is not unlike using a computer for "free" or reduced cost long distance telephone services. This technology has been improving, but it is still problematic. Common problems include "delay," which can cause two speakers to interfere with each other's sentences, "echoes," which are caused by signal reflections, and "jitter," which is caused by packets taking different routes through the Internet. Although the reliability of VoIP is lower than the reliability found in public switched telephone networks, eventual upgrades to service will make further the use of VoIP in distance education (http://www.cis.ohio-state.edu/~jain/cis788-99/voip_products/).

Another direction is the development of "virtual reference centers" that would not necessarily have to be located in any particular physical library. Current collaboratives among universities have created consortial reference centers accessible anywhere, anytime. The reference center librarian could direct the student to the nearest physical resource if that is what was needed or to an online full-text database based upon the student's educational profile, i.e., university, student status, and geographic location. The physical library may indeed become a repository for books and physical items, but the reference component may no longer be housed within that particular building.

SUPPORTING DISTANCE LEARNING

As the number of distance learners and distance programs increases, how do libraries support the needs of their students? Lowe and Malinski (2000) discuss how Toronto's Ryerson Polytechnic University handles the needs of its patrons by providing a cohesive and unified support infrastructure. Their discussion is based on the concept that in order to provide effective distance education programs and resources, there must be a high level of cooperation between the university, the departments involved, and the library.

At Ryerson, the Continuing Education Department was responsible for transitioning faculty from face-to-face classroom presentations to online classrooms. The department realized that the instructor and his or her online class were but a part of the whole. The department studied what types of support the students needed and identified technical, administrative, and academic help as three major areas of concern. Technical help was assigned to the university's computing services. Administrative help was available on the Web and through telephone access. Academic help, however, included writing centers, study skill programs, and library services. Ryerson's philosophy encompassed the concept that synchronization of all these components would assist in making the student's experience richer and give the student a higher degree of success.

The library at Ryerson was traditional in its services to the student, being able to serve the on-campus student who could walk in and ask a question, while distance learners did not have the same level of service. Books could be mailed, articles sent for, but the ability to "dig deeper" was missing. As the technology improved, students, for both distance and on-campus, were able to connect to the library website doing the basic functions of checking their records and requesting interlibrary loans. The library and the distance education unit worked to provide connectivity to resources that were important to the classes being taught online or at-a-distance. These types of library activities can make distance learning an even more successful and enriching experience. When a university system, as a whole, embraces a collaboration of all its components, both the students and the university reap the rewards.

CASE STUDY

At the University of South Florida (USF), knowledge of library services and resources is an important component of graduate coursework. The following case study reiterates the importance of collaboration between faculty and librarians in the development and support of distance education initiatives. Two authors of this chapter (BLL and AH), faculty at the USF de la Parte Institute, recently created two separate distance learning courses. The first course, *Foundations in Behavioral Health Systems*, required the transformation of an existing traditional classroom course to "fit" within an online environment. The second course, *Community-Based Prevention in Behavioral Health*, was developed specifically as a web-based course. Both courses were designed to fit within the new Graduate Studies in Behavioral Health Degree Program, a collaborative teaching initiative between the USF College of Public Health and the USF de la Parte Institute.

Conceptualization for an Online Environment

Converting the *Foundations in Behavioral Health Systems* course to an online environment first required a review of successful professor-student interactions. A mixture of traditional, didactic lectures, incorporation of related Internet sites, as well as supplemental readings linked to specific lectures were utilized in the design and transformation of this course to a web-based format.

Teaching for the first time on the Web, the course professors quickly discovered that a majority of the students, in excess of 50%, had never taken a Web-based course. Therefore, they needed to address these gaps in knowledge and help compensate for the students' lack of experience in taking web-based courses. In addition, since the professors are faculty in a mental health research institute, they were sensitive to the students' (often) overwhelming anxiety in coping with a semester-long web-based class. Student anxiety ranged from a perceived lack of general computer skills to significant trepidation concerning gathering information using the USF Virtual Library, as well as other academic, state, and professional Internet sites.

There were other issues that were considered in the design and development of these courses. For example, successful distance learning students, by definition, must be self-directed and self-motivated. Unlike a traditional classroom, the virtual classroom is primarily text-driven. Communication occurs almost solely in a written format, with print materials the primary sources for directions, announcements, regular and supplemental readings, class assignments, and mid-term and final examinations.

Virtual classrooms require a virtual library. Although it is incumbent upon faculty to provide links to significant Internet resources, some academic coursework is not adequately supported by links to selected web resources. Students need to know how to craft search queries that retrieve relevant and precise information. They need to know how to select appropriate resources. Based upon the past two years' experience and student feedback, students taking Web-based courses lacked immediate access to librarians for instruction on how to select and use academic resources for their coursework.

Finally, students often had difficulty structuring their daily and weekly schedules and balancing their time around class requirements. Many students mentioned they quickly became lost on the "Net" while researching a topic.

In their section on *Students and Student Services*, the Western Interstate Commission for Higher Education (WICHE) states: "Enrolled students have reasonable and adequate access to the range of student services appropriate to support their learning" (Krauth, 1996). The student service the professors identified as most critical was library services. Therefore, in the first lecture for each of the courses, they developed an overview on how to navigate the course on Blackboard (the online course software used by USF), the general use of the Internet within an educational environment, and general information literacy that included the creation of virtual library assignments for each lecture.

Another significant resource for all students is the use of the reserves held within libraries. Since the professors had used the paper reserve system for their traditional classroom courses, they were already familiar with acquiring class readings and sending them over to the library for placement on the reserve shelves. In the *Foundations in Behavioral Health Systems* course, they extensively utilized the Electronic Reserves component of the USF Virtual Library. The professors realized that many of the off-campus students may or may not have access to a large urban university library system similar to the one at the University of South Florida. However, in the *Community-Based Prevention in Behavioral Health* web course, a combination of electronic reserves and Internet resources (selected specifically for evidence of best practices in preventive behavioral health research) were used. The textbook for this course was *Healthy People 2010*, an online publication on the *Healthy People* site managed by the Office of Disease Prevention and Health Promotion, U.S. Department of Health and Human Services. Subsequent enhancements of the *Foundations in Behavioral Health Systems* course included more identified and refereed online resources, such as monographs found within the National Academy Press website.

Internet Use and Information Literacy

Using the Internet within an educational environment covers a wide range of activities and is closely linked with information literacy. The American Library

Association (1989) and Bruce (1997) defined information literacy as the effective use of technology and the ability to locate, evaluate, manage, and use the information found. However, Bruce also considered information literacy an important generic skill that allows a person to engage in effective decision making, problem solving, research, and continued learning.

In both of the web-based classes, the professors incorporated specific Internet-based readings for the lectures and assignments, including articles and databases available through the USF Virtual Library. They decided that it was critical to have students use the many full-text refereed resources available through the USF Virtual Library as well as learn how to successfully use the available databases. To help increase student awareness of the need for authenticating an Internet-based resource, an information literacy tutorial component and PowerPoint presentations on resources within the USF Virtual Library were included in the class assignments.

Assessment of the Courses

In public health as in behavioral health, the application of theory to practice is critical. This was repeatedly demonstrated through student feedback when students emphasized (via emails to the course faculty upon their completion of the course) that they had expanded their knowledge base and addressed "real-world" or pragmatic behavioral health service problems. In addition, students appreciated the inclusion of the virtual library exercises within their weekly assignments:

Student 1: *"...Being a novice to public health and its databases, I found the initial assignment on informatics to be instrumental. Likewise, I appreciated the sequencing of assignments to parallel the public health model itself (i.e., prevention, intervention, rehabilitation/working with specific populations). Sequencing the topics to match this was both helpful to my understanding, and interesting and thought-provoking as well..."*

Student 2: *"Overall, I really enjoyed this course. It provided me with a great introduction and overview of community and family health and prevention and intervention in Public Health. I especially liked the library searches (although not at the time) and the TILT tutorial, which helped me with my research in this class and others. The weekly homework assignments were in general a good application of the lecture material, which I also enjoyed. Lectures were an easy and informative read, unlike some of the articles. Although, as compared to the majority of my other classes, the readings were so much more applied and interesting!"*

As a result of student feedback and an increased comfort level with Web-based instruction, the professors have added a number of enhancements to the two

Web-based courses. Enhancements to student learning include: the addition of more online text in the form of articles, monographs, and white papers found on the Internet; increased use of media such as streaming video, demographic, statistical databases, and PowerPoint presentations; more group activity projects, and increased library activities as part of the weekly student assignments.

Thus, the case study presented underscores the dependence that both faculty and students in distance learning courses have on the use of the virtual library's resources and services throughout each of the two courses. It is incumbent upon university faculty to provide students with access not only to refereed, academic resources within the university library as well as those available on the Internet but also to instruction on how to use online resources to their best advantage. The USF Virtual Library was a necessary and critical component for distance learning courses.

SUMMARY

Distance education will only continue to develop. In order to support that educational initiative, it is vital that academic libraries establish ongoing supporting framework and commitment to those services traditionally provided by libraries. Students need to be able to access their "library." The virtual classroom needs not only a virtual library, but also access to the paper resources that have not yet been transformed into a digital format. The library must be able to deliver materials to students or assist them in finding alternate sources for physical resources. Libraries need to make sure that their students are identifiable, and work with the institution's ID card office in order to verify student information. Help desks, chat rooms, email programs, and live reference all contribute to the support of the distance learning programs.

Faculty members also require library support for their courses. For example, materials may be scanned and placed on the Web or videos may be "streamed" for online access. In addition, in some cases, the library may be the only location that can assist the faculty member with copyright clearance or information concerning the correct use of copyrighted materials. Finally, since faculty can no longer require DL students to go on "field trips" to a library's physical facility, it is important to provide information on how best to access the library virtually.

FUTURE ISSUES

Distance learning continues to flourish, especially for collaborative academic initiatives. With the advent of telecommunications technologies, there is a growing need for research examining the effective implementation and ongoing management of distance education. For example, much has been written about the social isolation of distance work. However, recent advances in groupware technologies have enhanced an individual's ability to stay connected for both work and social exchange through the use of synchronous and asynchronous remote communication (Li, 1998). Venkatesh & Speier (2000) speculate that these technologies have the ability to significantly transform the way organizations conduct their "business", span geographical boundaries, and at the same time potentially overcome the social isolation. However, they suggest that formal and extensive training on both distance technology and team communications are necessary.

The ephemeral nature of the Web is apparent as thousands of web pages move or cease to exist. For example, in a recent research study, nineteen percent of the 515 hyperlinks contained in online materials for three graduate-level biochemistry courses at the university had expired sometime between the creation of these courses in August 2000 and March 2002 (Kiernan, 2002). This "link-rot" impacts course development for distance education since the progressive disappearance of these materials presents a major problem for courses developed specifically to utilize "free" Web resources. For those course support pages developed by academic libraries within academic library catalogues, electronic reserves, or standalone pages, it is critical to maintain the intellectual content of these support pages. However, maintenance (and future development) comes at a continued cost in staff labour and software.

REFERENCES

American Library Association Presidential Committee on Information Literacy (1989). *Final Report*. Chicago: The Association.

Angaran, D.M. (1999). Tele-medicine and tele-pharmacy: Current status and future implications. *American Journal of Health-Systems Pharmacy, 56,* 1405-26.

Bruce, C. (1997). *Seven Faces of Information Literacy*. Adelaide, South Australia: AUSLIB Press.

Chickering, A.W. & Ehrmann, S.C. (1995). *Implementing the Seven Principles: Technology as Lever*. [Electronic Resource] Retrieved 03/08/02 from *http://www.aahe.org/technology/ehrmann.htm*. Accessed 12 December, 2001.

Coffman, S. (2001). Distance Education and virtual reference: Where are we headed? *Computers in Libraries, 21*(4):20.

Cordes, C. (1997, September 5). Federal Support for New Version of Internet Hinges on 5 Spending Bills: Next-generation network would be faster and would allow innovative applications. *The Chronicle of Higher Education,* Section: Information Technology, A38.

Cornell University Library. Timeline of the New York State College of Home Economics, 1900-1969. [Electronic Resource] Retrieved 03/08/02 from http://distancelearn.about.com/gi/dynamic/offsite.htm?site=http:// rmc.library.cornell.edu/homeEc/timeline.html.

Distance Learning (2002). 1728 Advertisement for Correspondence Course. [Electronic Resource] Retrieved 03/08/02 from http://distancelearn.about.com/library/timeline/bl1728.htm

Gapen, Kaye D. (1993). The Virtual Library, Society, and the Librarian. In Saunders, L.M. (ed.) *The Virtual Library: Visions and Realities.* Westport, CT: Meckler.

Kiernan, Vincent (2002). Nebraska Researchers Measure the Extent of 'Link Rot' in Distance Education. Chronicle of Higher Education, Distance Education. [Electronic Resource] Retrieved 04/10/02 from http://chronicle.com/free/2002/04/2002041001u.htm.

Krauth, B. (1996). Principles of Good Practice for Distance Learning Programs. *CAUSE/EFFECT* 19(1):6-8. [Electronic Resource] Retrieved 03/08/02 from http://www.educause.edu/ir/library/text/cem9613.txt.

Levin, B.L., & Hanson, A. (2001). Rural mental health services. In Loue, S., & Quill, B.E. (eds.). *Handbook of Rural Health.* New York: Kluwer Academic/Plenum Publishers, 241-256.

Lewis, L., Snow, K., Farris, E., Levin, D., & Greene, B. (1999). *Distance Education at Postsecondary Education Institutions: 1997-98.* Washington, D.C.: National Center for Education Statistics. [NCES 2000-013]. [Also available as an electronic http://nces.ed.gov/pubs2000/2000013.pdf].

Li, F. (1998). Team-telework and the new geographical flexibility for information workers. In Igbaria, M. & Tan, M. (Eds). *The Virtual Workplace.* Hershey, PA: Idea Group Publishing, pp. 301-318.

Lowe, W. & Malinksi, R. (2000). Distance Learning: Success requires Support. *Education Libraries,* 24(2/3):15-17.

McCollum, K. (1998, November 6). Faster, More Complex Networks Will Enhance Research Computing. *The Chronicle of Higher Education,* Information Technology section, A33.

National Center for Education Statistics. *Projections of educational statistics to 2011.* [Electronic Resource] Retrieved 02/28/02 from http://nces.ed.gov/pubs2001/proj01/chapter2.asp.

National Rural Health Association (1998). *The Role of Telemedicine in Rural Health Care.* Washington, D.C.: The Association.

National Telecommunications and Information Administration (1998). *The Na-*

tional Information Infrastructure: Agenda for Action. Washington, D.C.: The Administration.

O'Leary, M. (2000). Distance Learning and Libraries. *Online*, 24 (4): 4-96.

Oregon Community Colleges for Distance Learning. *The Strategic Plan of the Oregon Community Colleges for Distance Learning, Distance Learning History, current status, and trends*. [Electronic Resource] Retrieved 03/08/02 from http://www.lbcc.cc.or.us/spoccde/dehist.html.

Shea, Rachel H., and Boser, U. (2000). So where is the beef? *U.S. News & World Report*, 131(15):44-47.

Venkatesh, V. & Speier C. (2000). Creating an effective training environment for enhancing telework. *International Journal of Human Computer Studies*, 52(6):991-1005.

Yasnoff, W.A., O'Corroll, P.W., Koo, D., Linkins, R.W., & Kilbourne, E.M. (2000). Public health informatics: Improving and transforming public health in the information age. *Journal of Public Health Management and Practice*. 6(6):67–75.

PART III:

ADMINISTRATION
&
EDUCATION

Chapter XI

Issues for Library Management When Implementing Large-Scale Programmatic Change

Kathy Arsenault
Nelson Poynter Memorial Library at the
University of South Florida-St. Petersburg, USA

Ardis Hanson
The Louis de la Parte Florida Mental Health Institute at the
University of South Florida-Tampa, USA

Joan Pelland
Jane Bancroft Cook Library at the
University of South Florida-Sarasota/Manatee, USA

Derrie Perez
USF Library System at the University of South Florida-Tampa, USA

Beverly Shattuck
Hinks and Elaine Shimberg Health Sciences Center Library at the
University of South Florida-Tampa, USA

Change, by its very nature, is unpredictable, and often unmanageable, yet an organization's success depends on an ability to predict and control change in some way. To derive maximum benefit from new opportunities and to avoid

reactive situations, it is essential to manage organizational change. Further,
as change accelerates, the more difficult and stressful it is to manage.

The proliferation of change management literature in the library and
information field indicates that these issues are becoming increasingly
important as more academic libraries develop a virtual presence (Higuchi,
1990; Lee, 1993; Riggs, 1997; Meyer, 1997; Nozero & Vaughn, 2000). Nearly
a decade ago, Dougherty and Dougherty (1993) observed that the current
rate of change in the information field was higher than ever before, while
libraries' ability to respond quickly and decisively had never been more
constrained. Academic libraries, like other organizations, must respond
proactively to their changing environment in order to take advantage of the
opportunities for increasing their visibility, restructuring to meet the needs of
their users, and achieving their objective of remaining the preeminent source
of information within the academy.

This chapter begins with an overview of the theoretical perspectives of
change. Using Burke, Church and Waclawski's (1993) Managing Change
model, the authors will discuss the structure of change, the culture of change,
and the individual response to change within a case study framework.

THEORIES OF CHANGE

The literature reflects three major areas in organizational change: the structural
or planning aspect of change, the cultural aspect of change, and the individual human
reaction to change. Lewin (1958) looks at the patterns in the change process and
how best to manage effectively large system change, the evolutionary or revolutionary nature of change, and the characteristic patterns that typify change efforts in
organizations. His fundamental description of structural change has been incorporated into many process-oriented models of organizational change developed for
organizations to better understand and direct the process of systemic change
(Tichy, Hornstein & Nisberg, 1977; Schein, 1987).

Cultural change often affects organizational identity. Beckhard and Harris
(1987) focus on managing the transition concerning the organizational identity.
Members of an organization need to identify a desired future state and describe the
new role, function, or structure that the organization needs to adopt. They
recommend use of a transition management team and senior management to help
move forward and engage in activity planning. They further highlight the importance
of communication, leadership and emotional components of change.

Finally, Bridges (1986) is concerned about the experiences of individuals in the
change process. He has identified several personal transition stages, including the
release of individual identity, ambiguity, and establishing a new beginning.

Strategies To Manage Change

Strategies to manage change successfully abound in the business literature. There are process-oriented perspectives and strategic planning models (Beer, 1994). It is the case, more often than not, that effective and successful organizational change incorporates and manages both these perspectives concurrently. For example, Christensen and Overdorf (2000) consider infrastructure (which they define as processes and values, and organizational capabilities) as critical to manage change successfully. They suggest that managers create new processes and values to enable them to develop infrastructures that are more effective. The changing of institutional identity assists in the creation of processes and values. Newman and Chaharbagi (2000) emphasize the need for leadership when replacing a previous identity. However, it is equally important to establish a viable, working identity before replacing an old identity.

One cannot manage change if one lacks an understanding of why change does not happen. Beer and Eisenstat (2000) identify six mutually reinforcing barriers to implementing change. These were top-down or *laissez-faire* management style; unclear strategy and conflicting priorities; an ineffective senior management team; poor vertical communication; poor coordination across functions; and inadequate down-the-line leadership skills and development.

In addition to managing change, Geisler (1997, p.4) states that one needs to "marshal knowledge about changes, organizations, and corporate behavior—so that corrective actions may be undertaken to bring back balance and relative stability." However, all these authors agree that change is inevitable, it occurs at an increasingly faster rate, and it occurs unevenly in large institutions, particularly in higher education.

Riggs (1997, p. 3) said, "The libraries of colleges and universities are changing faster than their respective parent institutions. Essentially everything in and around the library is changing: services, technologies, organizational constructs, ownership and access policies, values and most of the rest." Traditional areas of responsibility for library administrators have included addressing patron needs, providing services and handling service provision networks, initiating collaborative arrangements, improving staff skills and abilities, and enhancing the image of the library (or how the organization is regarded by important oversight bodies) (Nutt & Backoff, 1992). In addition, library administrators must cope with new ways of funding and performing services (Spies, 2000). Morgan (1988) suggests that the gaps between current services, service provision vehicles, funding mechanisms, and skills often result in large-scale programmatic change via the use of innovative strategies, such as cross-functional teams and the creation of new units and programmatic areas.

Implementing Large-Scale Programmatic Change

Implementing innovative strategies often means dramatic organizational change. Innovation is not simply defined in terms of new products. Jarrat (1999) defines innovation as new ways of thinking of, generating, and coping with change. Implementing these innovations involves managing both the strategies and the elements of the organization that will have to be changed to enable the organization to anticipate, respond to, and shape future challenges (Nadler & Tushman, 1997). Even short-term change initiatives that focus on costs and/or changing established working practices have immediate and inevitable impact on the organization. They may not fundamentally change the core purpose of the organization; however, such may be highly traumatic for staff (Hailey, 1998).

Changes in strategic plans, such as the implementation of a virtual library project, require a realignment of the performance appraisal process to keep up with the goals and directions of the enterprise. Moving to more cross-functional work environments means that a 'top down' performance appraisal is no longer appropriate.

The judicious use of human resource interventions, the maintenance of organizational identity, and the supportive actions of its line managers help staff through the process of change (Hailey, 1998). Whether the change path involves rapid or gradual transformation, a crucial element of success is the commitment of line managers to people management. This, in fact, is more crucial than their commitment to the change itself. According to Hailey (1998), commitment to the management of people by supervisors ensures that staffs are counseled on a regular basis, both formally and informally; that their personal career development is discussed (with or without vertical career opportunities); and that they receive regular feedback on their performance. If these things are already in place, department heads and supervisors can easily facilitate change within their departments or units.

Middle managers, who see themselves as change agents, are perhaps even more important in encouraging adaptive change by staff. Their leadership philosophy is to do "real" work themselves, spend time on things that matter, and encourage and assist staff to do its best possible work (Penrod & Harbor, 1998). Further, their attitude toward accountability is to focus on a few key measures in critical areas and to promote the belief that they are accountable for their work (Katzenbach, 1996).

Whatever the method, successful organizations monitor their managers' capability in people management, and reward or sanction that performance accordingly. This results in a consistent departmental or supervisory response to change management, rather than an unpredictable response when supervisors either ignore a situation or try to incorporate initiatives into their busy workloads.

For example, department heads should avoid overwhelming senior supervisors with many different, and often contradictory, change initiatives. Instead, administrators should focus on a few clustered activities linked to an organizational need that makes sense to managers and their staff. Supervisors should be involved in the design of these change initiatives to increase investment in the change process.

Performance Measurement

Performance measurement systems can create an essential feedback and learning mechanism in support of key management decisions. When using a performance assessment system in the change process, all criteria should measure institutionally focused performance. A successful performance assessment system also functions as a communication and information system, particularly for senior staff and administration. Basically, performance assessment should allow staff members to know what is expected of them (through up-to-date job descriptions); continuing communication between supervisors and staff; recognition of staff for doing well; and staff development processes (Lubans, 1999). Effective people management assists line managers in handling change management, adding this capability to their managerial toolbox.

To enable the organization to accomplish its new purpose, administrators and managers must be aware of the implications of a major change in order to deal with all of the elements that must be addressed, including core competencies in existing and potential staff (Koper, 1997). It is critical to look for core capabilities used across multiple assignments and opportunities within the library. The literature on change management emphasises three broad generative skills repeatedly. These include a demonstration of interpersonal competence (Kanungo and Mendonca, 1996), personal integrity (McLagan and Nel, 1997; Collier, 1998), and the capacity to think systemically and in an integrated way about how work systems and people need to collaborate (Broderick and Boudreau, 1992; Buchanan and Boddy, 1992; Dodgson, 1993; Carnall, 1995;). If these skills are present (or can be developed) within existing staff, staff may obtain a variety of professional competencies for managing individual projects, team projects, and system-level initiatives.

CASE STUDY OF THE UNIVERSITY
OF SOUTH FLORIDA (USF)

In 1995, the USF Library Directors charged a group of librarians, the Virtual Library Planning Committee (VLPC), to develop a comprehensive virtual library plan. By July 1996, the *USF Libraries Virtual Library Project: A Blueprint for*

Development was complete. Four sections of the report described potential virtual services; collection and content; interface and infrastructure; and organizational structure (for more details on the evolution of the Virtual Library at USF, see Chapter 1 in this volume).

The USF Library System envisioned a two to three year plan to create its Virtual Library. It created a series of teams (totaling eleven by the end of the project), an oversight committee, and a project manager. Each team had a clearly defined charge, including continuous evaluation, and the development of a timeline for reporting and evaluation (Virtual Library Planning Committee, 1996). Further, the Project Manager, Project Groups, and Team representatives were to be accountable for reporting to their respective areas and libraries on their progress.

Managing Structural Change

Wide variations in management practice in academic libraries indicate the need for major improvements, particularly in terms of adopting a strategic approach to the planning and delivery of library and information services (Corral, 1995a). Marketing, business, and annual operational plans, with formal objectives for individual staff, follow strategic planning. A clear framework of strategic objectives and priorities, formulated through a participative planning process, will facilitate delegation of decision making and resource allocation to a level enabling quick flexible responses to identified customer needs (Corral, 1995b). As libraries become more 'virtual', academic library administrators must determine if the existing management and structure is both responsive to the changing user needs and utilizing technology to its best advantage (Spies, 2000).

Structurally, the USF Library System is unique among the rest of the Florida university system libraries. The five libraries are administratively decentralized, each headed by its own director, who is accountable either to his or her Dean/Vice President or to the campus Provost. For the Virtual Library project to be successful, a great deal of trust and communication would be necessary between the library directors and other library managerial positions during project implementation to avoid significant loss to the ongoing, daily work of the USF Libraries. In addition, this project would require a new way of working with the university administration, particularly when new positions (lines) would be requested that would be working for all the libraries, not just assigned as a staff position in the main library of the Tampa campus. It would also require a new perspective on budgets in order to acquire system-wide enhancements and resources. Acquiring these centralized resources would benefit all the libraries, be subject to library system-wide committee decisions, and have consensus of all of the library directors.

Managing Cultural Change

To manage change successfully, libraries must choose the appropriate change path and design its implementation to suit their own situations. This requires an understanding of key internal organizational features, such as staff identity, aspects of the organization they wish to preserve, the degree to which the organization as a whole is aware of the need to change, and the level of capability for change possessed at all levels within the library (Bryson, 1985). Today, many organizations are developing new cultures with leadership styles based on empowering people.

During 1995-2000, the USF Library System responded to rapid changes in the information environment, developing significant organizational changes necessary to implement a virtual library project. The libraries, operating as independent organizations, joined efforts to acquire the requisite capital, to build new organizational structures, and to work toward the shift in the organizational culture necessary to move the USF libraries into the virtual library environment. Parallel to creating new leadership styles at the administrative level, the library system altered its organization by developing small groups for project management, such as working groups, project groups, or teams across functional areas and library lines.

This culture shift was similar to the changes the library system encountered during the mid-1980s when NOTIS (the online library management system) was used to automate many circulation, acquisitions, and cataloging functions. Library administration assured their faculty and staff of their continued importance and value within the then new organizational structure. In both situations, it was the responsibility of the USF Library Directors to assist in creating an organizational environment that encouraged innovation.

Managing and Motivating Human Resources

From a management perspective, the establishment of the Virtual Library team process was an overall success. Members of the teams were enthusiastic; they communicated across teams and shared information. The team members were satisfied with their autonomy within the teams and their empowerment to tackle their team's charges, and, if necessary, to alter or change them to fit the parameters of the work. Further, both paraprofessional and professional staff worked together, lessening the artificial "class" structure often found in academic libraries. Another major benefit of the team process was the inclusion of staff from all of the USF libraries. This was the first time that many of the staff from the regional and specialty libraries felt they were true project partners with the main library staff.

Lessons Learned From the USF Virtual Library Project

Originally planned for a three-year implementation, the Virtual Library Project ran to five years. During this time, staff successfully implemented many activities outlined in the *Blueprint*. However, several sea changes occurred during that five-year period, including a Provost's Task Force to reorganize the USF Libraries, the death of one of the library directors, emerging supervisory issues, and significant changes within the operations of the teams. For example, several teams dissolved due to lack of a 'real' activity once their primary charges had been accomplished or due to dwindling team 'volunteers'. There was a growing realization among the library directors that the remaining virtual library teams had duties that needed to be integrated into ongoing library teams/departments (i.e., these activities were no longer 'projects' but daily library functions).

Most importantly, the library directors felt that the original *Blueprint* needed a close review considering the university's new USF Libraries strategic plan that resulted from Provost's mandate. This was crucial, since a strategic plan represents how the values, purpose, and operating principles in an organization are connected to its vision and strategy. Strategic objectives must be tied to the everyday operating environment and be measured through well-reasoned, logical performance criteria. (APQC, 1999). Library directors thus began the crucial process of reviewing the Virtual Library in light of new university missions and goals.

Although there were many positive outcomes and products in the development of the Virtual Library, there was one critical lesson learned: monitor the place of the team within the organization as the goals and structure of the organization change. To stay aligned, teams need to talk to one another and to the organization. By setting a clear direction, the organization also sets the boundaries within which teams work (Forrester & Drexler, 1999). Furthermore, according to Katzenbach and Smith (1993), teams require both individual and team accountability.

Sometimes, leaders of change also must be managers of change. Building job assignments and evaluation capacities into team positions is difficult and requires the use of concrete performance measures. However, without the accountability for staff time (within both regular and team assignments), organizations cannot have an accurate picture of the time, staff, and effort actually involved in projects or other aspects of organizational change. This is particularly true in the case of 'volunteer' projects.

There was a reluctance to build in or use the necessary administrative tools to measure work performed outside a staff person's normal job duties. For example, the Directors, the Implementation Team, and the Project Manager relied heavily on the volunteer status of the VL teams to accomplish the work necessary for the implementation of the Virtual Library. During the first year or two, people were enthusiastic. However, since participation in the Virtual Library was a volunteer effort, there were no mechanisms in place to ensure performance or delivery of product as the project continued into years three, four, and five.

This lack of administrative tools also made it difficult to place VL tasks in relation to ongoing library duties. Several supervisors and department heads felt that virtual library work infringed upon actual duties. They felt unable to ask for clarification of VL activities or to 'interfere' with VL work. From a larger management perspective, it was impossible to determine the actual number of work-hours involved in creating the virtual library or to review concrete workflow processes.

The 1996 goals stated in the *Blueprint* were misaligned with the successive years' goals of the USF Library system. It was evident to the directors that the Virtual Library would initially be a complement to, not a replacement for, the traditional library, at least for the near future. Maintaining the parallel structures and workflows of the Virtual Library teams and the traditional library departments seemed increasingly untenable.

Further, with the reclassification of the University of South Florida to a Research I university by the Carnegie Institute, the university's mission changed from a comprehensive university to a research university. The USF Libraries had to move to being a research library system and unique print resources were more essential than ever. The main research library, with the distinctive regional and specialized libraries, continues to build traditional collections unique to their constituencies as well as contribute to the growth of the collective electronic resources. The USF Library system's former mission to serve the comprehensive university alone was expanded to include development of both print and electronic scholarly collections of value to the state and national research communities. With this new mission, the USF Libraries began to plan for the collections and services appropriate for an institution that would eventually aspire to be accepted by the Association of Research Libraries.

This incongruence in goals and objectives between the USF Libraries and the original Virtual Library plan became a point of considerable tension among the library staff. "Us against them" mentalities and personal relationships forged among existing library departments and VL teams made workflow integration difficult. The recognition, travel opportunities, and new professional visibility available to certain VL team members became a source of resentment by traditional library employees who felt that their contributions were not valued. At the same time, certain VL team members may have felt that library integration would lead to a loss of status. Understandably, people who thought of themselves as 'agents of change' in 1996 perceived that the integration of the 'virtual library' into seamlessly organized USF Libraries represented a step backwards, both personally and institutionally.

Although the resulting tensions greatly complicated library-restructuring efforts, the recent integration of "virtual" activities with "traditional" activities has met with approval by many faculty and students who, ironically, did not see the two "libraries" as separate entities. In addition, the cross-functional team structure has been continued for those ongoing virtual library teams, although these teams now encompass a more inclusive perspective of the USF Library system. Library staff still self-identify those teams that appear most closely aligned with their interests and apply to join them. From a larger external perspective, the upcoming SACS (Southern Association of Colleges and Schools) accreditation has encouraged library system staff to see the total library system, not just portions of it.

Recommendations

There are six major lessons that administrators need to learn when working with organizational redesign or with team-based organizations. First, an organization's clarity of vision is critical and is subject to change based upon external forces, such as changes in the mission, vision, and values of the university. As the institution's priorities evolve, it is critical that administrators reevaluate and update a working document to ensure mission congruence.

Second, management should not underestimate the power of personal relationships. One of the most important aspects of inter-organizational networking is creating and sustaining the personal relationships between the parties (Blackler, 1995). For a team to be effective, a high-trust relationship needs to be developed. Members need to trust one another to be honest, capable, and committed to joint goals (Dodgson, 1994).

Third, do not let a team take itself too seriously since an innovation is not an ideology. Ironically, those who initially positioned themselves as change agents had a difficult time adjusting to the eventual integration of the Virtual Library Project.

Fourth, the rest of the organization should not be ignored. It is important to avoid resentment by making sure that other groups have equitable chances at perks and recognition, as well as meaningful challenges to accomplish. Edwards and Walton (2000) indicate that a number of factors (including perception, limited resources, departmentalization and specialization, nature of work activities, role conflict, inequitable treatment, violation of territory, and environmental change) are major sources of conflict in academic libraries.

Fifth, do not let the rest of the library ignore the team. One of the 'meaningful challenges' should be achieving the skills to fulfill the team's mission, e.g., all collection development librarians should work with virtual resources, all catalogers with metadata, and all reference librarians with innovative services and bibliographic instruction.

Finally, do not leave department/unit managers out of the loop, and make sure that goals are clear and clearly evaluated. Ray and Bronstein (1995) state that without measurable goals, there can be no team. All departments, divisions, and units should have clear, evaluative goals. An organization's precision and accuracy in marking progress should be clearly communicated to managers, staff, and teams. With clear communication of expected goals and outcomes, all members of an organization can focus on accountability, evaluating how well goals are achieved, and specifying exactly who is responsible for what (Forrester & Drexler, 1999).

CONCLUSION

There are potential advantages in organizational restructuring to achieve more effective collaboration in planning and delivering information services by libraries. The hierarchical, "top down" management style of the past is rapidly giving way to a system where employees take responsibility for their own actions and leadership comes from employee teams (Pierce & Kleiner, 2000). It does not mean that leadership always makes decisions at the lower levels, but rather it oversees the decisions that are made and evaluates their congruence with the direction of the organization. This has a direct effect on the organizational composition. Flatter and more flexible structures are emerging, moving away from traditional structures to multi-skilled, multi-tasked, and cross-organizational teams that more effectively tailor services and resources to particular patron requirements. Further, a strong leadership emphasis on team goals, clear expectations from team leaders, attention to team development, and an emphasis on coaching and challenging rather than directing is critical for successful change management when utilizing a team-based structure.

However, change requires a more thoughtful approach for the impact that major projects can and will have on the organizational culture and structure. Nearly two decades ago, Soudek (1983) formally defined the relationship between the organizational climate and professional behavior of academic librarians. In work building upon Kurt Lewin's programmatic equation ($B = f (PE)$ where $B =$ behavior, $P =$ personality, and $E =$ environment), Soudek combines the P and E elements of the equation to refer to organizational climate. A good organizational climate is high in individual autonomy, low in job structure, high in reward and recognition of achievement (personal or organizational), and high in consideration, warmth, and support (Soudek, 1983, p. 337). Successful organizational change should include these measures as outcomes of the change process.

FUTURE ISSUES

In the quickly evolving environment of academic libraries, Collier and Esteban (2000) see library leadership as being the systematic capability diffused throughout the organization to encourage creativity and to generate processes and practices that translate into organizational learning. Administrators exercise this through influence and intention, openness and communication, and autonomy and accountability. Successful leadership of libraries requires commitment, imagination, and energy, but above all the capacity to embrace change as a positive stimulus to organizational learning and development (Corrall, 1995a). In this way, learning and change can become legitimate aspects of organizational life.

According to Follett (1993) and Fielden (1993), the key tasks for academic library administrators are: to articulate future directions, based on a vision shared by all stakeholders and informed by continuing environmental appraisal; to secure the financial and other resources required to achieve agreed-upon goals; and to inspire and support colleagues as partners in exciting collaborative ventures. The information environment of the 21st century offers libraries the opportunity to play a central role in the academic community, but it will require bold and confident leadership along the way.

REFERENCES

APQC (1999). *Strategic planning: What works ... and what doesn't: Presentations from APQC's third knowledge management symposium.* [Electronic Resource]. Retrieved 12/12/2002 from http://www.apqc.org/free/whitepapers/dispWhitePaper.cfm?ProductID=672.

Beckhard, R. & Harris, R. T. (1987). *Organizational transitions: Managing complex change,* 2nd ed., Addison-Wesley, Reading, MA.

Beer, M. & Eisenstat, R.A. (2000). The silent killers of strategy implementation and learning. *Sloan Management Review,* 41(4):29-40.

Beer, M. (1994). Managing strategic alignment. In Berger, L.A. and Sikora, M.J. & Berger, D. R. (Eds). *The change management handbook: A road map to corporate transformation.* Burr Ridge, IL: Irwin, 33-48.

Blackler, F. (1995). Knowledge, knowledge work and organizations: An overview and interpretation. *Organization Studies,* 16(6):16-36.

Broderick, R., & Boudreau, J. W. (1992). Human resource management, information technology, and the competitive edge. *Academy of Management Executive,* 6(2):7-17.

Bryson, J. M. (1985). *Strategic planning for public and non-profit organizations.* San Francisco, Jossey Bass.

Buchanan, D. & Boddy, D. (1992). The Expertise of the Change Agent: Public Performance and Backstage Activity. Hemel Hempsted: Prentice Hall.

Burke, W.W., Church, A.H., & Waclawski, J. (1993). What do OD practitioners know about managing change? *Leadership & Organizational Development Journal,* 14(7): 3-11.

Carnall, C. (1995). *Managing change in organisations.* Hemel Hempstead: Prentice Hall.

Christensen, C.M & Overdorf, M. (2000). Meeting the challenge of disruptive change. *Harvard Business Review,* 78(2): 67-76.

Collier, J. (1998). Theorising the Ethical Organization. *Business Ethics Quarterly,* 8(4), 621-654.

Corrall, S. (1995a). An evolving service: managing change. In Dempsey, L. et al. (Eds.) *Networking and the future of libraries 2: managing the intellectual record.* Proceedings of an international conference held at the University of Bath, 19-21 April 1995. Library Association Publishing/UKOLN, pp. 45-61.

Corrall, S. (1995b). Academic libraries in the information society. *New Library World,* 96(3):35-42.

Dodgson, M. (1993). Organizational Learning: A Review of Some Literatures. *Organization Studies,* 14: 375-94.

Dodgson, M. (1994). Technological collaboration and innovation. In Dodgson, M. and Rothwell, R. (Eds), *The handbook of industrial innovation.* Aldershot: Edward Elgar Publishing.

Dougherty, R. & Dougherty, A. (1993). The academic library: a time of crisis, change and opportunity. *Journal of Academic Librarianship,* 18:342-6.

Edwards, C. & Walton, G. (2000). Change and conflict in the academic library. *Library Management,* 21(1): 35-41.

Fielden, J. (1993). *Supporting Expansion: A Report on Human Resource Management in Academic Libraries.* Bristol, England: The Councils.

Follett, B. (1993, December). *Report of the Joint Funding Councils' Libraries Review Group.* Bristol, England: The Councils.

Forrester, R. & Drexler, A. B. (1999). A model for team-based organizational performance. (Themes: Teams and New Product Development). *The Academy of Management Executive,* 13(3):36-50.

Geisler, E. (1997). *Managing the aftermath of radical corporate change.* Westport, Conn.: Quorum.

Hailey, Veronica Hope (1998). Transforming your organisation through people management. *Credit Control,* 19(8):25-33.

Higuchi, K. (1990). A delphi study on the future of academic libraries. *Library and Information Science,* (28):21-59 .

Jarratt, Alex (1999). Managing diversity and innovation in a complex organization. *International Journal of Technology Management,* 17(1,2):5-16.

Kanungo, R.N. & Mendonca, M. (1996). *Ethical dimensions of leadership.* Sage, London.

Katzenbach, J.R. (1996). New roads to job opportunity: From middle manager to real change leader. *Strategy & leadership*, 24(4): 32-36.

Katzenbach, J. & Smith, D. (1993). *The wisdom of teams: creating the high-performance organisation.* McGraw-Hill, New York, NY.

Koper, C. (1997). Managing change: The human resources component. *Optimum,* 27(4):48-53.

Lee, S. (1993). Organizational change in research libraries. *Journal of Library Administration,* 18(3-4):129-43.

Lewin, K. (1958). Group decision and social change. In Maccoby, E.E., Newcomb, T.M. & Hartley, E.L. (Eds), *Readings in social psychology,* Holt, Rinehart & Winston, New York, NY, pp. 197-211.

Lubans, J. (1999). "I've closed my eyes to the cold hard truth I'm seeing" -
Making performance appraisal work. *Library Administration and Management,* 13(2):87-99.

McLagan, P. & Nel, C. (1997). *The Age of Participation.* Berrett-Koehler Publishers, San Francisco, CA.

Meyer, R.W. (1997). Surviving the Change: The Economic Paradigm of Higher Education in Transformation. *The Journal of Academic Librarianship,* 23(January): 291-301

Morgan, G. (1988). *Riding the Waves of Change.* San Francisco, Jossey-Bass.

Nadler, D.A. & Tushman, M.L. (1997). Implementing new designs: managing organisational change. In Tushman, M.L. & Anderson, P., *Managing strategic innovation and change.* New York, NY: Oxford University Press, 595-606.

Newman, V. & Chaharbagi, K. (2000). The study and practice of leadership. *Journal of Knowledge Management,* 4(1):64-74.

Nozero, V.A. & Vaughan, J. (2000), Utilization of process improvement to manage change in an academic library. *Journal of Academic Librarianship,* 26(6):416-421.

Nutt, P. C. & Backoff, R. W. (1992) *The strategic management of public and third sector organizations.* San Francisco, Jossey-Bass.

Penrod, J.I. & Harbor, A. F. (1998). Building a client-focused IT organization. *Campus-Wide Information Systems;* 15(3): 91-102.

Pierce, T.N. & Kleiner, B.H. (2000). Changes affecting leadership and its importance in organisations. *Management Research News,* 23(7-8): 5-9.

Ray, D. & Bronstein, H. 1995. *Teaming up.* New York: McGraw-Hill.

Riggs, D.E. (1997). What's in store for academic libraries? Leadership and management issues, *Journal of Academic Librarianship,* 23(1):39-50.

Schein, E.H. (1987). *Process Consultation Volume 2: Lessons for Managers and Consultants.* Addison-Wesley, Reading, MA.

Soudek, M. (1983). Organizational climate and professional behavior of academic librarians. *Journal of Academic Librarianship,* 8(6):334-338.

Spies, P. B. (2000). Libraries, leadership, and the future. *Library Management,* 21(3):123-127.

Tichy, N.M., Hornstein, H.A., & Nisberg, J.N. (1977). Organization diagnosis and intervention strategies: Developing emergent pragmatic theories of change. In Burke, W.W. (Ed.), *Current Issues and Strategies in Organization Development,* Human Sciences Press, New York, NY, 361-83.

Chapter XII

Staffing the Transition to the Virtual Academic Library: Competencies, Characteristics and Change

Todd Chavez
Tampa Library at the University of South Florida-Tampa, USA

Change brought about by innovations in computing technologies has fundamentally altered the nature of work in academic libraries. In his description of the term informatica electronica, *Gilbert (1998) suggests that despite the way technology is changing how library staff do their work, it should not change the emphases on traditional services to patrons, such as accessing and retrieving information. This chapter also focuses on human changes that accompany the migration from print to electronic collections, from traditional to online services, and from the academic research library of a decade ago to the virtual library of today and tomorrow.*

INITIAL CONSIDERATIONS

The most important management decision to be made remains staffing the academic research library (Tennant, 1998). Historically, this has been a rather straightforward process, including the selection of a pool of candidates, each possessing similar experiences, skills, and competencies. A senior librarian would chair the search committee, with a selection of existing staff. Following one or more interviews, and perhaps a presentation, the library would solicit employment references, make the decision, tender the offer of employment, and the new employee would begin work.

In a nationwide survey, over 4,000 human resources professionals identified the two most significant issues facing their organizations (KnowledgePoint, 2001). Seventy-nine percent of the respondents stated that recruitment of qualified employees was their greatest challenge into the near future while 51% identified retention. Further elements contributing to the challenges of recruitment and retention included compensation, the need to demonstrate value for the employee, and poor management. Seventy-one percent of the human resources professionals stated that their employees cited improved communication as the most important factor contributing to retention rates. They also identified poor selection skills and practices as contributing to difficulties (KnowledgePoint, 2001).

Clearly, academic libraries are not exempt from many of the same pressures facing the respondents to the survey. In the past, it was possible to identify the specific skills and experiences that were desirable in an employee and either hire an individual with those skill sets or train an existing employee. Given the pace of change in today's academic library, this requires that library administration possess a crystal ball to predict which knowledge base and skills will remain important in the future (Tennant, 1998).

TECHNO-CHANGE AND THE CHANGING NATURE OF ACADEMIC LIBRARIES

Lynch and Smith (2001) reported on the results of a content analysis of 220 job announcements over a 25-year period (1973-1998) in *College and Research Libraries News*. Their research focused on the specific job characteristics listed in the position advertisements. They posited that position announcements in the *News* were probably representative of current trends and job requirements of the profession as a whole. Several significant trends were reported in this study.

The authors found that few traditional job elements persisted throughout the job announcements. First, although the requirement for a Master's degree in Library Science (MLS) from an American Library Association (ALA) accredited program in Library and Information Science was the most persistent (present in 80% of the advertisements), there has been a decline in M.L.S. requirements, particularly among the largest academic research libraries where specialized degrees are often required (Lynch & Smith, 2001). Association of Research Libraries (ARL) salary surveys for the period 1985 to 1998 reveal that a growing percentage of the professionals in these libraries were without the MLS (Lynch & Smith, 2001). Although the authors state that the knowledge, skills, and abilities formed from a library and information science (LIS) education continue to dominate the academic library workforce, an equally valid interpretation is that the ARL institutions are functioning as harbingers of future trends.

Lynch and Smith (2001) also found that computing technologies *as they relate to library and information science* were incorporated into all jobs and thus were present in all position announcements (emphasis added). The authors conclude that new hires alone cannot meet the academic library's increasing need for technological proficiency; rather, that the institutions must invest in a systematic program of continuing education and training.

In addition, Lynch and Smith discuss the increasing incidence of requirements for instructional experience, emphasizing a desire for teaching skills and knowledge of learning theories and methodologies and a growing and recent emphasis on departmental and unit team environments. Coupled with a concurrent emphasis on behavioral skills, such as effective oral and written communication, flexibility, and creativity, Lynch and Smith conclude that organizational cultures are changing. However, the changing emphasis on teams and increasing solicitation for behavioral skills supporting team organization and interaction is challenged by an apparent contradiction: position announcements for administrative jobs do not reflect the changes in organizational structure implied by the non-administrative position advertisements. What this apparent "disconnect" means for future organizations is not explored, but one may assume that some future crisis will emerge to challenge the existence of two divergent sets of expectations.

There are specific examples of the changing nature of work in the academic library. Nofsinger (1999) suggests that changes and innovations in computing technologies compel a systematic requirement for training and retraining for 21st century reference librarians in the following core competencies: reference skills, subject knowledge, communication skills, interpersonal abilities, knowledge and skills in technology, critical thinking skills, supervisory and management skills, and commitment to user services. For the cataloging side of the profession, Wendler (1999) cites the explosion in electronic publishing and the concomitant requirement for metadata as the impetus underlying the challenges to the cataloger's ability to order the chaos. It is clear that developments in computing technologies are changing the very nature of the academic library's mission and thus the staff's work.

Support staff is not immune to the effects of rapid technological change. Librarians tend to share many common competencies gained through the experience of graduate education in the discipline. This is not the case with paraprofessionals, who come to the academic library with a plethora of skills and experiences, diverse both in content and in level of accomplishment. Sheffold (2000) suggests that paraprofessional training and continuing education are quite often the first areas impacted by budget reductions. Organizationally, support staff are often left to operate the desks during important meetings and training opportunities for professional staff. Thus, the impact of change upon support staff is particularly serious.

Reporting on a case study of change within an academic library, Farley, Broady, Preston and Hayward (1998) characterize change as occurring on three levels: organizational, technological, and human. They caution the administrator to ensure that the concerns of all staff are examined and addressed prior to implementing change because "the negative impact of change on staff, even if successfully managed, must not be underestimated" (p. 151). Positing that academic librarianship has changed more over the last few decades than in its entire history, the authors cite four areas in which the change has been dramatic: economics, technology, higher education, and organization (p. 153).

HUMAN CHANGES

Technological change is the one constant for the academic library engaged in the transition from traditional format resources and services to future electronic collections and services. Nevertheless, the human dimension may well dwarf the technologically derived sources of change in terms of long-term impact upon the academic library. The most significant of these human changes include considerations of the changing demographics of the work force and management's response to these fundamental factors.

The demographic profile of a "typical" academic librarian (Bell, 1999; Cooper & Cooper, 1998) is white, female, and 45 years of age. Her undergraduate training is likely to be either in the arts and humanities or in the social sciences, with some graduate-level coursework in these disciplines. Regardless of where this typical librarian works, she is probably from the "reference side" of the profession. She possesses approximately 13 years of professional experience and earns $43,000 per year. This librarian is a member of a group who typically retires by age 63 (Matarazzo, 2000).

Consider the incoming library school graduate. At an average age of 36 years, this librarian is solidly "Generation X" (i.e., an individual born between 1961 and 1981). Contrasting significantly with the earlier generations, 'Xer's' are skill-focused, survivalists in orientation, used to rapid and unending change, and technologically competent (Cooper & Cooper, 1998, p. 20). Administrators and managers who are unaware of or unwilling to embrace these generational differences are positioning themselves for future difficulties. The generational changes between librarians have import in such areas as organizational culture, reward systems, training requirements and methods, and budget.

Morgan (2001, p. 58) highlights the importance of incorporating the human factor in any attempt to manage or adapt to change. He states, "What sometimes gets forgotten in all this [concern for change] is the human element involved in what is likely to be a heavily technology-driven future ... Research suggests that 90% of change initiatives that fail do so because human factors are not taken into account." Morgan's human factors include communication, staff involvement, and generational dynamics.

With human communication a recurring theme in much of the change literature, consider the effects of email in today's libraries. Hierarchical communication is dead. It is no longer necessary to make an appointment with the Dean of Libraries to place an idea or complaint directly on his or her desk. Lubens (2000) concludes that not only has email had a positive effect on staff productivity, it increases the staff's understanding of the organization. More importantly, it promotes good communications practices allowing staff to have immediate access to people and vital information to deal with change.

RESPONSE TO CHANGE

In an indictment of academic librarians' recognition of the fundamental results of the technological change experienced over the past decade, Herring (2001) accuses librarians of reaching "stasis," of creating or contributing to their own unemployment by becoming comfortable and complacent with the minimal adaptations made to date. He describes several external trends that threaten to make academic libraries irrelevant: 1) the "everything's-on-the-Internet" challenge; 2) competition with commercial information providers; 3) failure to be proactive in technological developments and innovations (i.e., allowing technology to drive library services and collections); and 4) a fundamental "disconnect" with the new generation of information consumer. Although Herring identified technological change as the catalyst underlying libraries' own undoing, he simultaneously makes it clear that obsolescence is not guaranteed – academic library professionals can make changes to the seemingly inevitable death of the library.

In an examination of the effects of technological change on academic library staff, Poole and Denny (2001) surveyed professional and paraprofessional personnel in 28 Florida community college libraries. They found that respondents were overwhelmingly positive about the changes that accompanied technological innovations, e.g., approximately 69% of the staff enjoyed the changes as contrasted to less than five% reporting that they disliked computers. From questions designed to assess the ability of training efforts to keep pace with the rate of technological change, Poole and Denny concluded that training needs were sufficient in Florida's two-year colleges. However, they identified the lack of management's commitment to involve staff in planning and decision making as a significant area of contention.

Herring (2001) states it is highly unlikely that anyone in the academic library community needs to be convinced of the challenge of change. Hudson (1999) suggests that managers first become clear as to the appropriate concepts to employ in this situation. She distinguishes between change that she defines as relating to a specific situation, and transition which is a psychological construct: change is "…a gradual process, internal to the individuals who are going through it…Transition is the process people go through to internalize the change" (p. 36).

Farley et al. (1998) identify four areas of human resource management that would minimize the negative effects of change: communication and information sharing, staff involvement and participation, training and development, and job design. Management should recognize that: 1) the traditional organizational structure in academic libraries is the opposite of what is needed to manage change and facilitate transition, and 2) "people are an organization's greatest asset but it would seem that few organizations truly believe this or act as if they do" (p. 162).

In addition to staff participation, Morgan (2001) champions adoption of a managerial style characterized by: 1) flat organizational models; 2) teamwork and project management; 3) strong links between library and institutional parent; and 4) a spread of accountability. He emphasizes developing and fostering a strategic awareness in all staff, ensuring that everyone understands the strategic goals they serve in the course of their daily work and getting a handle on the tendency for technology to drive people as opposed to the reverse (p. 60). Green, Chivers and Mynott (2000) similarly emphasize communication, developing peer relationships, staff involvement in decision making, appropriate recognition and reward, training, and staff development as being critical to effective, positive management of change and as motivational tools.

JOB SKILLS AND COMPETENCIES: ARE THEY PRACTICAL?

Should managers and human resources professionals serving the staffing needs of academic libraries rely upon job competencies – either formal (published) or informal (anecdotal) – to make selection and hiring decisions? Once an employment decision is made, can managers productively use these same competencies to evaluate and promote staff? These questions are deceptively simple. The answer to either query depends upon whether the competencies employed are statements of job skills, including lists of specific technological proficiencies, or by contrast, are stated in terms of desirable personal characteristics.

In an article describing desirable skills and competencies for librarians in the new millennium, Tennant (1999) lists knowledge of imaging technologies, optical character recognition, markup languages, cataloging and metadata, indexing and databases, user interface design, programming, Web technology, and project management. Although it is certain that different readers will argue for the continued validity of one or more of the skills listed, how relevant are all the skills that are listed in 2002? Arguably, skills with markup languages may no longer be essential given the quality of editing applications that accomplish the markup function for users who have word processing skills. At the USF Tampa Library, the experience is that such technologies as interface design and programming are best outsourced to individuals or organizations whose skills are at the "bleeding edge" of currency.

To illustrate the difficulty in employing skill lists for selection purposes, consider this recent example. After an extensive planning period, library management decided to establish a Geographic Information Systems (GIS) Research and Data Center. In January 2001, library management initiated a nationwide search for a qualified GIS Librarian to manage the center. The position announcement was carefully crafted to reflect the needs of the center with due consideration of minimal competencies. The library selected a candidate that matched the knowledge base and skills and assigned a start date of May 1, 2001. However, the following month, ESRI, the premier designer of GIS software applications used by all academic units at the USF Tampa campus, announced a major development in version eight of their GIS software application. In July 2001, the new GIS Librarian went to ESRI training to learn the new format. The lesson here? Skills in a particular application are good today and obsolete tomorrow. Flexibility and willingness to accept change are critical for success.

Now consider an extreme example of futuristic predictions regarding technological change in academic libraries and the competencies that would be required to bring this change to fruition. Gillett (1998) suggests that libraries use nanotechnology to produce information on demand from templates on a molecular level. In essence, he envisions "the library as factory"–a future as repositories of information templates in infinite variety. Based upon this view of the future, what are the job skills and competencies that academic librarians must possess to succeed in the world of "molecular information?" A shift from lists of job skills to competencies appears imperative.

The Association of South Eastern Research Libraries' *Competencies for Research Librarians* (Perez et al., 2000) outlines five competencies that define what is best in a research librarian. Perez et al. state that the successful research librarian possesses such attributes as "intellectual curiosity, flexibility, adaptability, persistence, and the ability to be enterprising" (p. 3). Woodsworth (1997) focuses on both particular technologies and personal characteristics when reviewing competencies for librarians who are best viewed as elements of a "global digital information infrastructure." These parallel Nofsinger's (1999) competencies for the reference librarian of the 21st century and Tennant's (1998) admonition regarding the importance of hiring and selection in academic libraries. Tennant also distinguishes between skills and traits and goes on to list such personal characteristics as capacity to learn quickly and constantly, flexibility, and innate skepticism as critical to the librarian of the future.

PERSONAL CHARACTERISTICS

Lynch and Smith (2001) noted the increasing incidence of behavioral characteristics in the position announcements they analyzed. Tennant (1998), Sheffold (2000) and Morgan (2001) have alluded to the importance of such personal characteristics as flexibility, enabling skills, and risk taking. Perhaps of more immediate importance, does the profession have a firm grasp on those personal characteristics and behaviors that are counterproductive to the transition from the traditional to the online environment?

Hudson (1999) suggests that conflict and stress are inevitable but need not be disastrous. It is important to recognize that failure to adapt to change need not be solely limited to unhappiness, lost workdays, or retention problems. The conflict and stress associated with change adaptation difficulties can cause violence or other unacceptable behaviors. Staff struggling to adapt to change and/or protect their own self-interests become stressed. Stress breeds conflict: stress, and conflict can result in abusive behaviors. This is the sobering side of the nature of change; it is a side of change that academic library managers must consider or be remiss in their responsibilities.

Bullying

Hannabus (1998) suggests that bullying is widespread in the workplace. Bullying takes a variety of forms: physical assault; gossip and rumor-mongering; ridiculing arguments in meetings; public criticism; overloading individual workers with assignments; denying annual or sick leave; abusing internal processes designed to alleviate management-worker tensions (e.g., grievances). Hannabus (1998) characterizes the classic bully as an individual with low self-confidence and low self-esteem, i.e., someone who is fearful that his or her inadequacies (perceived or real) will become evident. Bully-victim behaviors are symptoms of a more significant and pervasive problem (Hannabus, 1998).

Dealing with bullying requires a concerted effort by many in the organization. First, the victim must acknowledge that he or she is being bullied. Once a victim believes that he or she fully understands the dynamics of the situation, a meeting with management is in order to determine if the problem is one of bullying. Once that determination is made, the library should take assertive action. Bullies need to be confronted about their behavior since they need to understand the effect their actions have upon both the victim and the organization. Violent bullies should be removed from the workplace. Counseling sessions for all concerned may also be productive. To illustrate the importance of eliminating bullying, consider the following example. When a project team of volunteers was to be disbanded and integrated into the larger library system, most members of the team understood the need to make this change and actively facilitated the transition. However, one individual (opposed to change) publicly criticized colleagues, disrupted meetings, and threatened to file grievances, thus making the group's efforts to transform as difficult as possible.

Passive-Aggressive Behavior

Another common workplace phenomenon is the growing incidence of passive-aggressive behavior in the face of transition. McIlduff and Coghlan (2000) make it clear that passive-aggressive behavior is much more than a mere strategy adopted by individuals faced with the uncertainties that accompany change on this level. Described as "a pervasive pattern of passive resistance to demands for adequate social and occupational performances, beginning by early childhood and present in the functioning of the person in a variety of contexts" (p. 717), the term "passive" is the key to understanding the disorder. Passive-aggressive behaviors are exhibited in ways that do not directly offend other parties involved but do accomplish the intended goal of "getting back at authority figures for perceived ill treatment or injustice" (p. 718). These behaviors typically surface as a resistance to demands for performance.

Individuals immersed in passive-aggressive behaviors typically perceive change as threatening or unnecessary; assess the impact of the proposed change as a threat to themselves, the organization, and/or the clientele served; and respond to the change by dodging, opposing, or resisting the thrust of the initiative. Interventions, done in either a one-to-one setting or within a team environment, include: 1) calm but assertive communications describing the reason for intervention; 2) genuine efforts to understand the passive-aggressive individual's context; and 3) resolution to work through the problem, however long it may require (McIlduff & Coghlan, 2000). Toleration of passive-aggressive behavior will doom an organization to fail in its efforts to move forward.

Organizational Fit

First and foremost, academic libraries must attract, retain, and train staff to understand organizational culture. Staff must be capable of understanding the organizational culture, both as productive members and as prospective members seeking to join "the team." Accurate assessment of an organization's culture is critical to an employee's potential for success and a source of added stability to the organizational unit (Sannwald, 2000).

Ethics of Workplace Behavior

A second trait essential to successful adaptation to this changing environment is best described as a fully internalized and "automatic" sense of the ethics of workplace behavior, which is not the same as the principles of conduct that govern librarianship. The ethics of workplace behavior are personal rules of engagement that are designed to ensure integrity in all actions (Caville & Hoskins, 2001). Two examples of the ethics of workplace behavior are: "It is ethical to positively change the organization; it is unethical to damage it. It is ethical to go above and beyond expectations; it is unethical to do anything less" (pp. 11-13). Clearly, desirable staff are those who possess similar internal ethical standards.

Leadership

Metz (2001) argues that academic libraries are suffering from a general lack of leadership capable of leading in a discontinuous future. Defining a "discontinuous future" as one lacking sequence and cohesion, Metz challenges academic library leaders to recognize the significance of the transformation from print repositories to portals to electronic collections and thus develop new mind sets that value differences, redefine and eliminate historical limitations, manage expectations, and think discontinuously. He also stresses the importance of being a generalist possessed by many of the personal characteristics described in this chapter and simultaneously cautions against security in specialized skills.

Creativity

In a side-by-side comparison of inventories of desirable personal characteristics (Tennant, 1999, 1998; Oberg, 2000; Wilson, 1999), many similarities are immediately apparent: capacity to learn quickly (and constantly), skepticism, public service orientation, enabling skills, appreciation for colleagues, risk-taking philosophy, and so forth. Without exception in either form or meaning, one of the most desirable traits is creativity.

Creativity may well be the most essential of the personal characteristics discussed in this chapter. Defined as the "ability of providing an original or inventive response to a problem," (Yong, 1994), creativity is possible only when such traits as flexibility, risk taking, enabling, and comfort with change are present. More importantly, creativity can be assessed both during the selection process and after employment (Williams, 2001). Creative people possess four characteristics: 1) problem sensitivity ("the ability to identify the "real" problem"); 2) idea fluency ("the ability to generate a large number of ideas from which to choose"); 3) originality ("new ways to adapt existing ideas to new conditions"); and 4) flexibility ("ability to consider a wide variety of dissimilar approaches to a solution") (Yong, 1994, pp. 17-18).

Apart from attracting and selecting creative personnel is the matter of how to address existing employees, individuals who possess a rich and irreplaceable knowledge of the organization and are thus important to the successful continuance of the academic library's mission. Certainly, library management cannot simply abandon these individuals in an unswerving search for creativity, but we can train them. Williams (2001) endorses a program of creativity training including creative problem solving, creative self-statement (enhances creative performance), and "synectics," a brainstorming technique in which the user seeks to make the strange familiar and the familiar strange. It is clear that academic libraries can incorporate creativity training into their organizational repertoire, but the challenge is to ensure that negative behaviors such as bullying and passive-aggressive behavior do not combine to make the effort irrelevant. This is a particular challenge in an organization that is unsuccessfully dealing with the generational dynamics described by Cooper and Cooper (1998).

Yong (1994) and Williams (2001) also emphasize the need to ensure that managers receive training in appropriate methods for managing creative people, including such tools as role-playing and behavioral modeling. Among the areas wherein management may effectively and productively promote creativity are organizational culture and structure, work group design and use, job design, social support for the creative process, and recognition and evaluation.

CONCLUSION

It is clear that staff remains a library's most important asset in successfully transforming the traditional academic library into a 21st century organization. The need to devise selection strategies to attract the best personnel, to implement management practices and organizational structures conducive to retaining productive and creative staff, and to initiate training for valued existing personnel cannot be emphasized enough. While libraries cannot – and should not – abandon current hiring and selection practices in a wholesale manner, continued reliance on traditional lists of job skills separated into minimum and preferred qualifications will not facilitate employing the most desirable personnel available for a given function. The "life-time" employment system currently utilized in the majority of academic institutions may well work in direct opposition to elimination of the undesirable traits (bullying and passive-aggressive behavior) in favor of a creative workforce.

FUTURE ISSUES

To accomplish the goal of attracting and retaining creative personnel to academic libraries, it is essential that libraries broaden their perspectives on selection practices to incorporate measures of creativity heretofore unknown in the traditional academic search process. While it is unethical to wantonly disregard the rules of the organization, it is equally important to recognize that many institutional selection processes are antiquated leftovers from an age wherein diversity was the primary goal in selection. In this milieu, such considerations as creativity and flexibility take a backseat to representative candidate pools, and diverse search committees appear to be more essential than the ability of the membership to contribute to the selection process. It is important to recognize the wider implications of a desire for diversity: diversity of education, diversity in thought, and diversity in approach to change.

REFERENCES

Bell, C. (1999). Y210, succession planning in libraries: Finding the common ground. *PNLA Quarterly,* 64(1):20-21.

Caville, P., & Hoskins, A. (2001). Raising the bar on workplace behavior. *PNLA Quarterly,* 65(3):10-14.

Cooper, J. R., & Cooper, E. A. (1998). Generational dynamics and librarianship: Managing Generation X. *Illinois Libraries,* 80(1):18-21.

Farley, T., Broady-Preston, J., & Hayward, T. (1998). Academic libraries, people and change: A case study of the 1990's. *OCLC Systems and Services,* 14(4):151-164.

Gilbert, B. (1998). The more we change, the more we should stay the same: Some common errors concerning libraries, computers, and the Information Age. In M. T. Wolf, P. Ensor, & M. A. Thomas (Eds.), *Information imagineering: Meeting at the interface* (pp. 3-11). Chicago: ALA.

Gillett, Stephen L. (1998). Nanotechnology: The library as factory. In M. T. Wolf, P. Ensor, & M. A. Thomas (Eds.), *Information imagineering: Meeting at the interface* (pp. 219-227). Chicago: ALA.

Green, J., Chivers, B., & Mynott, G. (2000). In the librarian's chair: An analysis of factors which influence the motivation of library staff and contribute to the effective delivery of services. *Library Review*, 49(8):380-386.

Hannabus, S. (1998). Bullying at work. *Library Management,* 19(5):304-310.

Herring, M. Y. (2001). Our times they are a-changin', but are we? *Library Journal,* 126(17):42-44.

Hudson, M. P. (1999). Conflict and stress in times of change. *Library Management,* 20(1):35-38.

KnowledgePoint, Inc. (2001). Survey finds recruitment and retention the top issues facing employers. *Library Personnel News,* 14(2):8.

Lubens, J. (2000). "While I was busy holding on, you were busy letting go": Reflections on e- mail networks and the demise of hierarchical communication. *Library Administration & Management,* 14(1):18-21.

Lynch, B. P., & Smith, K. R. (2001). The changing nature of work in academic libraries. *College & Research Libraries* 62(5):407-420.

McIlduff, E., & Coghlan, D. (2000). Reflections: Understanding and contending with passive aggressive behaviour in teams and organizations. *Journal of Managerial Psychology,* 15(7):716-736.

Matarazzo, J. M. (2000). Library human resources: The Y2K plus 10 challenge. *Journal of Academic Librarianship*, 26(4):223-224.

Metz, T. (2001). Wanted: Library leaders for a discontinuous future. *Library Issues,* 21(3):1-6.

Morgan, S. (2001). Change in university libraries: Don't forget the people. *Library Management*, 22(1/2):58-60.

Nofsinger, M. N. (1999). Training and retraining reference professionals: Core competencies for the 21st century. *Reference Librarian,* 64:9-19.

Oberg, L. R. (2000). How to make yourself indispensable: A survivor's guide for the 21st century. *Library Mosaics,* 11(1):14-15.

Perez, D., Drake, M., Ferriero, D., & Hurt, C. (2001). Competencies for research librarians. *ASERL Web.* [Electronic Resource]. Retrieved 11/14/2001 from: http://www.aserl.org/statements/competencies/competencies.htm

Poole, C. E., & Denny, E. (2001). Technological change in the workplace: A statewide survey of community college library and learning resources personnel. *College & Research Libraries*, 62(6): 503-515.

Sannwald, W. W. (2000). Understanding organizational culture. *Library Administration & Management,* 14(1):8-14.

Sheffold, D. (2000). Support staff professional development: Issues for the coming millennium. *OLA Quarterly*, 5(4):7.

Tennant, R. (1999). Skills for the new millennium: Personal characteristics essential to digital librarians. *Library Journal,* 124(1):39.

Tennant, R. (1998). The most important management decision: hiring staff for the new millennium. *Library Journal,* 123 (3):102.

Wendler, R. (1999). Branching out: Cataloging skills and functions in the digital age. Journal of Internet Cataloging, 2 (1):43-54.

Williams, S. (2001). Increasing employees' creativity by training their managers. *Industrial and Commercial Training,* 33 (2):63-68.

Wilson, A. (1999). Ride the wave of the future: Be flexible in your job. *Library Mosaics,* 10 (6):7.

Woodsworth, A. (1997). New library competencies: Roles must be defined within the context of a global digital information infrastructure. *Library Journal* 122(7), 46.

Yong, L. W. (1994). Managing creative people. *Journal of Creative Behavior* 28(1),16-20.

Chapter XIII

Library Statistics and Outcomes Assessment

Rose L. Bland and Allison M. Howard
Hinks and Elaine Shimberg Health Sciences Center Library at the
University of South Florida-Tampa, USA

The objective of collecting library statistics is "to assess the quality and effectiveness of services [and resources] provided by the library" (Poll, 2001, p.307). A review of the literature shows that measurement of electronic resources is a concern, that standards are necessary, and collaboration with publishers is required. As libraries spend more of their valuable resources to provide access to the electronic environment, they need to turn their attention to the effective measurement of electronic resources. In order to do this, libraries must determine relevant statistics (including those that can be collected internally by the library), request vendors to provide standardized statistics, and finally, evaluate the data in the context of their unique setting to enable sound decision-making. Libraries also need to utilize user surveys in addition to local and content-provider statistics, to get a clearer picture of their user's needs and satisfaction with library services and resources. Although the task is daunting, obtaining reliable statistics in the electronic environment is needed and continues to be another challenging area in academic libraries.

This chapter will examine the various issues involved in gathering usage statistics for library electronic resources, including questions relating to why libraries collect statistics, what needs to be collected, and how data are collected. The chapter will also address the challenges encountered in collecting data, the perspective of content-providers, and the issues involved in data presentation. Finally, there will be a short review of several key initiatives on statistics for electronic collections.

OVERVIEW OF STATISTICS

Definitions

There is an immense need in the area of electronic resource measurement for concrete definitions. According to Hafner (1998, p.2), "Statistics is a collection of procedures or techniques that can be used to make sense out of numbers." A simple example is calculating the mean number of patrons attending classes on an electronic resource. Hafner (1998, p.4) then defines measurement as "the process that translates observations into data." A counter on a Website is a form of measurement. Statistics, therefore, is taking the data from the measurement process and applying a technique or procedure to give meaning to that data. In addition, the terms vendors, publishers, aggregators, and content providers refer to any supplier of electronic resources.

Why Statistics Are Collected

Libraries collect statistics for a variety of reasons. Statistics show how circulation trends have changed from year to year, explain how budget monies have been allotted, determine the most used resources, demonstrate need (including funding, programs, resources, new building, and equipment), and assess per capita spending. In addition, in times of budgetary shortfalls or windfalls, knowing what resources are of highest importance to primary constituents from a statistical perspective (not just from observation) assists in making difficult decisions and in communicating and defending those choices. Though electronic resources are a relatively new library category, usage data is critical. Without "measures for electronic services, libraries will be unable to compare traditional and electronic services for decision-making purposes" (Bertot & McClure, 1998).

Areas in which libraries collect statistics include: budget allocations; collection development; improvement of library services; marketing, promotion, and education; determining cost apportionments for multi-campus libraries and/or consortia purchases; reporting to accrediting boards and other agencies; assessing technology; and strategic planning.

Budgeting

Statistics show how much money is being spent in each area of the library, who and how many people are being served, and who is being underserved. Statistics also identify what types of collections get the highest usage and what services need to be increased. The use of statistics assists in identifying the kinds of education and promotion efforts needed to educate users to the availability of various resources, areas that require more staff time and attention, and resource duplication.

As users change how they access materials, operational costs (such as equipment needs and expenses, space requirements, and staffing needs) are affected. As libraries shift from print journals to electronic resources, staff spend less time shelving journals, handling bindery shipments, inserting erratum, mending pages, checking-in journals, processing, and claiming lost issues. The demand for highly skilled individuals increases and the need for lower-skilled jobs decreases. For example, when Drexel University's Hagerty Library migrated to a largely electronic journal collection, it discovered a need for "detail-oriented support staff who have advanced computer skills and who can adjust to continuous changes in procedures and methods" (Montgomery, 2000).

Collection Development

Statistics can identify which subject areas are getting the most use, which areas need enhancement, and the types of materials used. Statistics can further pinpoint the needs of teaching faculty, students, and research faculty, since the information needs and desired outputs of these different constituencies are likely to differ, not only from one another, but also across disciplines.

"Electronic publishing affects not only the ways in which scholars conduct their research, but also the selection process librarians utilize in acquiring these [electronic] products" (Svenningsen, 1998, p.18). Along with the standard evaluation criteria used in collection development, it is now necessary to think in terms of access technology. In addition to format (HTML, ASCII, PDF, Postscript), there are also questions regarding technical compatibility, training requirements, maintenance issues, licensing terms, the user interface, reliability of access, stability, and archival issues (Nisonger, 1997, p.60).

Library Services

The collection of data in this area allows the library to strengthen its current services and shift priorities as needed to meet additional service needs. When there is concrete information regarding how people use the library and its resources, the library can adjust its processes to provide more support to its users. Common service statistics center on issues related to utilization, demand, and availability.

They help identify peak periods of usage or "popular" services and ensure that appropriate levels of staffing and resources are available when and where they are most needed. Access is equally important, whether users are physically coming into the library or accessing the library's resources remotely. User satisfaction requires identifying any barriers a user perceives when accessing remote resources. Libraries need to recognize that access has changed over time and to identify the impact on the library, the staff, and the workflow as well as the library user. Since the availability of these resources involves people, time, money, and equipment even when the library is not open, increased funding may be a possibility (for a more thorough discussion on access issues, see Chapter 5 in this volume).

Marketing, Promotion, and Education

Since it takes between 16 months and three years for users to become accustomed to and effectively use new resources (Luther, 2001), marketing, promotion, and education of services and resources are vital. People need to know a resource exists before they can use it. Until a resource becomes very familiar, users may choose a recognized entity even if it is not the most appropriate, simply because it is known. Tracking a library's marketing and instructional efforts will tell administration and staff how pervasive an element the library is within an academic setting (a more thorough examination on marketing is provided in Chapter 8 in this volume).

Determining Cost for Multi-Campus Libraries or Consortia Purchases

In many multi-library universities, as well as in consortia, libraries pay for a portion of the resources purchased. The number of student, faculty, and staff full-time equivalents (FTEs), or who is going to use the resource the most, determines the percentage within a consortium. By tracking usage, the library can determine if a particular department or school is using a given resource as initially anticipated. Typical concerns include if the division of cost is fair, if the resource is used enough to warrant the cost expenditure, or if a different resource is appropriate for the given population. Without usage statistics, it is impossible to know what impact a resource has on the community of users.

Reporting to Administration and Accreditation Boards

Academic libraries have a number of external associations to which they report in addition to the reporting requirements of their own administration. Examples include the Association of Research Libraries (ARL), the regional Association of Southeastern Research Libraries (ASERL), and reporting boards, such as the Integrated Postsecondary Education Data System (IPEDS). Professional schools and academic departments within higher education, which have accreditation boards that approve their programs, ask the library for assistance when substantiating scholarly resources available to their program. Typical accrediting questions include what are the resources the library provides and in what formats, currency of the resources, and accessibility of resources. Nisonger (1997) raises some good points when he questions how libraries count their electronic journals. For example, a library may choose to count the journal if it purchases a subscription, licenses a subscription, or simply provides access via the World Wide Web, regardless of whether those journals are cataloged or archived. For those libraries where funding is tied to the size of their collection, issues such as ownership, access, and availability are critical. It becomes impossible to benchmark with like libraries if there is no prescribed method of gathering and reporting data.

Assessing Technology Needs

Determining technology needs can factor into infrastructure upgrade requests for university computing and/or administration. Basic computer system requirements include network specifications, technical support, training, maintenance, system upgrades, service contracts, and impending obsolescence. If the library or university acts as an Internet Service Provider (ISP), other important issues include the availability of remote access lines appropriate to users' needs, the number of users turned away, the quality of the Internet connection, and who shares the library network. Finally, libraries need to consider special client software, helper applications, or plug-ins for resource accessibility (Bertot & McClure, 1998; Nisonger, 1997; Svenningsen, 1998).

In addition to technology issues, security, privacy, and confidentiality are other areas of concern. Since many licensing agreements require that only authorized users have the ability to access a particular resource, there must be a way of authenticating the user. Although users are familiar with traditional library policies, libraries are now leading users to services outside their walls where user privacy issues are still evolving. If vendors do not provide information on their privacy policies, libraries should request information on what statistics are collected, how they are used, how long they are kept, and an explanation on how the users' privacy will be protected. Generally, vendors who offer customized services, such as table of contents and current awareness alerts, capture identifying information for those services. "Protecting the user's personal information is not just a courtesy; it is a legal obligation" (Luther, 2001).

Strategic Planning

Statistics are also a means of determining whether the library is meeting its mission and objectives. For example, if the mission statement refers to "collecting" resources, yet the library spends increasingly more money on "access" to resources but not the acquisition of them, it may be time to rethink where the library is going and if that direction is consistent with the mission statement of the library.

WHAT STATISTICS ARE COLLECTED

The challenge of statistics is not only in collecting the data, but also in knowing what data are necessary to collect, what are the questions to answer, the amount of time that is available to gather statistics, and what is available locally to be collected. In short, what do the data measure and what do they not measure? Shim et al. (2000) believe that it is better to collect a limited amount for a specific purpose than to collect a vast amount of data for no discernible reason. For example, it may be possible to create menus or redirect pages that allow certain statistics to be collected at the local level rather than rely on vendor statistics (see Appendix A for types of selected measures for collection and statistical analysis).

Traditional library statistics, such as door counts, numbers and types of questions asked, and items checked out, have been measured for years. Methodologies have been well established for their collection, interpretation, and utilization. Libraries keep track of which journal titles are reshelved as a measure of what titles are being used, photocopy activity to measure (to some degree) article level usage, and gate counts to measure library foot traffic. While not all of the measures are 100% accurate, they do provide a snapshot of library activity at a specific point in time. They indicate which journal titles are important in which disciplines and perhaps, depending on how staff tracks items, which discipline areas are using the most current issues, and which disciplines find the archival titles of more value. This leads to an understanding of information-seeking behaviors of different disciplines. These types of traditional measurements have relied on the concrete presence of a patron who had some sort of contact with the library and its staff.

When collecting statistics in a virtual library, the library can no longer look within its physical space and collect information on its resources and services. Remote access of resources becomes more difficult for the library to track. Since the needs of faculty, students, and staff differ considerably, it is essential to determine who is using which remote resources and to what degree. For example, are resources used now the same as they were in the print collection or have other titles become more heavily used, simply because they are available both remotely and in full-text? Also, the heavy usage of table of contents services may indicate that users want to know what a particular resource has available.

Since many of the electronic resources exist outside of the library on vendor sites, it is best that the vendor captures statistics at its level rather than at the library level. Since a library purchases and/or licenses resources from many vendors, the process of gathering statistics is quite challenging. Not only do vendors have diverse infrastructures, interfaces, and access methods, they also have differences in definitions, counting methodologies, and software packages. Unfortunately, according to Luther (2001), "Less than half of the publishers who offer journals in electronic form today are able to provide statistics on the usage of these journals."

Numbers are not the only things that are important. Decision-making looks at the context within which data (e.g., raw usage numbers) are gathered. Session length (time spent on a site) may or may not measure a number of variables, including value, system performance, or filtering tools (Rous, 2001). Low usage data may mean users are not aware of the resource or that they have had difficulty using it, rather than the resource is unnecessary. For example, low usage titles may be a vital part of a program or research department that brings in substantial grant monies. If so, could that department or research area function adequately without access to those titles? High usage numbers may reflect a number of things, including user interest, familiarity with the print version, the value of the collection, or the functionality of the search engine (Rous, 2001).

Finally, how much do usage statistics measure the value of the information? Traditionally, the value of an item is not based on usage, but rather determined by factors including the reputations of the Editor-in-Chief and Editorial Boards, imprint, faculty endorsement, caliber of research, and journal impact factors. Value is qualitative and is an important complement to quantitative data that are collected (Rous, 2001). For example, the ratio of usage to the number of articles published is an often-neglected measure. A list of the most used journals (determined by the number of articles downloaded) is not the same list when compared with the number of published articles in the journals (Luther, 2001)

HOW STATISTICS ARE COLLECTED

Before collection of data begins, there should be a clearly defined statement or question(s) to answer, definitions of the identified measure(s), and the rationale behind the reason for collecting the statistics. Generally, the question(s) dictate what data to gather. The resulting statistics, when analyzed, provide the necessary information for meaningful decision making. These questions will also help to establish procedures for their data collection. At a minimum, the procedure should state which individual(s) and/or vendor(s) are responsible for collecting the data, the frequency (weekly, monthly, quarterly), the instructions for the data collection (e.g., how to handle a title that has multiple accesses), and a clear description of the output format of the data (Shim et al., 2001).

It is important to note any special considerations concerning the collection of and the interpretation of data (Shim et al., 2001). One example is the counting of electronic books in an aggregator's database as electronic reference sources rather than as part of the aggregator's database. The procedure should clearly state how to count these resources and identify any staff-related issues associated with data collection. For instance, if a high degree of technical ability is necessary to compile statistics, it is important to specify that either staff will be trained to handle complicated analyses or that the analyses will be handled by the library's website host (Shim et al., 2001).

PROBLEMS IN DATA COLLECTION

Although collecting statistical data may seem like a simple task, the research indicates otherwise, since no standard has been widely adopted. Publisher and vendor statistics are not comparable with one another with any sense of accuracy, consistency, and reliability. There are numerous discrepancies in counting data elements, data definitions, software capability, and statistical processing methods. The good news is that both "librarians and publishers share a significant number of concerns about the development and interpretation of statistics" (Luther, 2001).

Rous (2001) identifies several problems in counting events and activities. These include whether to exclude demonstrations and training session hits from statistics of actual usage; determining the difference between an abstract vs. full-text, viewing a HTML file, downloading a PDF file, e-mailing, saving, or printing; and how to differentiate hits among spiders, crawlers and robots. Other questions include how to count the numbers of completed searches and even how to count double clicks in quick succession. Time-outs, which can vary from several minutes to 30 minutes or more, present another problem. Does inactivity on a resource skew usage statistics and tracking? In addition, some resources, such as those using Z39.50 clients, are incapable of providing statistics (Shim et al., 2001). Consortia resources further complicate usage statistics. For example, articles downloaded from a consortia resource may be from journals to which the library may or may not subscribe. It is important to ascertain if each participating library has access to consortia statistics as well as the statistics for its users.

Even with established standard definitions for "hit" or "session," results can still be ambiguous due to differences in communication software, network protocols, and system infrastructure (Luther, 2001). For example, most network logs do not count access via bookmarked sites stored in a local cache. Identifying multiple accesses, from multiple sites (e.g., library catalog, vendor website), is also difficult when providing an accurate count.

Another issue is how to compare resources that differ in so many ways.

Resources can include full-text, abstracts, citations, current journal issue, archival issues, whole books, or a mixture of several of these formats. There are often differences in resources that are available through a subscription and those accessible via a free service. Journal titles indexed cover-to-cover are not comparable with titles indexed selectively. It is no wonder that libraries and vendors have a difficult time collecting comparable statistics for electronic resources.

CONTENT PROVIDER PERSPECTIVES

Although content providers realize the importance of collecting usage data, providing such data is a new task (Luther, 2001). In addition, content-providers are concerned that libraries will cut the least used titles. From the vendor perspective, cancelled subscriptions require reevaluation and possible changes to the price structure. Rous (2001) notes that there is a movement toward pay-per-view or document delivery rather than subscription, which may affect smaller or more esoteric subsidized titles.

Content providers are equally concerned about the need for statistical standards to substantiate their product(s) and increase market share. Their sales departments, editorial boards, marketing departments, and system analysts and programmers need specialized statistics to support their product and service capacity. User privacy and confidentiality are also of significant concern to vendors (Shim et al., 2001).

Compiling statistics has created new demands for vendors as well. Many vendors, such as Elsevier and Academic Press, have identified the need to hire additional staff to write programs, meet with consortia (e.g., International Coalition of Library Consortia), design system architecture and query databases, and coordinate and implement statistical programs. They have also found it to be economically inefficient to create individually customized statistical reports. Steve Moss of the Institute of Physics Publishing estimated a price increase of about 2% for costs associated with gathering statistics (Nisonger, 2000)

Large-scale "mirrored" databases require compilation of multi-site statistics (Luther, 2001). To further complicate the issue, commercially prepared statistics software packages do not function consistently in all environments. Luther (2001) found that *NetTracker*, a software program used by the Institute of Physics, only counted HTML views but not PDF downloads. She also found that the software used by the American Institute of Physics was triple counting downloads in some cases and undercounting in other cases. Not only did the system not count searches and requests for abstracts, it only counted "requests for the full text of an article that require[d] either a subscription or pay-per-view access" (Luther, 2001). A caveat for vendors is to analyze their data carefully and provide documentation on collecting, counting, and recording statistics.

How Are Data Presented

Vendors and libraries benefit from a multi-purpose, standardized statistical format. Both, of course, would like data delivered electronically, on a regular basis, and in a downloadable format that does not require re-keying of the information. Formats with common, defined data elements would enable reports to be easily read, compared and understood, thus enhancing their value. The decision to compare or interpret the data is a serious one. Although general research methods are taught in graduate school, most "professionals in academic libraries are either too frequently unaware of the value of practical statistical utilization and/or use statistics incorrectly" (Frank, Madden, & Simons, 2001).

KEY INITIATIVES

In 1994, ARL stressed the importance of statistics by expanding its scope from simply describing research libraries to "measuring the performance of research libraries and their contributions to teaching, research, scholarship and community service" (Blixrud, 2001). This section will discuss several associations and organizations involved in the development of measurement standards and guidelines for electronic resources and services.

Developing Public Library Statistics and Performance Measures for the Networked Environment Study

Created out of an Institute for Museum and Library Services National Leadership Grant project, *Statistics and Performance Measures for Public Library Networked Services* (Bertot, McClure & Ryan, 2001), provides information on the development, maintenance, and reporting of network statistics and performance measures, and recommends specific data that should be considered for collection. The authors discuss managing data collection, how to reduce errors during measurement, and how to work with the statistics provided by content providers. Their manual also includes a number of sample forms, definitions, calculations, and analyses. For example, the chapter on user assessment discusses the use of questionnaires and focus groups and provides sample forms. Overall, the manual provides comprehensive information on what is collected, how to collect it, and how to deal with issues that influence measurement (http://www.ii.fsu.edu/Projects/IMLS/IMLS.abstract.html).

E-Metrics Project

An ARL New Measures Initiative, the E-Metrics Project created a "best practices" for measurement of electronic resources (Blixrud, 2001). The project created lists of minimum statistics and performance measures, a procedural manual, and a guide to collaborating with content-providers (Shim et al., 2001). Currently, the E-Metrics Project is concentrating efforts on locally defined major databases and collecting as many statistics as possible through redirect pages and proxy server logs (Shim et al., 2001) (http://www.arl.org/stats/newmeas/emetrics/).

EQUINOX: Library Performance Measurement and Quality Management System

Supported by the Telematics for Libraries Programme of the European Commission, the EQUINOX Project (1998-2000) focused on how to measure electronic resources and services with quality management in mind. The project had two main objectives: the continuing development of international agreements on performance measures by the inclusion of measures for electronic resources, and the development of an integrated tool for both quality and performance measurement by library managers. The project team identified 14 performance indicators that enhance and complement the indicators for traditional library services presented in *ISO 11620: Library Performance Indicators*. Further, the project team strongly recommended that these indicators be collected together (http://EQUINOX.dcu.ie/).

International Coalition of Library Consortia (ICOLC)

In 1998, the ICOLC released guidelines for the measure of electronic resources entitled *Guidelines for Statistical Measures of Usage of Web-based Indexed, Abstracted, and Full Text Resources*. Updated in December 2001, it is now entitled *Guidelines for Statistical Measures of Usage of Web-based Information Resources*. The guidelines include: minimum requirements for specific data elements, protection of user privacy and confidentiality, institutional or consortial confidentiality in regards to selling or releasing statistical usage by institution, definitions for data elements, access for consortium administrators to reports for the institutions they represent, and reports delivered in a web-based format (Luther, 2001). As of January 4, 2002, approximately 76 consortium members have adopted the ICOLC Guidelines (ICOLC, 2001) (http://www.library.yale.edu/consortia/2001webstats.htm).

LibQUAL+

Another ARL New Measures Initiative project, LibQUAL+ is defining and measuring library service quality from the user's perspective. The goals of the four-year project (1999-2003) include: the establishment of a library service quality assessment program, the development of a web-based tool to assess library service quality, development of mechanisms and goals for evaluating libraries, and identifying best practices in providing library services. Libraries will be able to identify where their services need improvement and benchmark the quality of their services with those of peer institutions. The SERVQUAL instrument, commonly used in the private sector to measure quality in customer service, is the model for the LibQUAL+ tool (Blixrud, 2001) (http://www.arl.org/libqual/).

National Commission on Libraries and Information Science (NCLIS) *2000 Public Library Internet Study*

The Public Library Internet Study (Bertot & McClure, 2000) focused on measurement questions related to "level[s] of connectivity, public access, training support and technology funding ... access and use patterns ... use of Internet-accessible resources including commercial product databases, [and] the ability of public libraries to report electronic database use" (Davis, 2000). In addition, the study addressed the needs of persons with disabilities to access the Internet in terms of software and hardware requirements. In conjunction with the Bertot and McClure study, a second report, *Electronic Access and Use Related Measures: Summary of Findings* (Davis, 2000), assessed other use related measures in electronic resources (http://www.NCLIS.gov/).

National Information Standards Organization (NISO) Forum on Performance Measures and Statistics for Libraries

In 2001, 65 participants (representing academic, public, school, government, and special libraries, associations, publishers, vendors, integrated library systems and the research community) participated in the review of the current ANSI/NISO standard *Z39.7: Library Statistics*. Major recommendations included the critical need for systemic data collection, guidelines for collecting qualitative and performance data, how to tie the value of libraries more closely to the benefits they create for their users, and different methodologies to measure network performance. A major recommendation from the conference participants suggested that NISO "serve as a clearinghouse for standards, guidelines, and other tools across diverse communities with closely related interests" (National Information Standards Organization, 2001) (http://www.niso.org/news/reports/stats-rpt.html#summary).

The Publishing and Library Solutions (PALS) Vendor-Based Usage Statistics Working Group

Created in 2000, the PALS working group is comprised of three organizations in the United Kingdom: Publishers' Association (PA), Association of Learned and Professional Society Publishers (ALPSP), and the Joint Information Systems Committee (JISC). The Working Group has created a common Code of Practice to enable publishers and vendors to record online usage statistics and deliver them in a consistent way to libraries. Major issues identified included gateways and hosts, sessions and searching, authentication, market elements (e.g., reporting data and levels of reporting), institutional identification, data integrity and accuracy, and types of reports (Publishing and Library Solutions usage statistics working group, 2001) (http://www.usagestats.org).

CONTINUING EDUCATION

There are many avenues to learn more about statistics, including formal academic programs, professional workshops, mentoring, and self-education. Many academic institutions offer statistics classes and allow individuals to audit classes. A number of national, state, and local library organizations also offer workshops on statistics as part of their continuing education programs or upon request.

Working with a mentor or tutor is an excellent way to receive individualized instruction. Graduate students, faculty, or librarians who have worked on measurement projects may be available to act as a mentor. In addition, tutorials on statistics are available on the Web. For example, *HyperStat Online*, points to sites with over 100 tutorials (Lane, 2001).

Finally, there are numerous books and journals available on the topic of statistics, with many articles specifically geared for librarians (Frank, Madden & Simon, 2001).

CONCLUSION

Capturing usage data for electronic resources that is consistent and reliable across content providers and libraries is extremely difficult. The many variables and differences in system architecture present a difficult challenge to identify best practice. Currently, best practice appears to be that libraries gather whatever statistics are feasible, keeping their methods as consistent as possible. By identifying their user population, defining and characterizing their data elements, and documenting local decisions and policies, libraries will be able to compare their procedures and policies with evolving national reporting and benchmarking standards. Further, although comparing usage statistics of various products from the same content provider is often considered reliable, the same is not true when comparing statistics across different content providers.

What is definitely clear is that measurement guidelines, vendors, and libraries need to remain flexible as technology changes. For example, when the ICOLC guidelines were first created in 1998, electronic resources, such as netLibrary™ did not exist (Shim et al., 2001).

Besides the collection of usage data, accurate interpretation is crucial. Accordingly, libraries should view all collected data in context. Libraries should have a clear understanding of their users' diverse information needs. Both qualitative measures and quantitative measures are essential for meaningful decision making.

FUTURE ISSUES

For future development of policies and procedures, interested librarians should continue to monitor ICOLC, LibQUAL+, and the ARL E-Metrics Project. Content providers and libraries should continue to identify areas where similar methodologies could be adopted. Measurement of usage and qualitative analysis of electronic resources in libraries is a thriving discipline and is likely to continue. New developments will no doubt be forthcoming and libraries would be wise to contribute their input. Awareness of what is happening in the field will help libraries keep abreast of new developments. Continued collaboration and open dialogue among content providers and libraries will serve to enhance future advancements of electronic resource measurement.

REFERENCES

Bertot, J. C., & McClure, C. R. (1998). Measuring electronic services in public libraries: issues and recommendations. *Public Libraries*, 37(3):176-180.

Bertot, J. C., McClure, C. R., & Ryan, J. (2001). *Statistics and performance measures for public library networked services*. Chicago: American Library Association.

Blixrud, J. C. (2001). *The Association of Research Libraries statistics and measurement program: from description data to performance measures*. [Electronic Resource]. Retrieved 11/14/2001 from http://www.ifla.org/IV/ifla67/papers/034-135e.pdf

Davis, D. (February 8, 2000). *2000 public library Internet study*. [Electronic Resource]. Retrieved 12/10/2001 from http://www.NCLIS.gov/news/

pressrelease/pr2000/bertot.html

EQUINOX *Library Performance Measurement and Quality Management System.* (2001, August 9). [Electronic Resource]. Retrieved 11/21/2001 from http://equinox.dcu.ie/

Frank, D. G., Madden, M. L., & Simons, N. R. (2001). The use of statistics by academic librarians: comments on a significant problem and suggestions for improvement. *Georgia Library Quarterly*, 38(2), 5-10.

Hafner, A. W. (1998). *Descriptive Statistical Techniques for Librarians.* Chicago: American Library Association.

International Coalition of Library Consortia (ICOLC). (2001). *Guidelines for statistical measures of usage of web-based information resources.* [Electronic Resource]. Retrieved 12/10/2001 from Yale University Web site: http://www.library.yale.edu/consortia/2001webstats.htm

Lane, D. M. (2001). *HyperStat Online.* [Electronic Resource]. Retrieved 11/11/2001 from Rice University Web site: http://www.ruf.rice.edu/~lane/rvls.html

LibQUAL+ General FAQ. (July 27, 2001). [Electronic Resource]. Retrieved 12/06/2001, from http://www.arl.org/libqual/geninfo/faqgen.html

Luther, J. (2001). *White paper on electronic journal usage statistics.* (2nd ed.) [Electronic version]. [Electronic Resource]. Retrieved 11/01/2001 from http://www.clir.org/pubs/reports/pub94/contents.html

Miller, R., & Schmidt, S. (2001, August 15). *E-Metrics: measures for electronic resources.* Paper presented at the 4th Northumbria International Conference on Performance Measurement in Libraries and Information Services. [Electronic Resource]. Retrieved 11/07/2001 from http://www.arl.org/stats/newmeas/emetrics/miller-schmidt.pdf

Montgomery, C. H. (2000). Measuring the impact of an electronic journal collection on library costs. *D-Lib Magazine,* 6(10). [Electronic Resource]. Retrieved 11/02/2001 from http://www.dlib.org/dlib/october00/montgomery/10montgomery.html

National Information Standards Organization (2001). *Report on the NISO forum on performance measures and statistics for libraries.* [Electronic Resource]. Retrieved 11/05/2001 from http://www.niso.org/news/reports/stats-rpt.html

Nisonger, T. E. (1997). Electronic journal collection management issues. *Collection Building*, 16(2):58-65.

Nisonger, T. E. (2000). Usage statistics for the evaluation of electronic resources. Report of a session at the 1999 ALA Conference. *Library Collections, Acquisitions, and Technical Services*, 24(2):299-302.

Publishing and Library Solutions (PALS) usage statistics working group (2001).

Working group progress report 10, August 2001. [Electronic Resource]. Retrieved 12/10/2001 from http://www.usagestats.org/

Poll, R. (2001). Performance measures for library networked services and resources. *The Electronic Library,* 19(5):307-314.

Rous, B. (2001, Spring). Usage statistics for online literature. *Professional/ Scholarly Publishing Bulletin,* 2(1):1-3. [Electronic Resource]. Retrieved 11/10/2001 from http://www.pspcentral.org/.

Shim, W., McClure, C.R., Bertot, J.C., Sweet, J. T., Maffré de Lastens, J.-M., Dagli, A., & Fraser, B.T. (2000). *ARL E-Metrics project: developing statistics and performance measures to describe electronic information services and resources for ARL libraries. Phase I report.* [Electronic Resource]. Retrieved 11/14/2001 from http://www.arl.org/stats/newmeas/ emetrics/phaseone.pdf

Shim, W., McClure, C. R., Fraser, B. T., Bertot, J. C., Dagli, A., & Leahy, E. H. (2001). *Measures and statistics for research library networked services: procedures and issues. ARL E-metrics phase II report.* [Electronic Resource]. Retrieved 11/14/2001 from http://www.arl.org/stats/newmeas/ emetrics/phasetwo.pdf

Svenningsen, K. (1998). An evaluation model for electronic resources utilizing cost analysis. *The Bottom Line: Managing Library Finances,* 11(1):18-23.

APPENDIX A: TYPES OF MEASURES TO BE CONSIDERED FOR COLLECTION AND STATISTICAL ANALYSIS FOR BOTH LIBRARIES AND CONTENT PROVIDERS

(Complied from Shim, McClure, Fraser, Bertot, Dagli, & Leahy, 2001, p. 94-95; Shim et al., 2000, p. 18-21)

Resources (hosted by library, institutional subscription, and/or consortia agreements)
- Number of electronic books
- Number of electronic full-text periodicals
- Number of electronic databases

Support Resources
- Number of public access workstations
- Number of staff providing electronic reference
- Number of staff providing technical assistance (resource updates, solving equipment problems, etc.)

Use
- Number of documents or citations viewed, downloaded, e-mailed, or printed from electronic databases
- Number of logins (sessions) to vendor-hosted electronic databases
- Number of logins (sessions) to locally-hosted electronic databases
- Number of people who participate in user instruction on electronic resources and services
- Number of queries (searches)
- Number of turn-aways (requests exceed simultaneous user limit)
- Number of electronic reference transactions
- Number of transactions by specific times of day (busiest times of the day, day of the week, weeks, months)
- Total connection time to electronic resources
- Response and access time

Users
- Percentage of undergraduate students using each type of electronic resource
- Percentage of graduate students using each type of electronic resource

- Percentage of faculty using each type of electronic resource
- Percentage of staff using each type of electronic resource
- Percentage of affiliated patrons using each type of electronic resource
- Percentage of others using each type of electronic resource

Cost

- Cost of electronic books
- Cost of electronic full-text periodical subscriptions
- Cost of electronic database subscriptions
- Library contribution to consortia for electronic resources

Performance Measures

- Analyzing cost per items viewed in individually subscribed databases
- Percentage of electronic books to all monographs
- Percentage of electronic materials use of total library materials use
- Percentage of electronic reference transactions of total reference
- Percentage of electronic titles to all periodicals
- Percentage of remote library visits of all library visits
- Ratio of public access workstations to defined population

Chapter XIV

Re-Engineering Library Education

Vicki L. Gregory
University of South Florida-Tampa, USA

The revolutionary changes in the educational curriculum for schools of library and information science being evinced by the exponential expansion of computer-based technologies require a reexamination of the skills and expertise needed to be acquired by the next wave of academic librarians. This is critical in order that they may continue to be able to provide information services and resources to the academic communities within which those librarians will practice their profession. In addition, it is important to meet emerging educational needs in terms of various multiculturalism and diversity issues that are arising today as well as a thorough understanding of research theory and practice. Implicit in these examinations is a need to review the way library school faculty will be teaching, using newer technologies including Web-delivery of courses, and how faculty should exhibit the skills needed in order to be able to deliver courses using the new technology-centered methods. Finally, this chapter will emphasize the importance of continuing education for future academic librarians and current professionals.

CURRENT AND FUTURE ROLE OF THE ACADEMIC LIBRARIAN

Butcher (1999) sums up the current role of the academic librarian of the future, for whom schools of library and information science are trying to provide an appropriate and relevant education in the swiftly changing present environment:

"Although much has changed in libraries in the last quarter century, the core of who we are and what we are remains the same. We continue to be a profession devoted to bringing users and information together as seamlessly as possible. Libraries have used technology to enhance and create services. They have recognized that changing expectations and lean budgets require organizations that call upon the talents of everyone. Librarians have become more engaged in teaching and research to serve the needs of students, faculty, and the profession better. Finally, librarians are crossing campus boundaries and entering wholeheartedly into the political process to insure that libraries have a voice in the redefinition of information access" (p. 353).

Thus, there are rapid changes in all types of libraries and the burgeoning of new technologies for librarians to learn. These changes, while increasing the knowledge base of graduate students to enter successfully into an academic library career, nevertheless remain rooted in the need to carry out the traditional librarian roles – though hopefully faster, cheaper, smarter, and more effectively. It is important to review the most significant of those roles and see how the new academic educational paradigms are affecting them from a library and information science education viewpoint.

COLLECTION DEVELOPMENT/MAINTENANCE

The traditional heart of the library has been, of course, its collections — from the time of the great Alexandrine Library of the Classical era, libraries have been, in essence, the repositories of learning and hence the materials through which that learning is transmitted. When those materials become literally ethereal, coming to the user electronically "through the ether" as the preferred method of delivery, will we continue to need collection development librarians at all in academic libraries? Although most conceptions of the emerging digital libraries of the future retain a key role for the information professional, some visionaries nevertheless question whether the typical librarian's present functions will be necessary. Will material selection, currently a key part of the professional librarian's role, continue to enjoy a place in the electronic environment in a fashion sufficiently analogous to the prominent role now occupied in the traditional print-on-paper oriented library?

Malinconico (1992) contemplated the possibility that it may soon be the computer technologist rather than the librarian who would be the keeper of the electronic keys to the gateway of academic information. This technologist would control and manage, through knowledge and domination of electronic information resources, the future of the information-seeking process as presently carried out by researchers in the typical academic library. Although this role is certainly important, and the "key" role of those who possess the necessary mastery of a technology in controlling the ends to which that technology is used should not be easily discounted, the centrality of the role of such persons can also be exaggerated. Nevertheless future academic librarians need to be cognizant of the opportunities and potential pitfalls of the electronic information environment in terms of their own career goals and plans.

Likewise, current students preparing for the future (and indeed the present) electronic library cannot be permitted to overlook the continued, lasting importance of print publications in the library's carrying out of its role. Thus, collection development courses at the Master's level must reflect an appropriately balanced approach, emphasizing the latest technology, not as an end in itself but rather as simply another tool to use in addressing the problems arising in acquiring adequate resources for a library collection, in whatever format is most appropriate for the particular library and for the "task at hand." Information resources and products continue to become more widely available and in increasingly diverse formats. Future academic librarians must be prepared to adapt and learn to become comfortable with these new formats.

As librarians and information professionals go about the process of acquiring electronic information resources, they must also be concerned with the issues of future accessibility and preservation of library resources. In the past, when a library acquired a book or set of serials, the acquisition librarian could be fairly certain that the materials would be there and available for some significant time for future library users (unless some portion of the materials was lost, stolen, or mutilated). Electronic materials, obtained through complex licensing requirements rather than through outright purchase, do not often come with that same assurance and present altogether different problems. Imagine a library whose books simply vanished from the shelves due to the mere passage of time. Collection development and preservation can be seen as aiming at the prevention of just such a thing. It is a concept that must remain an important part of the library school curriculum no matter how dominated and fascinated the field may become with electronic materials.

REFERENCE SERVICES

In most conceptions of the academic libraries of the future, academic reference librarians will continue to play many of the same reference roles that they have traditionally performed in collaborating with their library's users. They will continue to serve in an intermediary role to assist those users in finding needed information and to provide important "value-added" services through the production of instructional materials and guides to information resources. However, many of these functions, out of necessity, will be performed in media other than those that have been traditionally utilized. To cite a simple and obvious example, instead of developing traditional printed pamphlet guides to available resources, librarians will need to be able to produce locally on-line or Web-based resource guides. Collaboration and instruction may be expected to take place in a web-based "chat" environment or by email rather than through a face-to-face meeting over the reference desk. Abels (1996) puts the matter clearly into perspective when she points out that "complex reference requests will become more commonplace as electronic information services are expanded. Information professionals must be prepared to conduct effective reference interviews via e-mail" (p. 355). In other words, it doesn't get any easier for the reference librarian — but it will get more challenging and require a more thorough background. While Abels' work, which used library school students at the University of Maryland as intermediaries in her electronic reference study, was published in 1996, her predictions have turned out to be quite accurate. With the role of electronic reference now expanding beyond e-mail to other electronic forms of communication, one can only conclude that the transformation of the reference desk paradigm remains an ongoing process, likely only to accelerate in the coming years.

When addressing the role of reference, it is important to note that determining the service boundaries of all types of libraries is becoming more difficult given the dynamic nature of information resources available in our increasingly web-based, database-influenced environment. Academic reference librarians will, for instance, have to become comfortable helping users locate information that requires computational analysis. For example, federal census data, decennial and otherwise, is no longer a fixed product but a dynamic database of information that must be manipulated in order to be discerned and analyzed. Increasingly, information in all fields will no longer take the form of a static product but rather a dynamic, restless sea of information. Reference librarians will be required to access a myriad of databases containing information that must be manipulated in order to be obtained and used, rather than simply viewed as in the older style, fixed-print media.

Academic librarians of the future must therefore acquire teaching skills as well as informational skills. They will need to be able to teach information literacy skills as students discover that just finding some on-line information on a topic and pushing the "print" button is not enough. In the electronic information world, librarians must be prepared to evaluate resources in a somewhat more in-depth way than was necessary when they could often depend upon refereed print journals for the majority of their information.

Increasing use of distance education programs by most institutions of higher education will also add to the skills required of the average academic librarian. They will need education and training in the delivery of information to distant users, which necessarily includes some basic knowledge of the various technological problems involved as well as the purely informational problems with which they may feel more comfortable. In addition, academic librarians will need to become fully informed concerning the copyright and intellectual property issues that affect the ability to use and loan electronic materials that are only leased by or licensed to, and not necessarily owned by, the library.

TECHNICAL SERVICES

In addition to all the vagaries involved with the classification and cataloging of traditional print materials, technical services librarians today, and doubtless more so in the future, will have to be prepared to cope with all the varieties, flavors, and forms that electronic resources may take. These will include both those resources housed locally, such as CD-ROMs, and those obtained from remote sources, such as online journals, electronic books, maps, graphical materials, and various other multimedia resources. Technical services professionals are increasingly dealing with many different formats and kinds of materials that may defy classification and are often not traditionally cataloged. Other approaches, such as indexing and abstracting techniques and the development of in-house library-constructed databases, as well as webliographies, may be undertaken as methods of organizing the access and retrieval process.

Future graduates planning a career in the technical services side of academic librarianship should place a much greater focus (than is presently typically allowed for in the library school curriculum) on the technological aspects of information provision. Concurrently, library and information science schools need to take steps to provide programs and courses that will build student skills in document creation for the digital library environment. Unfortunately, this cannot serve as a replacement for the traditional knowledge and skills involved in cataloging and classification, but rather an additional literacy that students will need to acquire. As a minimum, students will need to gain a hands-on knowledge of the architecture of the infrastructure and databases behind a digital library. Library and information science schools would best accomplish this goal through the development of an additional specific course, rather than trying to make room in the already overstuffed basic "organization of knowledge" class that most schools currently offer.

Future academic librarians will also need additional technical and systems skills to allow them to deal successfully with metadata concepts, and to learn at least the basics of markup languages such as XML (Extensible Mark-up Language) and SGML (Standard Generalized Mark-up Language). Although it has never really been cost effective to make computer programmers out of professional librarians, a theoretical knowledge of such topics, coupled with some hands-on experience, is important and can pay significant dividends in ensuring that academic librarians will be able to manage the applications technology being made in the organization of library resources. Additionally, the theoretical knowledge acquired by librarians would assist them in working with programmers and systems developers of products, services, and applications on a local level.

So, how can this be accomplished? Vellucci (1997) sums up the current situation with regard to the cataloging curricula typical in schools of library and information studies:

"Educators want to ensure that students are prepared for future careers, yet no one is sure of how the future delivery of information will be cast, or what exact role the cataloger might play within that veiled future. Cataloging teachers continue, therefore, to examine factors likely to influence the organization of information, and to incorporate appropriate changes into their courses. But how many new concepts and skills can be added before a course is overloaded? And what can be deleted with assurance that it will not leave a significant gap in knowledge? The inevitable result is not only the restructuring of a specific course, but a rethinking of the entire context of the cataloging curriculum to accommodate new areas of study, while retaining the fundamental theory and critical thinking process that will enable students to adapt to their changing futures, and, in some cases, provide a leadership role in the area of knowledge organization"(p. 36).

In many ways, the increasingly electronic nature of our information resources puts more stress on the effective organization of access to them, i.e., technology is, again, making the librarian's job harder, not easier. In the early days of electronic resources and online catalogs, many felt that keyword searching would be all that would be necessary for future access to materials. In the reality of the digital information environment, we have found that the deluge of electronic resources has put more stress upon organizational systems, and the skills used to develop them, than has ever been the case.

LIBRARY ADMINISTRATION

All librarians need education in library management, and this is especially true in the case of academic librarians. Even new professional librarians often acquire subordinates, generally student assistants. Suddenly, he or she discovers the need to acquire skills in management techniques as well as library management theory. Library management will only become more complex as we move toward more of an electronic existence. Consider, for example, telecommuting with a staff librarian conducting electronic reference from outside the library building. Learning both the traditional skills of face-to-face management and the skills necessary to deal with a workforce and user base that is often working or accessing library materials or staff remotely is extremely important for future academic librarians.

Lynch (2000) discusses the major issue of funding and collections for academic library administration:

> "In a world of shared resources on the network, it is possible to centralize more of the management, organization and description, and preservation of content, and economic considerations encourage such centralization. Yet there are legitimate needs for local control and for responsiveness to local institutional needs.....[which include] resolving the systemic funding problems in an environment where costs for traditional materials are increasingly unsustainable and where libraries are simultaneously being confronted with the need to invest in the support of a range of nontraditional networked information resources."

These administrative concerns require students to learn, for instance, about licensing issues for electronic information resources as well as more complicated budgeting techniques. They will not only be required to know about technology but must be aware of the pitfalls in dealing with the impact of technology on all areas of the library's operations. Technology requires librarians to conceptualize and operate within a much larger framework than that in which librarians operated in the traditional print environment. The idealized relatively monastic isolation of the traditional print library, where silence was the golden rule, is definitely ancient history. Flexibility and creativity are going to be necessary traits and skills for future academic librarians.

MULTICULTURALISM AND DIVERSITY

The rapidly changing nature of the population of the United States means that all future librarians must be conversant with major issues concerning multiculturalism and diversity. These concerns are not only with race and ethnicity issues but also with gender, age-related, and disability issues. Given the overall student population makeup of our schools of library and information studies, it is very probable that their graduates will need to provide services for people who are of a different racial or linguistic background than their own. With the rapid aging of the U.S. population, they will also have to be prepared to provide more services to elderly patrons. The delivery of information to meet the needs of persons with disabilities is exacerbated by new electronic technology. For example, to develop web pages for persons with visual or perceptual impairments, students will have to meet federal guidelines for access to electronic information. Students need to be aware of how to bridge the gap between their background and abilities and those of library users.

THE ROLE OF RESEARCH

Academic librarians must understand the research process and be able to conduct their own research and/or participate as a member of a research team. To adequately understand the needs of faculty and doctoral student research, the academic librarian needs to be able to "talk the language" of research. This skill greatly enhances the credibility of the librarian in the eyes of the researcher. From the Association of Research Libraries/Online Computer Library Center (ARL/ OCLC) Strategic Issues Forum (1999) came "The Keystone Principles," three short statements summarizing the core values of academic and research libraries. Principle 3 states "The academic library is the intellectual commons for the community where people and ideas interact in both the real and virtual environments to expand learning and facilitate the creation of new knowledge."

On a university campus, an academic librarian is often expected to publish in order to receive promotion, tenure, or merit pay increases. In addition to thinking of research as a requirement, it is important to think about research in terms of improving library services. There are, and have been, many practical applied research projects that have the possibility of greatly improving academic library services and performance if academic librarians had adequate training in research. This is where research faculty and staff can collaborate with librarians to increase the knowledge in the field of librarianship. These collaborations would enable librarians to be more confident in the development of sound empirical or applied research studies as well as in the use of quantitative and qualitative methodologies. Also, librarians can benefit from the support and knowledge of faculty who have published extensively, learning what are success factors to ensure publication, and the opportunities for collaboration on research publications (Bahr & Zemon, 2000; Kochan & Mullen, 2001).

TEACHING MODES

In the foreseeable future, it is apparent that more and more instruction will be in a distance mode with Web delivery, video-conferencing and other technological means of providing instruction. A current burden on many library and information science faculty members is how to adapt a course, originally designed for a face-to-face classroom encounter, to a web-based encounter. Although the goals, objectives, and major assignments for a class might remain the same, the overall means of delivery puts more pressure on faculty members to devise new ways of delivering material. Both virtual" and print reserve materials may become problematic as distance from the home site increases. Compounding the traditional instructional component is the additional element of computer support. Increasingly, when something goes wrong with the computer on a student's end, the faculty member is expected to be able to do computer troubleshooting over the telephone or by email. Although it is common for programs and universities to provide technical support, the faculty members usually find themselves caught up in the technical support problems much more so than when their classes are taught in the traditional manner. Of course, when the academic computing staff person or the faculty member is unavailable, the next major organization on the campus that fields these questions is the library. Academic librarians must deal with technical, computing, and/or network issues as well as assisting the beleaguered student (or faculty member). So, although these issues primarily affect the teaching of library and information studies classes, they also have a major impact on the services demanded of the academic library.

Another way that academic librarians are going to be affected by new modes of teaching technology is in their work in bibliographic instruction. As colleges and universities increasingly engage in distance education, librarians will have to be more active participants by delivering bibliographic instruction in a web-based format. Experience in one or more web-based classes while in library school will help future academic librarians respond appropriately and sympathetically to a diversity of users' needs. Experience with learning in a distance mode will help them understand the needs of distant learners when they take a professional position. Schools of library and information studies are beginning to offer classes in services to distant learners, which is another way for students to gain insight into the problems and challenges involved with delivering instruction at a distance.

CONCLUSIONS AND FUTURE ISSUES

Compounding the problems with redesigning a graduate library and information science program is the fact that many students do not end up employed in the type of library matching their academic preparation. The initial professional degree is, therefore, general in nature. In the past this has worked fairly well because most libraries had more similarities than differences. In today's electronic world, however, that assumption is not always true.

It may be that the traditional 39 to 42 semester-hour Master's degree will no longer suffice for future academic librarians. At the very least, a commitment to continuing education will be an absolute necessity. The library profession has always stressed continuing education, but, except for times when revisions to the current cataloguing code are introduced or the library purchases a new automation system, many librarians have undertaken minimal formal continuing education. To be able to keep up with the fast-moving changes in technology and new models of delivery of information, continuing education has become a necessity, not a luxury. However, this also means that academic libraries will need to budget for the continuing education of their staff. If not considered as a luxury, but rather a necessity, librarians should expect some financial assistance from their institution for their continuing education efforts.

The other possibility is for library and information science schools to create advanced certificates beyond the Master's degree, with a concentration in academic libraries. After five years or so on the job, returning for such an educational program would update skills and allow librarians to focus on particular areas where they need enhanced educational experiences. In this age of technology, such a program could be site-independent with all, or the majority, of the courses offered via the Web; thus, the professional librarian would not need to journey to an institution of higher education to take such courses.

Whichever path is taken, it is clear that change is the order of the day for academic librarians and the curricula that prepare them. Librarians must prepare themselves to deal with change as their constant companion – at least for the foreseeable future.

REFERENCES

Abels, E.G. (1996). The E-Mail Reference Interview. *RQ*, 35(Spring): 345-358.

Association of Research Libraries and the Online Computer Library Center. (1999). ARL/OCLC Strategic Issues Forum: The Keystone Principles. Accessed November 1, 2001, http://www.arl.org/training/keystone.html.

Bahr, A.H. & Zemon, M. (2000). Collaborative authorship in the journal literature: perspectives for academic librarians who wish to publish. *College and Research Libraries*; 61(5): 410-19.

Butcher, K. (1999). Reflections on Academic Librarianship, *Journal of Aca-*

demic Librarianship, 25(5): 350-353.

Kochan, F. K. & Mullen, C. A. (2001). Issues of Collaborative Authorship in Higher Education. *Educational Forum*, 65(2):128-135.

Lynch, C. (2000). From Automation to Transformation: Forty Years of Libraries and Information Technology in Higher Education. *EDUCAUSE Review,* 35 (1):60-68.

Malinconico, S.M. (1992). What Librarians Need to Know to Survive in an Age of Technology. *Journal of Education for Library and Information Science*, 33 (Winter): 226-227.

Vellucci, S.L. (1997). Cataloging Across the Curriculum: A Syndetic Structure for Teaching Cataloging. *Cataloging and Classification Quarterly*, 24(1/2): 35-59.

About the Authors

Ardis Hanson is the director of the research library at the Louis de la Parte Florida Mental Health Institute at the University of South Florida (USF). Interested in the use of technology to enhance research, she has presented at the USF Symposium on 21st Century Teaching Technologies and Internet2 showcasing innovative software applications. She is an adjunct instructor in the School of Library and Information Science and the College of Public Health at USF. Ms. Hanson was a member of the Virtual Library Planning Committee, the Implementation Team, the Interface Design Project Group, and the Metadata Team.

Bruce Lubotsky Levin, Dr.P.H., is Associate Professor and Head, Graduate Studies in Behavioral Health, the University of South Florida de la Parte Institute & College of Public Health. He currently serves as Editor of the *Journal of Behavioral Health Services & Research*, and is Senior Editor of *Mental Health Services: A Public Health Perspective* (Oxford University Press, 1996) and *Women's Mental Health Services: A Public Health Perspective* (Sage Publications, 1998). His research interests include managed behavioral health services, mental health policy, graduate behavioral health education, and mental health informatics.

***

John Abresch has a Masters of Arts degree in Geography and has worked as a Geographic Information Systems analyst in both the private and public sector on many research projects using both urban and environmental applications of GIS. Currently employed as a paraprofessional in the Technical Services Department at the Tampa Library of the University of South Florida, Mr. Abresch is pursuing a graduate program of study in Library and Information Science.

Nancy Allen is a reference librarian at the Jane Bancroft Cook Library, which serves New College of Florida and The University of South Florida at Sarasota/

Manatee. She also teaches an undergraduate library research skills course. A former member of the Virtual Library Marketing Team, Ms. Allen now serves on the USF Libraries Marketing Committee.

Kathy Arsenault is library director at the University of South Florida St. Petersburg, where she served as collection development librarian from 1982-2001. Before coming to USFSP, she was employed by the Minneapolis College of Art and Design, Brandeis University and Princeton University. She is a graduate of Wellesley College and Simmons College School of Library Science.

Rose L. Bland is the Assistant Director of Systems at the University of South Florida, Shimberg Health Sciences Library in Tampa Florida. She received her Library, Media, and Information Science Masters degree from the University of South Florida. Rose is a member of the Florida Health Sciences Library Association and Southern Chapter/Medical Library Association. She has presented at Computers in Libraries and the Southern Chapter/Medical Library Association on the topic of technostress.

Merilyn S. Burke heads the Access Services department of the Tampa Library at the University of South Florida. Her undergraduate degree in history and her masters in Library Science were obtained from the University of Rochester. Her professional experience includes academic and health sciences libraries. Prior to the emergence of online distance education, she was the head of the SUS (State University System) Extension Library of Florida. Her current job duties include responsibility for ILL, circulation, ereserves, copyright, stack maintenance, and security. She is a member of the Tampa library's distance learning team.

Beverly Caggiano is the Associate Director, Technology, of the University of South Florida Library System. Ms. Caggiano has many years of experience as UNIX systems administrator in the corporate sector for Price Waterhouse. In addition to her work on UNIX systems, Ms. Caggiano has developed several innovative systems, including an electronic reserves system at the university. Further, she has implemented a content management system for the USF Virtual Library pages and is in the midst of planning the systems side for the installation of a new library management system.

Todd Chavez - Following his graduation from the University of South Florida's School of Library and Information Science, Todd Chavez accepted a position as assistant to the Head of Access Services at the USF Tampa Library. During this time, he worked to incorporate a variety of technological innovations into the organization. Mr. Chavez now serves as Assistant Director for Human Resources at the USF Tampa Library. Prior to coming to the Tampa Library, Mr. Chavez managed Barnes & Noble bookstores for over ten years.

Charles L. Gordon is Senior Monographs Cataloger at the University of South Florida Tampa Library. His experience includes managing a university film library, serving as cataloger for an academic medical library, and cataloging rare books for an art museum library. He has also taught as an adjunct instructor at the USF School of Library and Information Science and served on the Virtual Library Metadata Team. Mr. Gordon is a graduate of Marshall University with a degree in secondary education with fields of specialization in Spanish and Library Science and the University of South Florida with a Masters of Arts in Library Science.

Vicki L. Gregory is Professor and Director of the School of Library and Information Science at the University of South Florida where she teaches courses in collection development, information science, and library networks. Prior to beginning her teaching career, she was the Head of the Department of Systems and Operations at the Auburn University at Montgomery Library. She is the author of four books, including *The State and the Academic Library (Greenwood Press) and Selecting and Managing Electronic Resources* (Neal-Schuman). Current professional association positions include the Director of the Florida Library Association and serving as Deputy SIG Cabinet Director, a board level position, for the American Society for Information Science and Technology.

Kim Grohs is the Systems Librarian at the Jane Bancroft Cook Library serving New College of Florida and The University of South Florida at Sarasota/Manatee. She previously held the position of Director of Information and Access Services. Mrs. Grohs was a member of the Virtual Library Planning Committee and the Implementation Team. She led the Marketing Team and the Electronic Reserves Team. She co-presented a poster session on the Virtual Library at the 1997 ACRL Conference in Nashville, TN. In addition, Mrs. Grohs served as an adjunct instructor in Information Services for the School of Library and Information Science at USF.

Susan Heron is the Head of the Cataloging Department of the University of South Florida Libraries (USF). Previously she was Head of Technical Services at the University of San Diego, Head of Cataloging at San Diego State University, Project Coordinator for Database Conversion at Temple University, and a Library Liaison with the Research Libraries Group. Ms. Heron was a member of the Virtual Library Implementation Team as well as the Metadata, Digitization, Thesis and Dissertation, and Electronic Reserve Teams.

Allison M. Howard is the Catalog Librarian at the Shimberg Health Sciences Library at the University of South Florida in Tampa, Florida. Previously she was the Special Project Cataloging Librarian at Western Psychiatric Institute and Clinic, and the Cataloging Library Specialist at Falk Library, both at the University of Pittsburgh. She received her Master of Library and Information Science degree from the University of Pittsburgh. Ms. Howard is a member of the Medical Library Association, the Southern Chapter of MLA, the Florida Health Sciences Library Association. She is currently serving as the Chair of Florida Center of Library Automation's Technical Services Planning Committee.

William Kearns, Ph.D., is the director of the Louis de la Parte Florida Mental Health Institute Computer Support Center. Dr. Kearns has published 28 research papers and book chapters. He is the university representative to the national Internet2 Project, a consortium of 185 Carnegie "Comprehensive Research" category universities. In addition, he recently developed the first high bandwidth digital video application created by a Florida university to be demonstrated at an Internet2 national meeting (March, 2000). His interests include high performance networking, streaming media, and human factors psychology.

Tina Neville is currently employed as the Head of Reference at the University of South Florida, St. Petersburg Library. Ms. Neville was a member of the USF Libraries Virtual Library Planning Committee and, since 1996, has served as the facilitator for its Electronic Collections Team. She has also chaired the American Library Association, RUSA / CODES, Computer-Based Methods and Resources Committee and the Tampa Bay Library Consortium's Electronic Resources Task Force. Ms. Neville has a Bachelor of Arts degree in zoology and bacteriology from Ohio Wesleyan University and a Master of Arts in Library and Information Science from the University of South Florida.

Joan Pelland is library director at the Jane Bancroft Cook Library which serves both New College and the University of South Florida, Sarasota-Manatee. Prior to her role as director, she served as Director of Technical Services & Collection Management from 1989-1991. Before coming to New College, she was employed by the Loyola (New Orleans) University Law School Library and the Rockefeller Library at Brown University. She is a graduate of Simmons College School of Library & Information Science and Brown University.

Dr. Derrie Perez serves as Acting Dean of the USF Library System and was Interim Director of USF Tampa Library. Currently she is the secretary of the National REFORMA, the National Association to Promote Library and Information

Services to Latinos and the Spanish-Speaking, and is on the Editorial Board for the *College & Junior College Journal*. At USF, she has been co-chair of the Virtual Libraries Task Force, member of the Strategic Planning Task Force on Enhancing USF Libraries, as well as a member of the Task Force on the Multi-Campus Environment.

Patricia Pettijohn is Collection Development Librarian at the Louis de la Parte Institute Research Library at the University of South Florida. Ms. Pettijohn is a member of the University of South Florida Electronic Collections Team and the State University System Electronic Collections Social Sciences Committee. Her areas of interest include collection development, qualitative research, and women's studies. Ms. Pettijohn also has experience as a book editor for *The WomanSource Catalog & Review* and as a coordinator for documentary film.

Caroline Reed is a Reference Assistant at the Jane Bancroft Cook Library which serves New College of Florida and the University of South Florida at Sarasota/Manatee. She is a candidate for a Masters of Library and Information Science degree at the University of South Florida in Spring 2002. Ms. Reed serves on the Virtual Library Electronic Collections Team and previously was a member of the Metadata Team. Prior to coming to the University of South Florida, Ms. Reed was a Library Specialist at the University of the Virgin Islands, St. Thomas Campus.

Beverly A. Shattuck is Director of the Shimberg Health Sciences Library and Media Center at the University of South Florida in Tampa, which serves the Colleges of Medicine, Nursing, Public Health, the School of Physical Therapy, and health care researchers and providers throughout Florida. Before coming to USF in 1989, she was Assistant Director of the Lamar Soutter Medical Library at the University of Massachusetts Medical Center in Worcester, Massachusetts. She is a member of the Medical Library Association, Southern Chapter of the Medical Library Association, Florida Health Sciences Library Association, and Special Libraries Association. She was a founding member of the USF Virtual Library Planning Committee. Ms. Shattuck received a BA degree in anthropology from the University of Maine, a Masters in Business Administration from Anna Marie College and a Master of Science degree in Library Science from Simmons College.

Amy Tracy Wells, M.L.S., has worked on issues related to metadata and the development of digital libraries for the past nine years at the Internet Scout Project (University of Wisconsin-Madison), the National Institute of Standards and Technology, and the Library of Congress, She has co-authored federally funded initiatives totaling over $3.6 million and is the senior editor and contributor to *The*

Amazing Internet Challenge: How Leading Projects Use Library Skills to Organize the Web (1999). She is a past recipient of the Louis Shores-Oryx Press Award and the Machine-Assisted Reference Section Recognition Award. She received her Masters in Library and Information Science from the University of South Florida and is currently pursuing doctoral work at Michigan State University. She is also Co-Principal of Belman-Wells, an economic and information services partnership.

Index

The International Journal of Distance Education Technologies (JDET)

The International Source for Technological Advances in Distance Education

ISSN:	1539-3100
eISSN:	1539-3119
Subscription:	Annual fee per volume (4 issues): Individual US $85 Institutional US $185
Editors:	Shi Kuo Chang University of Pittsburgh, USA
	Timothy K. Shih Tamkang University, Taiwan

Mission

The International Journal of Distance Education Technologies (**JDET**) publishes original research articles of distance education four issues per year. JDET is a primary forum for researchers and practitioners to disseminate practical solutions to the automation of open and distance learning. The journal is targeted to academic researchers and engineers who work with distance learning programs and software systems, as well as general participants of distance education.

Coverage

Discussions of computational methods, algorithms, implemented prototype systems, and applications of open and distance learning are the focuses of this publication. Practical experiences and surveys of using distance learning systems are also welcome. Distance education technologies published in JDET will be divided into three categories, **Communication Technologies, Intelligent Technologies, and Educational Technologies**: New network infrastructures, real-time protocols, broadband and wireless communication tools, Quality-of Services issues, multimedia streaming technology, distributed systems, mobile systems, multimedia synchronization controls, intelligent tutoring, individualized distance learning, neural network or statistical approaches to behavior analysis, automatic FAQ reply methods, copyright protection and authentification mechanisms, practical and new learning models, automatic assessment methods, effective and efficient authoring systems, and other issues of distance education.

For subscription information, contact:

Idea Group Publishing
701 E Chocolate Avenue
Hershey PA 17033-1212, USA
cust@idea-group.com

For paper submission information:

Dr. Timothy Shih
Tamkang University, Taiwan
tshih@cs.tku.edu.tw

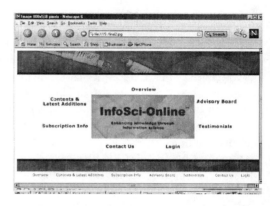

World Libraries on the Information Superhighway:
Preparing for the Challenges
of the New Millennium

Patricia Diamond-Fletcher, University of Maryland, Baltimore Co.
John C. Bertot, University at Albany, State University of New York

The global economy and the Internet are creating an international perspective on the management and use of information. Libraries, as repositories of knowledge, are key institutions for guiding the transition to a global networked information environment. The issues specific to the effective development and use of a truly international networked information environment are critical in these formative years of the Internet.

Libraries of all types—public, academic, business and other special libraries—are creating a variety of responses to the many issues of a global networked information environment.

Best practices in Internet service deployment in libraries around the world are a valuable information sharing tool for other libraries. *World Libraries on the Information Superhighway Preparing for the Challenges of the New Millennium* shares these practices as it addresses issues such as funding for Internet services, staffing and training for global networked information, transborder issues, copyright, privacy and technology applications in this must-read volume.

ISBN 1-878289-66-7 (soft cover) • US$74.95 • 320 pages • Copyright © 2000

> "This book provides a fascinating look at the past and current impact and the future potential of IT in libraries worldwide. Much can be learned from this international group of authors who describe their journeys along the information superhighway."
>
> —*Ruth V. Small, Syracuse University*

It's Easy to Order! Order online at www.idea-group.com or call our toll-free hotline at 1-800-345-4332!
Mon-Fri 8:30 am-5:00 pm (est) or fax 24 hours a day 717/533-8661

Idea Group Publishing
Hershey • London • Melbourne • Singapore • Beijing

An excellent addition to your library